Service Level Management in Cloud Computing

Melanie Holloway

Service Level Management in Cloud Computing

Pareto-Efficient Negotiations, Reliable Monitoring, and Robust Monitor Placement

Mit einem Geleitwort von Prof. Dr.-Ing. Ralf Steinmetz

 Springer Vieweg

Melanie Holloway
Darmstadt, Germany

Dissertation Technische Universität Darmstadt, 2016
u.d.T.: Melanie Holloway: „Service Level Management in Cloud Computing. Pareto-Efficient Negotiations, Reliable Monitoring, and Robust Monitor Placement".

Hochschulkennziffer D17, Darmstadt

·

ISBN 978-3-658-21521-7   ISBN 978-3-658-18773-6   (eBook)
DOI 10.1007/978-3-658-18773-6

Springer Vieweg
© Springer Fachmedien Wiesbaden GmbH 2017
Softcover reprint of the hardcover 1st edition 2017

This Springer Vieweg imprint is published by Springer Nature
The registered company is Springer Fachmedien Wiesbaden GmbH
The registered company address is: Abraham-Lincoln-Str. 46, 65189 Wiesbaden, Germany

Dedicated to the loving memory of
Dr. Christopher John Holloway
1949 – 2016

Preface

Cloud computing is a major IT paradigm of our time. It has changed the way how IT resources are shared and used. By shifting the tasks and responsibilities for managing these resources to the provider side and by delivering these resources as a service to consumers on-demand over the Internet, several new challenges arise and affect cloud adoption. One major issue for cloud consumers is the loss of control over non-functional properties of the cloud resources. Today's cloud providers aim to address that issue by offering quality guarantees in terms of service level agreements and perform for themselves corresponding monitoring solutions.

Dr. Melanie Holloway thoroughly **analyzes the shortcomings** of existing approaches related to the process of service level management **from the consumer's perspective**. Based on her results, she develops new approaches for service level agreement negotiation and monitoring by integrating in a very elegant way concepts from the fields of economics, computer science, mathematical optimization, and statistics.

Since service level agreements offered by today's cloud providers are usually fixed (i.e. static), consumers of cloud services are not able to efficiently align their individual business requirements with the non-functional properties of the cloud resources. Therefore, appropriate approaches for automatic IT-based negotiations of individual service level agreements are required. Having this as her target, Dr. Melanie Holloway elaborates a new very elegant negotiation mechanism which allows to approach Pareto-efficient agreements taking into account the results of concurrent negotiations with multiple providers. In contrast to existing approaches, the negotiating parties are able to achieve such an **efficient solution without revealing private information** and not depending on the proposed values of the other involved parties. By simulations, Dr. Melanie Holloway demonstrates the high quality of her negotiation mechanism.

In order to verify whether the formerly negotiated service level agreements are maintained on the provider side, cloud consumers are also in the need of reliable monitoring solutions. In her thesis, Dr. Melanie Holloway focuses on availability monitoring techniques, since most of today's service level agreements only define some type of guarantees. As a major contribution, she presents a **monitoring approach** that places monitoring units on the provider and the consumer side. This is done in conjunction with two mathematical models. These models provide decision support for monitoring configuration in two ways: While the first model enables to determine an appropriate monitoring frequency and the required sample size in order to obtain monitoring results at a certain level of confidence, the second model facilitates the adjustment of the monitoring frequency in the presence of network impairments. The work of Dr. Melanie Holloway is the first one I have come across which considers the **accuracy of the monitoring data in conjunction with the monitoring frequency** taking into account key issues in the underlying network. Dr. Melanie Holloway shows the accuracy of her models by performing testbed experiments based on a prototypical implementation of her monitoring approach.

The whole work also demands a reliable monitoring infrastructure. In this respect, Dr. Melanie Holloway identifies the new robust cloud monitor placement problem and formalizes this problem as a mathematical optimization model. This is the first time that probabilistic reliability values of all involved entities within one monitoring infrastructure are considered. Based on her mathematical model, Dr. Melanie Holloway shows the exact solution. Due to the exponential time complexity of the computation of the exact approach, she further proposes two heuristics with polynomial time complexity. In simulations, Dr. Melanie Holloway shows that a random placement of monitoring units is not appropriate and that her solution approaches are all able to reduce the maximum overall downtime of the monitoring units by more than ninety percent.

Concluding her thesis, Dr. Melanie Holloway focuses on a scenario in which a broker acts as an intermediary between cloud providers and cloud consumers. The broker offers her solution approaches as a service and increases market efficiency by successfully mediating service level agreement negotiations and by acting as a trusted third-party whenever cloud service monitoring is used. In doing so, the thesis contributes to a foundation for market-based cloud service provisioning.

This work was performed at the TU Darmstadt as part of the **E-Finance Lab**, an industry-academic partnership between Goethe University Frankfurt, TU Darmstadt and the partners Deutsche Börse, DZ Bank Gruppe, Finanz Informatik, IBM, 360 Treasury Systems, Interactive Data Managed Solutions, and usd AG located at Goethe University Frankfurt.

Let me conclude mentioning the following: I had the pleasure to supervise the thesis and to work with Dr. Melanie Holloway. She managed to have a lot of interaction with experts related to several issues of her work: At this point I just want to mention Dr. Amr Rizk and Dr. Dieter Schuller who provided valuable feedback at various stages of this outstanding thesis.

Darmstadt, April 2017   Ralf Steinmetz

Acknowledgments

First of all, I would like to express my sincere gratitude to my advisor Prof. Dr.-Ing. Ralf Steinmetz for giving me the opportunity to work as a research staff member at the exciting Multimedia Communications Lab (KOM) and complete my Ph.D. under his supervision. I would like to thank him for his continuous support, guidance and understanding, especially during the personal hard times at the end of writing this thesis. In addition, I would like to thank my co-advisor Prof. Dr.-Ing. Michael Zink from the Electrical and Computer Engineering Department at the University of Massachusetts in Amherst for his valuable comments and encouragement. Besides my advisors, I would also like to thank my other thesis committee members, Prof. Dr.-Ing. Klaus Hofmann, Prof. Dr.-Ing. Rolf Jakoby, and Prof. Dr.-Ing. Anja Klein for letting my defense be an enjoyable moment and for providing me with interesting comments and suggestions. Moreover, I am very grateful for the generous support from my mentor Dr.-Ing. Nicolas Liebau.

Special thanks also go to my (former) group heads Dr.-Ing. Amr Rizk and Dr.-Ing. Dieter Schuller for their precious support and fruitful discussions, especially during the final stage of my thesis. Furthermore, I would like to thank my (former) group members of the Service-oriented Computing research group and the Adaptive Overlay Communications research group for their helpful feedback and for creating a friendly and cooperative working environment: Dr.-Ing. Sonja Bergsträßer, Rahul Dwarakanath, Dr.-Ing. Julian Eckert, Dr.-Ing. Christian Groß, Ronny Hans, Rhaban Hark, Dr.-Ing. Boris Koldehofe, Dr.-Ing. Ulrich Lampe, Prof. Dr.-Ing. André Miede, Dr.-Ing. Michael Niemann, Dr.-Ing. Apostolos Papageorgiou, Björn Richerzhagen, Nils Richerzhagen, Dr.-Ing. Dominik Stingl, Olga Wenge, and Dr.-Ing. Sebastian Zöller.

In addition to the colleagues mentioned above, I would also like to thank Lena Depres, Dr.-Ing. Mojisola Erdt, Dr. phil. Paul Gebelein, Dr.-Ing. Christian Gottron, Fabian Kaup, and The An Bin Nguyen for their support, for being my co-authors and office mates, and for the wonderful lunches during the last years. I am also very grateful to the administrative and legal staff members of KOM for providing the perfect surrounding conditions for our research and for being very helpful in all organizational issues: Matthias Bastian, Marion and Klaus-Peter Ehlhardt, Britta Frischmuth-Zenker, Jan Hansen, Monika Jayme, Frank Jöst, Sabine Kräh, Silvia Rödelsperger, Jan Schnurr, Gisela Scholz-Schmidt, Karola Schork-Jakobi, and Christian Theiß.

Last but not least, I would like to thank my family. Words cannot express how grateful I am to my parents Ursula and Rolf Siebenhaar, my sister Dr. phil. Stefanie Mehler, and my parents-in-law Sabine and Dr. Christopher Holloway for their continuous support, encouragement, and faith in me writing this thesis.

Finally, my deepest gratitude goes to my husband, Dr. rer. nat. Steven Holloway, for his endless confidence, support and patience, and for being the best that ever happened to me in my life. ♡

Darmstadt, April 2017   Melanie Holloway

Contents

Acronyms

AJAX	Asynchronous JavaScript and XML
API	Application Programming Interface
ARPANET	Advanced Research Project Agency Network
CEP	Complex Event Processing
CNP	Contract Net Protocol
CPU	Central Processing Unit
EC2	Amazon's Elastic Compute Cloud
ESB	Enterprise Service Bus
GRiP	Greed, Risk, and Patience
HTML	Hypertext Markup Language
HTTP	Hypertext Transfer Protocol
IaaS	Infrastructure as a Service
ID	Identification Number
ILP	Integer Linear Program
IoS	Internet of Services
IP	Internet Protocol
ISO	International Organization for Standardization
ISP	Internet Service Provider
IT	Information Technology
ITIL	Information Technology Infrastructure Library
ITU	International Telecommunication Union

MDA	Monitoring Data Aggregator
MILP	Mixed-Integer Linear Program
MLA	Monitoring Level Agreement
MRS	Marginal Rate of Substitution
MTTF	Mean Time To Failure
MTTR	Mean Time To Repair
NIST	National Institute of Standards and Technology
OASIS	Organization for the Advancement of Structured Information Standards
OLA	Operational Level Agreement
PaaS	Platform as a Service
PCs	Personal Computers
P2P	Peer-to-Peer
QoS	Quality of Service
REST	Representational State Transfer
RCMPP	Robust Cloud Monitor Placement Problem
RSS	Really Simple Syndication
RTO	Retransmission Timeout
RTT	Round Trip Time
SaaS	Software as a Service
SLA	Service Level Agreement
SLM	Service Level Management
SLS	Service Level Specification
SMI	Service Measurement Index
SNMP	Simple Network Management Protocol
SOA	Service-oriented Architecture

SOAP	Simple Object Access Protocol
SOC	Service-oriented Computing
S3	Amazon's Simple Storage Service
TCP	Transmission Control Protocol
TTF	Time To Failure
TTR	Time To Repair
UDDI	Universal Description, Discovery and Integration
URI	Uniform Resource Identifier
URL	Uniform Resource Locator
VM	Virtual Machine
VPC	Virtual Private Cloud
WSDL	Web Service Description Language
XML	Extensible Markup Language
XSD	XML Schema Definition Language

1 Introduction

Soon after the advent of Information Technology (IT), the desire to share computing resources and stored data with other users emerged. Starting from standalone Personal Computers (PCs) and isolated mainframes, PCs being part of local networks, the era of sharing resources over a network was initiated (cf. [207]). The evolution of IT continued with the ability of local networks to connect to each other, thereby forming global networks, leading to today's Internet. Over time, requirements for the utilized computing resources and corresponding architectures have been increasingly driven by business needs. Traditionally, IT started with a supportive role for business activities with the aim of increasing efficiency, which then evolved into a strategic role over time, enabling new business models [93]. The business-driven evolution of IT is a direct response to increasing dynamics and high competition in the market leading to rapidly changing business requirements, forcing IT infrastructures to adapt correspondingly quickly [149]. With the allocation of a more strategic role, principles of service-oriented design originated and the corresponding paradigm of a Service-oriented Architecture (SOA) following these principles evolved. Basically, a service-oriented approach incorporates reusable, autonomous services encapsulating a certain business functionality that can be loosely-coupled in order to create dynamic business processes (cf. [55, 149]). In doing so, enterprises can easily adapt their business processes according to changing business requirements with a small amount of management effort. In 2007, the vision of a global Web-based service marketplace based on the SOA paradigm evolved, the so-called Internet of Services (IoS), facilitating the retrieval and usage of electronic services for Internet users [175]. However, at that time, enterprises could not, in practice, tap the full potential of service-oriented design, even less so on a global scale. The envisioned Web-based service economy could then not be turned into reality. In general, barriers might include issues involving security, reliability, divergent national laws, flexible enterprise and Internet infrastructures, and the identification and creation of appropriate services [68]. Furthermore, several requirements have to be met in order to realize the vision of the IoS [174]. First of all, semantic and technical interoperability between the services is necessary to enable automatic discovery and composition. Second, intermediaries in the form of service brokers, for example, must reside in the market to allow them to undertake a global search for services. Finally, the realization of the IoS also depends on adequate means to cope with technical service descriptions, e.g., in the form of service registries, so that services can be easily found and understood. Besides the envisioned IoS, a much older vision of providing computing resources as a utility, similar to other utilities such as electricity or water, has been around since the era of mainframes and several different IT paradigms have been proposed for this purpose (cf. [25, 147]). The latest of these is cloud computing, which incorporates the delivery of arbitrary computing resources as a service over the Internet. The computing resources range from infrastructure-based services in the form of virtual machines or data storage, for example, over platform-based services, providing runtime environments or development systems, to various applications on the Software as a Service (SaaS) level. Within the so-called "cloud", computing resources are pooled in large data centers, operated by cloud providers and located at several locations worldwide. The computing resources are provided and released on-demand and enable cloud service consumers to adapt rapidly to changing business requirements. In conjunction with its universal and flexible infrastructure, the characteristics of cloud computing appear to better fit the envisioned global Web-based service economy.

However, the IoS faces similar challenges in the cloud era, as in 2007, that are currently addressed in research. These challenges incorporate interoperability and portability for service deployment across different providers, the negotiation of quality guarantees and service monitoring, as well as appropriate techniques to ensure security and availability [136]. Former SOA research problems, such as efficient service discovery (e.g., [119, 178, 179]) and QoS-aware service selection (e.g., [176, 177]), also have to be re-considered in a cloud context. Solving all these challenges would lay the foundation for market-based cloud computing with brokers as intermediaries acting on behalf of consumers. To date, cloud computing is already considered to be a major computing paradigm of our time and, according to Cisco, cloud data centers will process more than 86% of workloads by 2019 [35].

1.1 Motivation

Cloud services are highly configurable and are provisioned on-demand, both with minimal management effort due to a shift of responsibility to the cloud provider (cf. [131]). At the same time, however, this shift of responsibility implies a loss of control for cloud consumers. Besides functional requirements, cloud consumers also have non-functional requirements for their utilized cloud services, such as a required level of availability, to meet certain business constraints. In order still to provide a certain level of control to a consumer, a so-called Service Level Agreement (SLA) can be established. Basically, an SLA represents a contract between providers and consumers specifying certain quality guarantees for a particular service as well as penalties for the cloud provider for the case that terms of an SLA are violated. To date, cloud service SLAs are mainly static and usually only consider availability (e.g., [5]). These static SLAs are not sufficient from a business perspective. Since the efficiency of today's business processes mainly depends on the performance of the utilized IT, cloud service performance is critical. Therefore, enterprise cloud consumers require individual SLAs according to their specific business constraints. However, manual negotiations are time-consuming and are not appropriate in the presence of a large number of consumers and providers. In addition, this is not in line with the idea of on-demand cloud service provisioning, so that an automation of SLA negotiations is required (cf. [215]). Having agreed on certain SLAs, the provider's adherence to these SLAs at runtime must also be observed in order to detect SLA violations and to obtain a proper compensation. Typically, providers offer their own monitoring solutions for assessing cloud service quality at runtime and often impose the burden of SLA violation reporting on their customers [152]. However, this cannot be considered to be an independent evidence base from a consumer's perspective. This perception is emphasized by a joint cloud market maturity study of the Cloud Security Alliance and ISACA in 2012, according to which the degree of confidence of consumers that providers effectively measure performance against SLAs, is very low [41]. Therefore, consumers are also in the need of appropriate means to monitor cloud service performance independently from a cloud provider.

The aforementioned issues concern the two major activities, *SLA negotiation* and *SLA monitoring* of Service Level Management, which constitutes a process within an organization that comprises specific activities in order to guarantee consumers a certain level of quality for each delivered IT service [167]. Generally, *SLA negotiation* represents the activity of negotiating quality guarantees in terms of thresholds for certain parameters of an IT service and results in a contract, in case of an agreement. Having agreed on SLAs, *SLA monitoring* represents the subsequent activity of measuring the performance of an IT service against the prior negotiated SLAs.

1.2 Broker-based Service Level Management

So far, several approaches for SLA negotiation and SLA monitoring have been proposed in related research works. Concerning SLA negotiation, related approaches usually propose an automation of SLA negotiation using autonomous software components, denoted as *agents*, acting on behalf of the negotiating parties by exchanging messages in order to reach an agreement (e.g., [43, 46, 59, 117, 143, 190, 217, 225]). Furthermore, several works present a broker-based approach (e.g., [190, 195, 216, 224, 225]). These solutions contribute to a foundation for market-based cloud computing, with brokers as intermediaries acting on behalf of consumers, and thus, further help to approach the IoS. In electronic markets, intermediaries may act as experts and/or information source and, thus, may be essential to increase market efficiency as follows [33]: When acting as experts, intermediaries are able to assess the quality of an electronic product and consumers can benefit from their expertise. However, even with no expertise in evaluating a providers' quality, an intermediary can become a trusted source for information by relying on consumers' experience. Finally, intermediaries enhance market efficiency by successfully mediating trades, since there is less chance to find appropriate sellers or buyers, given a large number of providers and consumers. Concerning SLA monitoring, intermediaries may also act as trusted third parties, when they perform monitoring tasks independently from a cloud provider on behalf of cloud consumers.

Having stated the reasons above, this thesis focuses on a scenario, in which a broker residing in the market provides the two major activities of Service Level Management (SLM) *SLA negotiation* and *SLA monitoring* as a service to cloud consumers. Hence, the broker negotiates SLAs with public cloud providers on behalf of consumers for desired cloud services and provides monitoring services later on. In this thesis, we exemplarily consider cloud services on the SaaS level due to their increased business relevance and complexity. Concerning SLA monitoring, we focus on availability, since it constitutes one of the very few parameters for which guarantees are offered by today's cloud providers, as mentioned above. Nevertheless, our contributions can also be slightly adapted to suit other types and parameters of cloud services.

1.3 Research Goals and Challenges

Focusing on enterprise cloud consumers, the following three research goals have to be addressed, in order effectively to realize an automated SLA negotiation and independent SLA monitoring in the context of the envisaged broker-based scenario:

- *Pareto-Efficient SLA Negotiation:* Enterprise cloud consumers aim to obtain individual quality guarantees according to their specific business constraints and aspire to achieve the best available outcome given their time and cost constraints. In such a business context, rational parties will strive for economically efficient, so-called *Pareto-optimal*[1] agreements (cf. [61, 118, 165]). Basically, an agreement is considered to be Pareto-optimal, if none of the negotiating parties can be better off without rendering another party worse off (e.g., [46, 214]).

- *Reliable SLA Monitoring:* Monitoring results obtained from the envisaged non-provider-based assessment of cloud service quality must be reliable in order to enable consumers to verify whether the prior negotiated SLAs are maintained. This is especially important when business critical applications are involved.

- *Robust Monitor Placement:* Finally, not only the monitoring information itself must be reliable, but the underlying infrastructure must also be *robust*. The monitoring units should work correctly, although components can be subject to failure with a certain probability.

---

[1]   Note that we use the terms "Pareto-optimal" and "Pareto-efficient" interchangeably in this thesis.

Consequently, we address the following main research question in this thesis: *How to control cloud service performance from an enterprise cloud consumer's perspective in an efficient and reliable manner?*

Existing approaches for SLA negotiation and SLA monitoring reveal several short-comings for the envisaged broker-based scenario as outlined in the following. Concerning automated SLA negotiation, the majority of existing approaches focusing on Pareto-efficient outcomes is based on the shortest-distance to the opponent's last proposal (e.g., [46, 117, 194, 224, 225]). However, these mechanisms may not necessarily lead to a Pareto-optimal solution and the *strategic behavior* of the negotiating parties is limited [117]. The limited strategic behavior refers to the fact that the values proposed by a negotiating party depend on the former values proposed by the opponent. In other works, a mediator is applied since finding Pareto-efficient solutions in a scenario with incomplete information is very difficult (e.g., [30, 117, 118, 143]). For this purpose, the negotiating parties have to reveal their private preferences to this central entity, an assumption that cannot be made in a business scenario. All in all, *none of the existing approaches considers Pareto-efficient outcomes, given the conditions of the envisaged scenario, i.e., in which a broker negotiates concurrently with multiple providers over multiple issues of a particular service, while maintaining the strategic behavior and the privacy of the negotiating parties.*

Regarding SLA monitoring, most of the existing approaches only focus on provider side monitoring (e.g., [37, 51, 52, 86, 113, 122, 129, 192]). These approaches are usually intended to be implemented by providers for internal management purposes and require access to the provider's infrastructure (e.g., [51, 129]). The results obtained from these approaches can also be (additionally) provided to consumers (e.g., [192], Amazon CloudWatch[2]). However, monitoring data obtained in this way cannot be perceived as a reliable evidence base for consumers in order to monitor the adherence of cloud providers with prior negotiated SLAs. Hence, reliable monitoring capabilities outside the control sphere of a cloud provider are required. This introduces additional complexity in the monitoring tasks since cloud consumers only have limited access to a cloud provider's infrastructure. So far, only a few approaches exist to address the problem of SLA monitoring from a consumer's perspective (c.f., [32, 133, 158, 180]). However, *none of the existing monitoring approaches explicitly considers the reliability of monitoring information.* In order to obtain reliable monitoring results, a monitoring approach must be *location-aware*, since only incidents within the control sphere of a cloud provider may constitute SLA violations, *resource-aware* in order to determine the correct SLA clause, and *accurate*. The latter means that monitoring tasks have to be configured in such a manner that the observed values for the SLA parameters represent the real values as closely as required.

---

[2]   https://aws.amazon.com/cloudwatch/

With regard to monitor placement, most of the existing approaches only consider a network to be resilient if it continues to work correctly, given a maximum number of concurrent node and/or link failures (e.g., [106, 140, 148, 153, 164]). However, in order to maximize the reliability of the monitoring infrastructure, setting upper bounds on the number of failures is not sufficient. Furthermore, the monitoring infrastructure must exhibit sufficient resource capacities in order for monitor units to work correctly and not to interfere with other cloud services. Resource constraints have only been considered in very few approaches in related research works aiming, for example, to obtain a cost-minimal monitor placement or a resilient Virtual Machine (VM) placement in the presence of host failures (cf. [16, 127, 158, 159]). In summary, *none of the existing approaches jointly considers the reliability of all the components involved in monitoring as well as resource constraints, while placing monitor units given an individual redundancy level for each cloud service to be observed.*

1.4 Contributions

Having stated the aforementioned research goals and challenges, the main objective of this thesis is to design and build a new SLM solution focusing on the two major tasks SLA negotiation and SLA monitoring in the context of our envisaged broker-based scenario. For this purpose, we first investigate the shortcomings of existing approaches. Given the insights from related work, we derive the requirements for a new SLM solution and propose the conceptual design of our envisaged Service Level Management broker CSLAB.KOM. Based on the conceptual system design, this thesis makes the following three major contributions:

Concerning our first research goal, we propose *a mechanism for Pareto-efficient concurrent multiple-issue negotiations*, referred to as CSLAB-Neg.KOM, which follows a new two-phase meta-strategy. In order to realize that meta-strategy, our negotiation mechanism comprises a negotiation protocol and corresponding negotiation strategies. In detail, we develop a negotiation protocol, which enhances the well-known Alternate-Offers protocol and propose a strategy based on the Greed, Risk, and Patience (GRiP) levels of the negotiating parties (denoted as GRiP-based strategy), which is applied during the second phase. In addition, we propose a corresponding negotiation algorithm, which defines the behavior of the negotiating parties when following a GRiP-based strategy. During the first phase of the meta-strategy, we apply existing time-dependent strategies due to the time constraints of the negotiating parties. In contrast to related approaches, our negotiation mechanism allows approaching Pareto-efficient outcomes while maintaining the strategic behavior and the privacy of the negotiating parties (cf. Section 1.3). Concerning the evaluation, we assess the contractual performance in terms of the Pareto-efficiency and success rate as well as the computational performance in terms of the execution time and the number of exchanged messages. For this purpose, we perform simulations, in which we exploit realistic data from cloud providers. In order to validate the target performance of the negotiation mechanism in terms of Pareto-efficiency, we develop an ex post Pareto-efficiency reference model that allows the computation of a representation of the set of Pareto-optimal solutions as baseline.

In order to address our second research goal, we develop *an approach for reliable consumer side availability monitoring*, denoted as CSLAB-Mon.KOM. In contrast to existing approaches, we explicitly address the reliability of the monitoring results. For this purpose, our approach is *location-aware* in order to distinguish real SLA violations within a cloud provider's control sphere from other incidents, *resource-aware* in order to identify the violated SLA clause based on the affected resources, and *accurate* so that the monitoring results reflect the real state of the observed cloud service as closely as required. For the latter, the contributions are twofold. Firstly, we provide decision support for determining an adequate monitoring frequency in conjunction with the required sample size in order to achieve monitoring results at a certain level of confidence. Secondly, decision support is provided for computing a minimum timeout period in the presence of a certain level of packet loss in order to avoid a decrease in accuracy due to an increase in timed-out measurements. In the evaluation, we demonstrate the applicability of our approach in practice and that it provides accurate monitoring results by conducting testbed experiments based on a prototypical implementation of our approach and a real cloud service.

Regarding our third research goal, we propose *strategies for robust cloud monitor placement*, referred to as CSLAB-Loc.KOM. For this purpose, we first formalize the considered Robust Cloud Monitor Placement Problem (RCMPP) as a mathematical optimization model. Since the RCMPP constitutes a non-linear, multi-objective optimization problem, we propose a set of transformations in order to turn the RCMPP into a linear, single-objective optimization problem based on a worst-case perspective. The resulting problem can then be solved by applying off-the-shelf algorithms resulting in the exact solution approach CSLAB-Loc-Exa.KOM. Since the exact solution approach exhibits exponential time complexity, we develop a heuristic opening procedure CSLAB-Loc-Start.KOM, which yields polynomial time complexity. In addition, we propose a heuristic improvement procedure CSLAB-Loc-Imp.KOM, which permits further improvement of the quality of the solution to the opening procedure, while still exhibiting polynomial time complexity. We evaluate our strategies for robust monitor placement with respect to computation time and solution quality. In this regard, the exact solution approach CSLAB-Loc-Exa.KOM serves as a baseline in terms of solution quality. In order to provide a baseline in terms of computation time, we create a random placement procedure CSLAB-Loc-Rand.KOM. We conduct simulations in order to assess the performance of our placement strategies by incorporating realistic data from cloud providers and Internet performance statistics.

1.5 Structure of this Thesis

The remainder of this thesis is structured as follows:

Chapter 2 - *Background* - introduces definitions, concepts, and technologies representing the foundations for this thesis. It comprises the characteristics of cloud computing, the objectives and activities of Service Level Management, the contents of SLAs, and the objectives and principles of automated negotiations and monitoring.

Chapter 3 - *Related Work* - gives an overview of related approaches concerning Pareto-efficient concurrent multiple-issue negotiations, reliable consumer side monitoring, and robust monitor placement. In this regard, we analyze and discuss the shortcomings of existing approaches and point out the differences to our work.

Chapter 4 - *Basic System Design - CSLAB.KOM* - specifies the basic system design of our new SLM solution. Based on our results obtained in Chapter 3, we justify our major design decisions. Specifically, we describe the design of our envisaged SLM broker, the requirements for the two main SLM activities, SLA negotiation and SLA monitoring, and we introduce our basic negotiation model and monitoring approach.

Chapter 5 - *Pareto-Efficient Negotiations - CSLAB-Neg.KOM* - presents our first contribution for Pareto-efficient concurrent multiple-issue negotiations. Given the basic negotiation model presented in Chapter 4, we first introduce an ex post Pareto-efficiency reference model serving as a baseline for our negotiation mechanism. Subsequently, we describe our Pareto-efficient negotiation mechanism comprising a negotiation protocol, negotiation strategies, and a negotiation algorithm.

Chapter 6 - *Reliable Monitoring - CSLAB-Mon.KOM* - introduces our second contribution for reliable consumer side availability monitoring. Based on our basic system design in Chapter 4, we enhance our basic monitoring approach in order to achieve reliable consumer side availability monitoring. In detail, we describe the major activities of data collection and aggregation and discuss and address the influence of the monitoring frequency and packet loss on accuracy.

Chapter 7 - *Robust Monitor Placement - CSLAB-Loc.KOM* - describes our third contribution comprising strategies for robust monitor placement. Within this chapter, we first formalize the considered monitor placement problem as a mathematical optimization model. Since the resulting model constitutes a non-linear, multi-objective optimization problem, we suggest a number of transformations, so that the resulting model can be solved using off-the-shelf-methods. Subsequently, we introduce our strategies for robust monitor placement encompassing an exact solution approach (CSLAB-Loc-Exa.KOM), an opening heuristic (CSLAB-Loc-Start.KOM), and an improvement heuristic (CSLAB-Loc-Imp.KOM).

Chapter 8 - *Evaluation* - presents the setup and corresponding results of the evaluation of our Service Level Management solution. Firstly, we analyze the Pareto-efficiency of our negotiation mechanism using a simulation framework. Secondly, we describe the prototypical implementation of our consumer side monitoring approach and validate its accuracy by setting up a small testbed. Finally, we evaluate our heuristic approaches for robust monitor placement with regard to computation time and solution quality using our exact optimization approach as baseline.

Chapter 9 - *Summary and Outlook* - summarizes the content and major findings of this thesis, points out the contributions, and revisits the research goals. The thesis closes with an outlook briefly sketching related issues that could be addressed in future work.

2 Background

This chapter introduces the fundamentals and major terms of this thesis. Since cloud-based services are the focus of the present work, Section 2.1 discusses different definitions of cloud computing and describes the main characteristics of cloud-based services. Furthermore, Section 2.1 elaborates on the technologies enabling cloud-based services and describes related paradigms. In order to provide an overview, explaining how guarantees for certain quality levels of cloud-based services can be obtained and how it can be ensured that they are maintained during service usage, Section 2.2 outlines the activities of Service Level Management. Furthermore, it introduces the term Service Level Agreements and elaborates on how they relate to Quality of Service (QoS) parameters well known from the area of communication networks. Section 2.3 presents mechanisms and concepts on how to automate the negotiation of quality guarantees. Finally, Section 2.4 describes objectives and principles when it comes to measure the current performance of a cloud-based service against these guarantees.

2.1 Cloud Computing

2.1.1 Definition

Although cloud computing has become a major computing paradigm of our time, no widely accepted definition exists, as yet. Basically, the term *cloud computing* was coined by today's famous cloud providers Amazon and Google in late 2006 (cf., e.g., [147, 218, 221]). Although it is controversial, which of them was the first propagating this new computing paradigm, the term *cloud computing* itself has its origins in industry. Research in academia started later in 2007 [218]. Nevertheless, the underlying idea of provisioning computing resources as a utility is not new and has been a vision since the era of mainframes (cf., e.g., [25, 147, 221]). Early in 1961, John McCarthy envisaged that *"'computation' might someday be organized as a public utility"* [147]. In 1969, the same vision was again uttered by Leonard Kleinrock, a chief scientist of the Advanced Research Project Agency Network (ARPANET) project, the predecessor of today's Internet [111]:

> *"As of now, computer networks are still in their infancy, but as they grow up and become sophisticated, we will probably see the spread of*

'computer utilities', which, like present electric and telephone utilities,
will service individual homes and offices across the country."

Kleinrock already envisioned some of the main characteristics of cloud-based services today, namely, that computing resources will be provided on-demand with ubiquitous access in the form of web-based services (cf., e.g., [25, 111]). These characteristics already emphasize some of the main advantages of cloud computing from a consumer's point of view. Since cloud-based services are provided in a manner similar to other common utilities, such as electricity, consumers do not have to maintain their own complex IT infrastructure anymore and only pay for the services based on their usage [25]. In addition to the advantages on the consumer side, there are also several advantages on the provider side. Some of them have already been mentioned in one of the first definitions of cloud computing by Ian Foster (co-inventor of the grid computing paradigm as a preceding paradigm of cloud computing) and others in 2008 [72]:

"A large-scale distributed computing paradigm that is driven by economies
of scale, in which a pool of abstracted, virtualized, dynamically-scalable,
managed computing power, storage, platforms, and services are delivered
on demand to external customers over the Internet."

According to Foster et al., the most important aspects in this definition are that clouds are *"massively scalable"*, provide *"different levels of services"*, are *"driven by economies of scale"*, and that *"the services can be dynamically configured [...] and delivered on demand"* [72]. All these aspects provide major advantages to service providers and consumers. By offering services at different levels and enabling their dynamic configuration, a high level of customization of cloud-based services can be achieved. Furthermore, massive scalability allows the consideration of varying business requirements and the handling of unforeseen peak behavior. Last but not least, by aggregating cloud computing resources into large-scale resource pools, economies of scale can be realized on the provider side. That is, cost savings can be achieved by conducting the same operations more efficiently on a larger scale [85]. Cloud service providers are then able to pass on these cost savings to their customers. All these advantages make cloud computing highly attractive to the industry. Nevertheless, the characteristics of cloud computing, especially the high dynamics, scalability, and flexibility, also raise several new challenges (cf., e.g., [9, 17, 130, 197, 221]) that have been addressed in academic research since 2008. A major number of these scientific works is based on the definition by the National Institute of Standards and Technology (NIST). The thesis at hand also follows the NIST definition, which reads as follows [131]:

"Cloud computing is a model for enabling ubiquitous, convenient,
on-demand network access to a shared pool of configurable computing

resources (e.g., networks, servers, storage, applications, and services)
that can be rapidly provisioned and released with minimal management
effort or service provider interaction. This cloud model is composed of
five essential characteristics, three service models, and four deployment
models."

The NIST definition incorporates all the aspects of cloud computing mentioned above. Moreover, it also provides a further characterization of cloud computing by defining its essential characteristics, service models and deployment models, which are described in detail in the following.

On-demand self-service   According to their demand at particular timeslots, consumers are able to obtain computing capabilities, such as software, storage, or CPU time, automatically from a service provider without human interaction [45, 131]. The automated resource provisioning also enables service providers to adapt rapidly to dynamic changes, such as flash crowd effects [221].

Broad network access   Unified access to computing capabilities over the Internet permits the usage of heterogeneous clients, such as mobile phones or laptops [131, 197]. In addition, many of today's cloud providers place their data centers at different locations worldwide in order to improve network performance [221].

Resource pooling   The computing resources are aggregated to large-scale resource pools and dynamically shared among multiple consumers based on their demand. In doing so, virtual computing resources assigned to different consumers can be co-located on the same physical machine, referred to as multi-tenancy [131, 197]. In general, consumers are not aware of the exact location of their leased resources, but may specify location preferences at a higher level, e.g., country or data center [131].

Rapid elasticity   From a consumer's perspective, there seem to be unlimited resource capacities within a cloud and additional/less resources can be rapidly acquired in line with a consumer's demand by, e.g., scaling up or scaling down [45, 131]. More dimensions of scalability are typically distinguished: scale-up/-down and scale-out. While the former requires an application following a concurrent programming model and only allows the resources to be scaled-up to the resource capacities of a single machine, scale-out requires an application following a distributed programming model and allows the combination of the resources of multiple machines resulting in a single virtual machine [76].

Measured service   Resource usage is tracked by metering capabilities allowing for an automated control and optimization of resources and providing transparency for cloud providers and consumers [131]. Typically, a pay-per-use model is applied, which lowers operating costs for both, providers and consumers, but increases the complexity in controlling these operating costs from a provider's perspective [221].

The essential characteristics in the NIST definition represent generic properties of cloud-based systems. However, within a cloud-based system, the computing resources provided to consumers differ. Basically, different levels of services are offered, such as *"computing power, storage, platforms, and services"* [72], and several proposals for a universal classification of these service models have been made so far (cf., e.g., [45, 57, 131, 160, 220, 226]). Among all these proposals, the NIST definition specifies the following three service models, which are the most common. Additional service models are usually a special case of one of these.

Software as a Service   On the Software as a Service (SaaS) level, applications running on a cloud provider's infrastructure are provided to consumers. Access to these applications can be gained through either thin client interfaces (e.g., a web browser) or program interfaces. Besides being able to configure certain application settings, consumers are neither able to control the underlying cloud infrastructure, such as the network, server, or operating system, nor individual capabilities of the application [131]. Popular examples are the Customer Relationship Management software of Salesforce[1] and Google Docs[2] [197].

Platform as a Service   According to the NIST definition [131], the Platform as a Service (PaaS) level comprises capabilities to develop and deploy applications that are build *"using programming languages, libraries, services, and tools supported by the provider"*. Similar to SaaS, consumers do not have control over the underlying cloud infrastructure, but, in contrast, are able to control the deployed applications and may possibly configure settings of the hosting environment. Popular examples are Google App Engine[3] and Microsoft Azure[4] [197].

Infrastructure as a Service   The Infrastructure as a Service (IaaS) level incorporates the provisioning of fundamental computing resources, such as processing power, networks, and data storage, that can be used by consumers in order to deploy and run applications and operating systems. Again, consumers do not control the

---

[1]   http://www.salesforce.com/crm
[2]   http://www.docs.google.com
[3]   http://cloud.google.com/appengine/
[4]   http://azure.microsoft.com

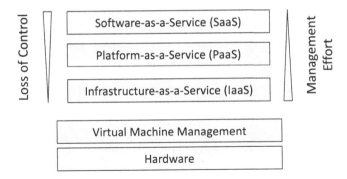

Figure 2.1: Cloud service stack and service models

underlying cloud infrastructure[5], similar to SaaS and PaaS, but are able to manage applications, operating systems, data storage, as well as selected network components, such as a host firewall [131]. Although the IaaS model provides more flexibility to consumers than PaaS, it also implies an increased management effort on the consumer side regarding, e.g., updates of the operating system. Popular examples are Amazon's Elastic Compute Cloud (EC2)[6] and Amazon's Simple Storage Service (S3)[7] [197].

The three service models form a layered model in a cloud architecture as depicted in Figure 2.1 and are located on top of a virtual machine management layer, which is responsible for the management of the virtualized computing resources above (cf. Section 2.1.2), and the physical hardware. In general, when moving from the bottom (i.e., IaaS) to the top (i.e., SaaS) of this layered model, the loss of control for consumers increases while the management effort decreases. In addition to the different service models, clouds can be further distinguished based on their ownership, target user group(s), and location (cf. [197]) resulting in the following deployment models as proposed by the NIST definition [131].

Public cloud   A cloud infrastructure that is provided to *"the general public"* and that is located on the premises of a certain cloud provider. That provider owns, manages, and operates the cloud and may be an organization from the industrial, academic, or governmental sectors, or a combination of these [131]. The economic benefit of utilizing resources from public clouds is often described as turning capital expenditure into operational expenditure [9]. However, consumers also loose fine-grained control over issues such as data, network and security concerns [221].

---

[5]   It should be noted that the term 'cloud infrastructure' in this thesis denotes the physical infrastructure of a cloud and, thus, is different from the virtual IaaS layer.

[6]   http://aws.amazon.com/ec2/

[7]   http://aws.amazon.com/s3/

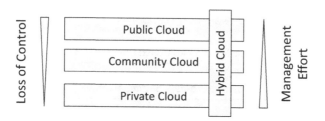

Figure 2.2: Cloud deployment models

Community cloud A cloud infrastructure that is provided exclusively to a specific community comprising consumers of different organizations sharing similar concerns. One or more organizations being part of that community, a third party, or a combination of both may be the owner, manager, and operator of that cloud and it may be located on or off the premises of the collaborating organizations [131].

Private cloud A cloud infrastructure that is provided exclusively to a single organization that may comprise multiple consumers, such as different business units. The organization itself, a third party, or a combination of both may be the owner, manager, and operator of that cloud and it may be located on or off the premises of that organization [131]. Running a private cloud offers the highest level of control over aspects such as performance, security concerns, reliability, and mission-critical tasks, but does not allow, for example, to eliminate up-front investments in contrast to public clouds [45, 221].

Hybrid cloud A cloud infrastructure that is a combination of two or more of the other deployment models. Each of the clouds being part of the hybrid cloud remains a discrete entity, although being able to move data and applications to the other clouds by applying appropriate (i.e., standardized or proprietary) technology [131]. The hybrid cloud deployment model can be beneficial in specific scenarios (cf. [45, 131, 197]). In case of a bursting scenario, for instance, a private cloud can acquire more resources from a public cloud. Also, in order to optimize resource utilization, a hybrid cloud permits keeping core business activities in a private cloud, while moving other, less critical activities into a public cloud.

Besides these four, most common deployment models, as depicted in Figure 2.2, also a fifth type, namely, a Virtual Private Cloud (VPC) is mentioned in literature. Zhang et al. [221] describe a VPC as *"a platform running on top of public clouds"* that permits own network topologies and security settings (e.g., firewall rules) to be established by exploiting virtual network technology. That is, the underlying communication network is also virtualized in addition to servers and applications. In doing so, a traditional private network infrastructure can be easily rebuild within a public cloud infrastructure while keeping the privacy of the resulting communication network.

According to Dillon et al. [45], a VPC is a mixture between a private and a public cloud. On the one hand, it utilizes resources from a public cloud provider. On the other hand, it provides a secure connection to these resources from an organization's corporate infrastructure and isolates these resources from other public cloud resources. The authors mention Amazon Virtual Private Cloud[8] as the first example for this kind of deployment model.

2.1.2 Enabling Technologies

In general, cloud computing is considered to be a paradigm (cf., e.g., [25, 72, 130, 147, 207, 218, 220, 221]) and, thus, it is not bound to a specific implementation. Nevertheless, it is based on certain technologies (cf., e.g., [25, 72, 209, 221]). Existing works often make no explicit distinction between enabling technologies and other computing paradigms that are related to cloud computing. However, since enabling technologies refer to the concrete realization of a cloud-based system and computing paradigms refer to abstract principles and certain concepts of an IT-based architecture, an explicit separation between both concerns is made in the following. While enabling technologies are described in this section, related paradigms are discussed in the subsequent Section 2.1.3. Concerning enabling technologies, the work by Erl et al. [57] contains the most comprehensive enumeration and description of these technologies.

According to Erl et al. [57], the following cloud-enabling technologies can be distinguished. The authors state that although each of these technologies existed before cloud computing gained momentum, some of them further evolved with the advent of cloud computing.

Broadband Networks and Internet Architecture   The existence of global networks, such as the Internet, enables remote provisioning of computing capabilities by cloud providers and permits ubiquitous access to these capabilities for cloud consumers [57, 131]. Hence, the quality of cloud-based systems depends highly on the performance of these networks. Therefore, enterprise consumers are faced with the decision whether to choose a private cloud deployment in their own data center and access its capabilities through the organization's own network or to choose a public, Internet-enabled cloud deployment model. In the former case, the network is usually completely managed and controlled by the respective organization. In the latter case, the cloud provider assumes these responsibilities and can provide ubiquitous access to the computing capabilities through an Internet connection (cf. Section 2.1.1). While a private cloud deployment is less affected by connectivity, bandwidth, or latency issues when accessing the computing capabilities through a corporate network, public

---

[8]   http://aws.amazon.com/vpc

cloud deployments facing these issues usually provide superior Internet connectivity at additional network usage charges [57].

Data Center Technology   Aggregating IT resources in large data centers allows power-sharing, IT resources, and IT personnel and, thus, allows for higher efficiency [57]. Typically, IT resources in a data center comprise servers, storage, networking components, and software (cf., e.g., [57, 131]), and can be physical or virtual in nature. The physical resources build the physical infrastructure of a data center, which serves as a hosting environment for virtual resources. The virtual resources represent physical resources that are virtualized in order to, e.g., facilitate corresponding management tasks, such as their allocation, operation, release, monitoring and control [57].

Virtualization Technology   Virtualization is an inherent technology of cloud-based systems and, thus, already mentioned in several definitions of cloud computing (cf., e.g., [72, 131]). The concept of virtualization allows the abstraction from the details of physical resources and the consideration of these as resource pools. In doing so, a logical view on the physical resources can be established and they can be managed as a whole. Hence, (multiple) virtual resources can be dynamically assigned to them on-demand according to particular business requirements [12, 221]. In general, different kinds of resources can be virtualized, such as servers, storage, networks, power, and software [12, 27, 57]. A virtualized server is denoted as Virtual Machine (VM) and multiple of these logical VMs can be hosted in parallel on a single physical machine [25, 221]. Major advantages of this kind of abstraction are as follows [25, 72]. First of all, virtualization permits encapsulation, so that, e.g., different operating systems can be run on different VMs residing on the same physical machine. A second major advantage is improved resource utilization, since each VM can utilize a different amount of the underlying physical resources. Finally, virtualization enables dynamic resource provisioning, which comprises the automation of activities such as starting, stopping, deploying, and migrating VMs. In general, different techniques for server virtualization exist, from which hardware-based virtualization is the most common [27]. The logical layers in case of hardware-based virtualization are depicted in Figure 2.3. An implementation of this type of virtualization is based on a so-called hypervisor. Basically, a hypervisor represents a meta operating system with minimal system requirements. It establishes a VM management layer between a host and the guest operating systems running different applications in order to distribute the physical resources among the different VMs and to coordinate their hardware access [12, 27, 57].

Web Technology   Since cloud computing is based on the existence of broadband networks, Web technology is used for implementing and managing cloud services and their functionality is exposed to consumers through Web-based interfaces [26]. Web

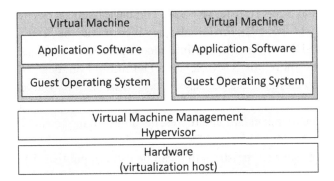

Figure 2.3: Logical layers of hardware-based virtualization (based on [12, 57])

standards encompass the Uniform Resource Locator Uniform Resource Locator (URL) to identify and locate Web-based resources, the Hypertext Transfer Protocol (HTTP) to exchange requests with a resource host, and the Hypertext Markup Language (HTML) and Extensible Markup Language (XML) to express Web-based data and metadata, respectively [57]. Besides these well-known Web technologies, a set of new, so-called Web 2.0 technologies has gained momentum. Web 2.0 enables building interactive and flexible applications based on new technologies, such as Asynchronous JavaScript and XML (AJAX), Really Simple Syndication (RSS), and well-known service technology such as Web services [26, 72]. In doing so, Web 2.0 allows the provision of Desktop-like applications over the Web. A popular example of a Web 2.0-based cloud application is Google Docs[9][26].

Multi-tenant Technology A multi-tenant application enables a user (denoted as tenant) to use the same application concurrently with multiple other users without interfering with the other users due to isolated operational environments. A dedicated instance is provided to each user with, e.g., a customized user interface, individual application logic, and own data. The users are sharing various artifacts, such as middleware and databases, while adhering to certain security levels so that tenants are not able to access private data of other users. The isolation of the operational environments allows the implementation of metering capabilities that track each tenant's usage separately and supports the scalability when the number of tenants increases. SaaS typically implements this kind of application [57].

Service Technology Clouds have adopted service technologies in order to provide a predefined Application Programming Interface (API) for using, configuring, and programming cloud services [57, 72]. These service technologies comprise Web services

---

9   https://www.google.com/intl/en/docs/about/

and Representational State Transfer (REST). The basic Web service technologies are
as follows (cf., e.g., [4, 55, 57]). First of all, they incorporate the Web Service Description Language (WSDL) to describe the interface, operations, and message types of a
Web service. Furthermore, the XML Schema Definition Language (XSD) is used to
specify the data structures of the message types within a WSDL document. Simple
Object Access Protocol (SOAP) (formerly denoted as the Simple Object Access Protocol) constitutes another standard and represents a messaging format for requests and
response messages. Finally, Universal Description, Discovery and Integration (UDDI)
is a specification for service registries that can be used to publish WSDL documents
and to query for particular Web services. Further, enhanced Web service technologies
denoted as WS-* extensions or WS-* stack exist concerning additional areas, such
as message-level security and reliable messaging (cf., e.g., [55, 57, 154]). Besides
the traditional Web service technologies, REST evolved as an alternative approach
for implementing services. REST was originally introduced as a new *"architectural
style for distributed hypermedia systems"* by Roy Thomas Fielding in his doctoral
dissertation in the year 2000 [65]. RESTful Web services are perceived to exhibit less
complexity due to the fact that they leverage core Web technologies, such as HTTP
and the Uniform Resource Identifier (URI) for global addressing [57, 154]. Erl et al.
[57] further mention service agents and service middleware in the context of service
technology. According to the authors, both can be operated in a cloud-based environment. Service agents represent active or passive event-driven programs that take
further actions, such as monitoring and reporting, based on the contents of intercepted
messages. In contrast, service middleware, such as an Enterprise Service Bus (ESB)
and an orchestration platform, is designed in order to accomplish tasks like service
brokerage and service composition.

2.1.3 Related Paradigms

The idea of providing computing resources as a utility is not new (cf. Section 2.1.1)
and several other computing paradigms (cf., e.g., [12, 25, 26, 45, 72, 130, 205, 209])
have been proposed, further approaching this vision prior to the emergence of the
cloud computing paradigm [25]. Among these paradigms, service-oriented computing
and grid computing are the most related to cloud computing and, thus, they will be
elaborated in more detail in the following.

Service-oriented Computing   The concept of delivering computing resources in
the form of different *"as a Service"* models (cf. Section 2.1) already indicates a
relationship of cloud computing to service orientation. Indeed, Service-oriented Computing (SOC), where services represent the main blocks for building applications,
can be considered to be a reference model for cloud-based systems [26]. However,
although sharing certain concepts, both paradigms differ. Therefore, a few research

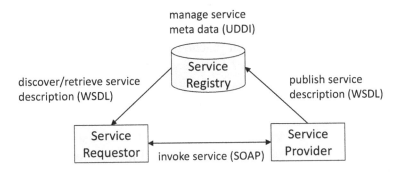

Figure 2.4: Interaction in an SOA using Web services (based on [54], p. 75)

works are discussing how cloud computing can benefit from service-oriented computing (cf. [45, 213]). The term service-oriented computing is often used synonymously
with the term 'service-oriented architecture' (SOA) [55] and SOA is also perceived as
a foundation for cloud-based systems (cf., e.g., [12, 209]). However, while service-
oriented computing comprises several basic design principles around service-oriented
solution logic, SOA represents an architectural paradigm supporting the realization
of these principles [55]. The Organization for the Advancement of Structured Information Standards (OASIS) defines SOA as *"a paradigm for organizing and utilizing
distributed capabilities that may be under the control of different ownership domains"*
and services as *"the mechanism by which needs and capabilities are brought together"*
[145]. Hence, an SOA shall facilitate the integration and orchestration of multiple
functional capabilities in the form of services from different organizations. In doing
so, SOA is not bound to a specific technology, but often implemented using Web
services (cf., e.g., [12, 55, 196, 209]). The basic interaction between organizations
following the SOA paradigm is typically represented in the form of a triangle and
depicted in Figure 2.4 assuming an implementation using Web service technology.
In detail, a service provider may advertise a service by registering a corresponding
service description in a service registry. The service can then be discovered by service
requesters searching this registry. Having retrieved the service description containing the location of the desired service, the service can then be invoked by directly
exchanging messages with the respective service provider. Basically, a service en-
capsulates a certain business logic and abstracts from the underlying implementation
by providing well-defined interfaces resulting in autonomous units (cf., e.g., [53]).
As a consequence, services can be loosely coupled in order to build larger business
processes. Thus, SOA enables the creation of flexible business process infrastructures
that can be easily adapted according to changing business requirements. Summarizing,
SOA defines a uniform architectural model for offering, discovering, and interacting
with distributed capabilities encapsulated as services and allows the creation of new

services from existing ones [145]. In comparison to SOC and SOA, cloud services also encapsulate a certain business logic as a re-usable, autonomous service, which is provided over the Web and expose their functionality through Web service technology, such as SOAP and REST (cf. Section 2.1.2). Hence, SOC and SOA are most related to the SaaS model. However, most of the current cloud applications are provided as entire (single-purpose) applications that do not require the flexibility that SOA provides (cf. [196]). Although following SOC and SOA principles is not mandatory in order to build cloud applications, SOA can serve as a blueprint, such that cloud applications can reach their full potential when being composed of loosely-coupled services (cf., e.g., [26, 196, 209]).

Grid Computing   The *grid computing paradigm* was coined in the mid 1990s by Ian Foster and others and describes a distributed computing infrastructure that provides computing power on-demand, originally intended for resource sharing among scientific collaborations [70, 72]. According to Foster et al. [71], the underlying concept aims at *"coordinated resource sharing and problem solving in dynamic, multi-institutional virtual organizations"*. A virtual organization, thereby, denotes *"individuals and/or institutions"* that adhere to clearly defined resource usage policies while sharing computing resources, such as computers, data, and software, as if these resources belong to the same organization [71, 72]. The description of the underlying concept of grid computing already reveals some characteristics shared with cloud computing. In a grid, different computing resources are also aggregated to large, logical resource pools with networked access (cf. [56]) and provided on-demand. In contrast to cloud computing, these resources generally belong to different administrative domains, which are geographically distributed and the resources are heterogeneous in capacity and dynamic so that their availability varies (cf. [72]). The architecture of a grid is based on the definition of standard protocols and the provisioning of middleware like the Globus Toolkit [69], considered to be the de facto standard implementation [72]. The middleware provides features such as load-balancing and autonomic configuration management and cloud computing is therefore perceived as a descendant of grid computing [56]. However, in comparison to cloud computing, grids have not initially been driven by commercial offers, so that grids are either build by sharing idle resources or users pay a fixed rate for each service [205]. Hence, in contrast to clouds, grids do not fully realize the idea of providing resources as a utility, similar to, e.g., electricity based on a pay-per-use model. Finally, hardware virtualization is also not part of the grid computing paradigm. As a consequence, grids do not support performance isolation, so that performance issues of one user or virtual organization can interfere with the performance of other users, which is one of the reasons that prevented grids adoption [209].

2.2 Service Level Management

2.2.1 Definition

Basically, Service Level Management (SLM) comprises specific activities of an organization with the aim to ensure an agreed level of quality for each of its provisioned IT services to service consumers [167]. In general, SLM is part of the IT governance of an organization. According to the IT Governance Institute, IT governance is the responsibility of the business management for specifying and managing structures and processes within an organization in order to align the organization's IT with the organization's strategy and objectives [100]. Hence, IT governance provides a generic framework for an organization's IT. Several concrete frameworks specifying best practices in the field of IT governance have been defined so far, among which the Information Technology Infrastructure Library (ITIL) is considered to be the de facto standard for IT service management. In ITIL, SLM is explicitly defined as a separate process of the service design phase, which encompasses the design of new services and the adaptation of existing services (cf. [19]). An official definition of SLM is provided by ITIL as follows [167]:

> *"The process responsible for negotiating achievable service level agreements and ensuring that these are met. It is responsible for ensuring that all IT service management processes, operational level agreements and underpinning contracts are appropriate for the agreed service level targets. Service level management monitors and reports on service levels, holds regular service reviews with customers, and identifies required improvements."*

It can be deduced from the ITIL definition, that two of the main activities of SLM are the negotiation and monitoring of service level agreements (SLAs), which are also the focus of the present work. Moreover, SLM aims to maintain and improve the quality of an IT service continually and, thus, also incorporates reporting on service levels, studying the generated reports with customers during service review meetings, and taking appropriate corrective or improvement actions if required (cf. [22, 167]). The reports are compiled based on measurements obtained from monitoring services and allow to assess whether the agreed service level targets have been met or not during a certain period of time. Besides SLAs, also agreements with internal and external providers have to be made in order to ensure compliance with the corresponding service level targets defined in an SLA. An internal agreement, denoted as Operational Level Agreement (OLA), are made between or within IT departments and external agreements, denoted as underpinning contracts, are made with external or third-party vendors or suppliers (cf. [22, 167]).

The generic activities performed during the lifecycle of an SLA are grouped into five different phases by Keller and Ludwig [109] as depicted in Figure 2.5. Although their

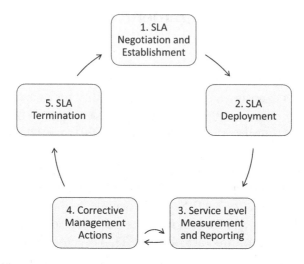

Figure 2.5: SLA lifecycle model (based on [109])

lifecycle model has been established in the context of Web services, it is applicable to IT services in general and to cloud services as well, since service technology is considered to be an enabling technology of cloud computing (cf. Section 2.1.2). The five phases according to Keller et al. [109] are described in detail in the following:

- *1. SLA Negotiation and Establishment:* An SLA is negotiated with regard to certain parameters and the resulting SLA document is made available for deployment.

- *2. SLA Deployment:* The validity of an SLA is checked, configuration information is accordingly generated, and the system configures the respective components.

- *3. Service Level Measurement and Reporting:* SLA parameters, such as availability or execution time, are computed by retrieving corresponding metrics, the measured parameters are compared against the agreed thresholds specified in the SLA, and the associated management system is notified.

- *4. Corrective Management Actions:* In case, that an SLA violation has been detected, corrective actions are executed in order to resolve the violation.

- *5. SLA Termination:* An SLA is terminated, either when certain conditions are satisfied or an expiration date has been reached as specified in the SLA.

The five phases are considered to form a loop in this thesis, since consumer requirements may change, which makes it necessary to negotiate new SLAs for a given service or service properties may change allowing to provide improved SLAs to consumers. In addition, corrective management actions performed in the fourth phase may either be successful or not. Depending on the preferences of the contractual parties, the system can proceed with service level measurement and reporting afterwards or an SLA can be terminated.

2.2.2 Service Level Agreements

As described in the previous section, SLAs are the focus of SLM in order to guarantee a certain level of quality for a given IT service. Basically, different definitions exist for the term *service level agreement*. According to Marilly et al. [128], for example, an SLA can be defined as follows:

> *"A Service Level Agreement (SLA) is a contract between Service Providers or between Service Providers and Customers that specifies, usually in measurable terms, what services the Service Provider will furnish and what penalties the Service Provider will pay if he cannot meet the committed goals."*

Hence, an SLA is a binding agreement that specifies what a service provider guarantees to deliver and can be offered to other service providers or to consumers. Furthermore, these guarantees have to be defined in such a manner that the adherence to these guarantees can be monitored later on during service usage. Therefore, the goals represented by these guarantees are usually expressed in the form of thresholds for certain parameters, so that the current values of the corresponding parameters can be determined at runtime. Often, financial penalties are imposed for the case that a service provider deviates from an agreed SLA. A more detailed definition of an SLA can be found in ITIL (e.g., [22, 167]):

> *"An agreement between an IT service provider and a customer. The SLA describes the IT service, documents service level targets, and specifies the responsibilities of the IT service provider and the customer. A single SLA may cover multiple IT services or multiple customers."*

It can already be deduced from the definition in ITIL that SLAs can be defined in different ways. Indeed, ITIL further distinguishes *customer-based SLAs* that are defined for a set of services of a certain customer and *service-based SLAs* that are defined for all customers using a specific service (cf., e.g., [19, 22]). Furthermore, ITIL mentions a combination of these two types resulting in a so-called *multi-level SLA approach*, in which elements of services that concern all customers are defined in a *corporate-level SLA*. Besides these different types of SLAs, the definition in ITIL also already indicates that an SLA consists of different parts incorporating the service itself, service level targets as well as responsibilities of the contracting parties. Among these parts, the part addressing service level targets, also often referred to as service level objectives, is denoted as Service Level Specification (SLS). According to Marilly et al. [128], the SLS contains metrics and corresponding thresholds to be guaranteed for technical parameters, such as network availability, latency, or throughput, and specifies according measurement methods, periods, and provided reports. The authors further mention the possibility to define an SLS template and to instantiate this template for a specific customer by setting the desired value for each threshold. Formal SLA specification languages are suitable for this purpose. In the field of Web services, different standards of such a formal language evolved for specifying SLAs in a machine-readable format as a prerequisite towards automated SLA management. The most popular ones are WSLA [109] developed by IBM and WS-Agreement [8] specified by the Open Grid Forum. In the field of cloud computing, automated SLA management is still an open issue (cf. Section 1.1). However, several approaches in research exist exploring the application of these Web service-related standards to cloud computing, for example, how WSLA can be adapted to a cloud computing context (cf. [152]).

2.2.3 Quality of Service

Service level targets specified within an SLA express some guarantees given by a service provider and usually concern technical, i.e., non-functional properties of a particular service (cf. Section 2.2.2). Hence, SLAs assure that a service exhibits a certain overall quality, also often referred to as Quality of Service (QoS). However, no single, common definition exists for the term QoS in general. Furthermore, QoS is not necessarily bound to software-based services and existing definitions mainly differ with respect to the considered application area. A generic definition of QoS in the field of communication networks is given by Schmitt et al. in [173]:

> *"QoS is the well-defined and controllable behavior of a system with respect to quantitative parameters."*

The definition by Schmitt et al. indicates that QoS goes beyond a set of well-defined quantitative parameters of a service. Moreover, these parameters can be controlled in such a manner that they lead to a desired behavior of a system. Another definition for QoS by the International Telecommunication Union (ITU) that has also been published in a standard provided by the International Organization for Standardization (ISO) is given as follows [101]:

> *"A set of quality requirements on the collective behavior of one or more objects. Quality of service may be specified in a contract or measured and reported after the event. The quality of service may be parameterized."*

The aforementioned definition reveals the relation of QoS to service quality. Following that definition, QoS implies a particular behavior of certain objects under consideration, similar to the definition by Schmitt et al., thereby fulfilling specific quality expectations. Moreover, QoS, and accordingly the desired behavior, can be described by the use of parameters, in terms of quality attributes expressing certain quality requirements. These quality attributes can be subject of a contract, i.e., part of an SLA, and can be monitored at runtime. Since the perception of QoS highly varies depending on the subject under consideration, several different QoS attributes have been considered in different application areas, such as communication networks (cf., e.g., [81]), multimedia (cf., e.g., [198, 199]), peer-to-peer systems (cf., e.g., [34, 92, 200]), and Web services (cf., e.g., [15, 158]). Since Web services are an enabling technology for cloud computing (cf. Section 2.1.2) and also realize the concept of Internet-based service delivery, the non-functional properties for Web services also apply to cloud-based services. However, there are some attributes that are either new or of major importance in the field of cloud computing. Thus, the Service Measurement Index (SMI) has been proposed by the Cloud Services Measurement Initiative Consortium in order to provide a set of standardized key performance indicators for comparing cloud-based services with respect to their business and technical requirements [42]. Besides non-functional properties concerning a service, the SMI also contains functional properties as well as attributes that apply to the cloud service provider. Therefore, a model for cloud-based services focusing only on non-functional properties of a service is presented in the following (cf. [89]). The model adapts the classification of non-functional properties for Web services by Berbner [15] and incorporates non-functional attributes of the SMI framework [42]. The resulting model of non-functional properties of cloud-based services is depicted in Figure 2.6 and the different properties will be elaborated on in more detail in the following.

Performance When it comes to performance in the context of computer systems, a variety of metrics exists (cf., e.g., [103]). In the field of Web services, performance is expressed by the speed in order to complete a service request [157]. Usually, that speed is represented in terms of the amount of time required from sending a request until receiving the response, denoted as *response time*, and the number of successful requests within a certain time interval, denoted as *throughput* (cf., e.g., [132, 157]). Response time, in turn, can be further split into *execution time* and *latency* (cf., e.g., [133]). While execution time encompasses the time for processing a request on the server side, latency comprises the time required for a one-way delivery of a message, i.e., a request or response, over the network (cf., e.g., [133, 150, 157]).

Assurance This category incorporates attributes that express the degree to which a service will behave as expected [42]. Concerning non-functional properties, *availability*, *reliability*, and *robustness* are usually considered (cf. e.g., [42, 80, 150, 157]).

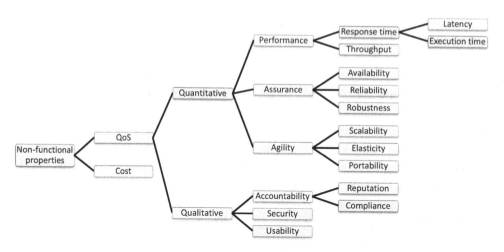

Figure 2.6: Non-functional properties of cloud-based services (based on [15, 42, 89])

Availability represents the probability that a service is up and running and can serve service requests. Basically, different metrics exist to express availability, such as the percentage of uptime or mean uptime (cf., e.g., [74, 80, 103, 132]). Reliability indicates, whether a service is able to work correctly over a certain time interval. Hence, it is very much related to availability and can be measured by the number of failures over a certain period of time, the probability of failures, or the mean time between or to failures (cf., e.g., [80, 103, 157]). Robustness represents the ability of a service to continue working correctly under unforeseen circumstances. Such circumstances may occur, for example, due to unexpected input that is invalid, incomplete or interferes with other input [157]. In the field of computing, no common metric for robustness exists and each work defines its own measure focusing on different aspects [219]. In the present work, the terms robustness and resiliency are used interchangeably.

Agility   In contrast to former computing paradigms, cloud computing provides a very high level of flexibility allowing for dynamic resource provisioning according to a consumer's demand (cf. Section 2.1.1). In this regard, the well-known attribute *scalability* and the two new attributes *elasticity* and *portability* are mentioned in the literature and characterize this agile behavior. Basically, all these attributes are indicators for the ability of a service to adjust quickly to changing user requirements with minimal disruption [42]. Scalability expresses, whether a service is able to sustain increasing workloads while maintaining adequate performance at an acceptable cost in terms of, e.g., response time or resource consumption [18, 94]. Further dimensions of scalability, namely scale-up/-down and scale-out, are distinguished in the context of cloud computing (cf. Section 2.1.1). Elasticity represents the degree to which a service is able to adapt to changing workloads by automatically adding or removing resources that closely match the consumers' demand at each point in time [94]. Hence, elasticity is closely related to scalability. In order to allow for scalability, additional resources are occupied or have to be provisioned and elasticity represents the ability to determine and to switch to that required amount of resources in an automated manner. Portability indicates, whether a service can be easily moved to a different cloud provider [42]. In cloud computing, the foundation for portability is established by the use of virtualization technology. However, while the option of moving VMs within a cloud is usually given, a successful migration to another cloud provider depends highly on the interoperability between the two clouds and still represents an obstacle in today's cloud environments (cf. [123, 156]). Nevertheless, several activities[10] exist, which address the development of cloud standards.

Accountability   Within the SMI framework, this category addresses properties concerning the cloud service provider (cf. [42]). Nevertheless, the two attributes *reputation* (in the SMI framework denoted as "ease of doing business" expressing client satisfaction) and *compliance* can also be applied to a cloud service itself. In this regard, reputation is a measure of collective trustworthiness in a community based on the individual referrals or ratings derived from personal experience or second hand referrals of the community members [108]. Hence, reputation reflects the degree of satisfaction of all consumers with a particular cloud service and their strength to recommend this service. Compliance indicates the adherence to legal and regulatory requirements, such as standards, policies, processes, and established SLAs (cf., e.g., [42, 80, 150]). It is obvious, that the level of compliance may also have an influence on the reputation.

Security   Concerns related to security are considered to be major obstacles in cloud adoption (cf., e.g., [64]). This is mainly due to the fact that the utilization of cloud-based services is accompanied with a shift of responsibility to the cloud provider. Furthermore, cloud computing enables the portability of cloud-based services as well as related data to other locations. In this regard, virtualization has a major impact on cloud security. First of all, VMs are stored as a file, so that they could be moved to a different host or network without the knowledge of a consumer. Second, multiple VMs can be run on the same host, so that an attacker could gain access to other VMs on that machine [184, 203]. Solutions for cloud security basically aim to address concerns, such as access control, confidentiality, data integrity, as well as threat and vulnerability management (cf., e.g., [42, 80, 84, 132, 150]).

Usability   This category represents how easy it is to use a service. It comprises attributes, such as accessibility indicating whether a service can be used by consumers

---

10   An overview of the activities can be obtained from `http://cloud-standards.org/`.

with disabilities, installability expressing the effort to get a service ready for use, and learnability representing the effort to learn how to use a service [42].

Cost   In contrast to all other aforementioned attributes, cost is not considered to be a QoS attribute (cf., e.g., [80]). Cost further represents a separate important non-functional property when comparing different cloud-based services. In this regard, cost shares a competitive relationship with QoS in terms of customer or provider utility, since a higher quality is usually associated with a higher price, and vice versa. In general, several options for pricing in cloud computing are possible. Among them, pay-as-you-go and subscription pricing are the most widespread models in cloud computing today [120].

The model in Figure 2.6 distinguishes qualitative and quantitative non-functional attributes of cloud-based services. While the latter can be expressed using numerical values, the former are usually described in terms of existing or non-existing properties, unless a quantification of the corresponding properties is conducted. However, there currently exists no commonly accepted quantification method for the qualitative attributes. Hence, only quantitative non-functional properties and cost are considered in the present work. Numerical values are required in order to be able to compare the non-functional attributes of different services against each other when negotiating SLAs and to detect SLA violations later on in terms of deviations from the negotiated thresholds.

In the field of communication networks, the concept of QoS evolved, since the prevailing service in the Internet has been, and still is, *best effort*. That means that, all packets are treated equally without providing any resource guarantees, which is critical for applications that require a minimum amount of resources in order to operate effectively, such as video conferencing or Internet telephony [212]. In addition, the applications provided over the Internet ranging from simple mail services to business-critical, transaction-based SAP systems highly differ in their requirements with respect to the underlying network [173]. In order to enable QoS in the Internet, different architectures and mechanisms allowing for resource assurance and provisioning of different levels of service according to customer requirements have been developed [212]. Ferguson and Huston [63] point out that such mechanisms allowing to treat one customer's traffic differently than another customer's, can also provide economic advantages, which can be exploited by developing according economic models. The same applies for the provisioning of customized quality guarantees in terms of SLAs for cloud-based services (cf. Section 1.1).

2.3 Automated Electronic Negotiations

Negotiations are generally conducted in case of conflicting interests. In cloud computing, conflicting interests occur between consumers and providers, since consumers want to obtain cloud services that exhibit a certain level of quality at low costs, while providers aim to maximize their profit [185]. To date, dynamic negotiations of SLAs are not supported or only offered with restrictions by today's cloud providers [25]. However, automated negotiations have been considered in several research works in different areas, such as service-oriented computing (e.g., [43, 143, 169]), grid computing (e.g., [23, 121, 206]), and cloud computing (e.g., [6, 25, 216]), all envisioning market-based service provisioning.

2.3.1 Negotiation Mechanisms

Following other research works as mentioned above, an automation of negotiations can be realized by applying negotiation mechanisms. Such a negotiation mechanism usually comprises a negotiation protocol and negotiation strategies of the negotiating parties. Basically, a negotiation protocol specifies the rules for interaction, i.e., the types of participants, negotiation states, events changing states, and actions that are valid in particular states [104]. A selection of commonly-used negotiation protocols in the field of automated electronic negotiations (cf., e.g., [3, 43, 46, 117, 121, 161, 223, 225]) is depicted in Figure 2.7 and described in the following.

Take It Or Leave It   This is a very simple negotiation protocol over a single round. One party proposes an offer with a fixed content and the other party can accept it or not [104].

Alternate Offers   This is a multi-round negotiation protocol proposed by Rubinstein [166]. The parties alternate in making offers and counter-offers until the parties come to an agreement or decide to break off negotiations. This protocol serves as a foundation for many other works (e.g., [117, 190, 216]).

Extended Contract Net Protocol   The Contract Net Protocol (CNP) as proposed by Smith [193] was originally designed for task distribution. Using this protocol, a central node specifies a task and offers the task to all contractor nodes in a system. The contractor nodes then respond with an offer and the central node assigns the task to the contractor node with the best offer. In contrast, the extended CNP, also being used in several research works (e.g., [3, 43]), combines a multi-round alternate-offer phase with a two-phase commit phase, so that proposals are initially accepted preliminarily, and then have to be finally accepted in order to reach an agreement.

Besides negotiation protocols, negotiation strategies define the sequence of actions planned to make during a negotiation [126]. Hence, negotiation strategies represent the decision models of the negotiating parties and are based on their objectives, their method to valuate proposals, and their tactics applied during negotiation. Usually, the negotiating parties' objective is to reach an agreement while maximizing their individual utility. Thereby, their reserve utility defines the lowest utility level, below which they are not willing to continue to negotiate. Tactics define how an offer is generated for a single issue based on a particular criterion and the tactics for all issues are combined to form a strategy [58]. In the present work, we use the terms 'tactic' and 'strategy' interchangeably, if a strategy only comprises a single tactic. Three different types of tactics are usually distinguished: *time-dependent tactics*, in which the negotiating parties have (individual) time limits and make concessions during negotiation based on that deadlines; *resource-dependent tactics*, in which negotiating parties also make concessions depending on the remaining amount of available resources; and *behavior-dependent tactics*, in which a negotiating party is not under pressure and imitates the tactics of its opponent in order to prevent being

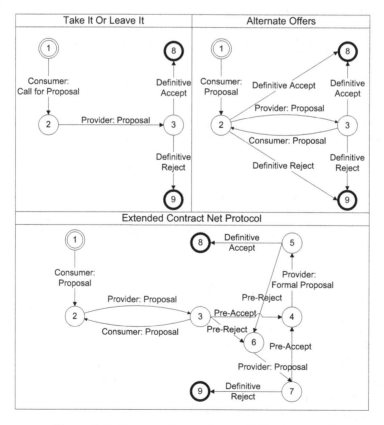

Figure 2.7: Commonly-used negotiation protocols

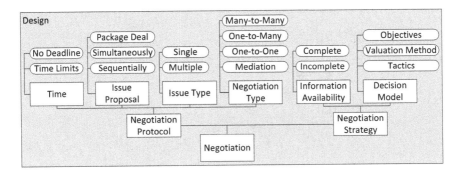

Figure 2.8: Aspects of negotiation design

exploited [58]. Such types of tactics are applied in case of self-interested, competitive parties negotiating without any information on their opponents' preferences while also keeping their preferences private. However, the negotiating parties may also entrust the task of determining an agreement to a third-party mediator, which usually obtains a part of their private information for that purpose (e.g., [143]). In case of a complete information setting, a mediator is able to determine an optimal solution. Hence, the quality of the negotiation outcome also depends on the amount of information that is available. A mediator-based negotiation is only one of the possible negotiation types. Depending on the number of participating parties, one-to-one (so-called bilateral), one-to-many, and many-to-many negotiations are typically distinguished, where the last two types can also be arranged as concurrent negotiations in a bilateral manner [126]. Negotiations can also be distinguished concerning the number of negotiated issues. Basically, a negotiation can concern single or multiple parameters (so-called issues), where the latter can be either negotiated sequentially, simultaneously, but independently of each other, or as a package deal considered as a bundle [62]. The aforementioned aspects of negotiation design are summarized in Figure 2.8.

2.3.2 Utility Theory and Pareto-Efficiency

During a negotiation, the negotiating parties have to decide whether a received proposal is acceptable to them or not. Furthermore, in case of multiple proposals, when negotiating over several rounds and/or with multiple participants, the negotiating parties must be aware of the conditions under which a certain proposal is preferred over the others. For this purpose, each negotiating party has its individual valuation method (cf. Section 2.3). Usually, utility functions, which assign a numerical value to each proposal, thereby expressing a user's utility, are applied as valuation method (cf., e.g., [59, 118, 121, 143, 168, 190, 195, 217, 222, 224]). In doing so, the concept of utility is used when comparing several alternatives in order to determine the level of satisfaction, denoted as utility, provided by each alternative [202]. Nevertheless,

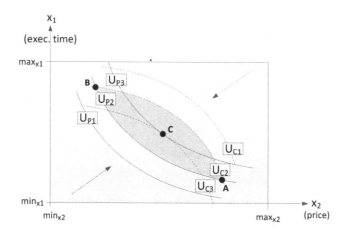

Figure 2.9: Pareto-efficient solutions and room for improvement

negotiations can also be conducted without having explicit utility functions. According to Chalamish and Kraus [30], the minimal requirement on a suitable valuation method is to express a user's preferences in such a manner that a party is able to compare and rank alternatives. However, the authors state that the advantage of using utility functions is that exact numerical values are associated with each result, so that they also indicate to which extent a certain result is preferred over another.

When negotiations are conducted over multiple issues, trade-offs are possible between the different issues. By making a trade-off, the value of a certain attribute is decreased while the value of another attribute is increased, so that the overall utility for one or both negotiating parties increases [59]. As a consequence, several offers with different attribute values can be composed that exhibit the same utility from a proposing party's point of view, but provide different levels of utility to the opponent. In microeconomics, this situation can be expressed by using indifference curves. Basically, an indifference curve expresses the preferences of a certain party and represents different combinations of attribute values where each combination provides the same level of utility to that party (cf., e.g., [214]). In this regard, the Marginal Rate of Substitution (MRS) mathematically describes the exchange ratio of the attributes. In detail, at a given point of an indifference curve, the absolute value of the slope of the curve corresponds to the MRS (cf., e.g., [214]). Now, in order to compare different solutions against each other, the notion of Pareto efficiency is usually applied. Basically, a solution is denoted as Pareto-optimal or Pareto-efficient, if there is no other solution that makes a party better off without making another party worse off (cf., e.g., [46, 126, 214]. In order to determine such efficient solutions, intersection points of the negotiating parties' indifference curves can be analyzed. This demands convex indifference curves, which are usually assumed (cf., e.g., [214]). Such a situation is illustrated in Figure 2.9, in which the solid and dashed lines represent the indifference curves of the provider and consumer, respectively. Each indifference curve thereby expresses a certain level of utility provided to the consumer (i.e., U_{Ci}) or to the provider (i.e., U_{Pi}). Assuming, for example, that a consumer negotiates with a provider over the two attributes execution time as x_1 and price as x_2 of a given service. In that case, proposals on lower indifference curves (i.e., a lower execution time and a lower price) would be more beneficial from a consumer's perspective and proposals on higher indifference curves (i.e., a higher execution time and a higher price) would be preferred from the provider. Hence, both parties have to make concessions in order to reach an agreement. Although, the solution points A and B are intersection points of a consumer's and provider's indifference curve, they do not represent an efficient solution. When moving from these points to other intersection points within the dark gray area, improvements are still possible for the consumer and provider. Solely in tangent points of the indifference curves, such as solution point C, no further improvement can be made, so that tangent points represent Pareto-efficient solutions (cf., e.g., [214]).

2.4 Monitoring

Besides the negotiation of SLAs, holistic SLM also incorporates measuring the values of the SLA parameters at runtime in order to assess whether a provider adheres to the agreed thresholds as specified within an SLA or not (cf. Section 2.2). The objectives and principles related to the corresponding task of service monitoring are explained in detail in the following. Prior to that, a definition of the term *monitoring* is applied.

2.4.1 Definition

As with the term QoS, no single, common definition of the term monitoring exists. However, there are certain activities that most of the existing definitions have in common. In the field of distributed systems, Dodd and Ravishankar [47], for instance, define monitoring *"as the measurement, collection, and processing of information about the execution of tasks in a computer system"*. Hence, monitoring deals with the observation and analysis of certain activities in a system. A more detailed definition concerning monitoring for performance analysis in computer systems is provided by Jain. According to Jain [103], monitoring is a key activity in performance measurements and monitors, that are applied for this purpose, can be defined as follows:

> *"A monitor is a tool used to observe the activities on a system. In general, monitors observe the performance of systems, collect performance statistics, analyze the data, and display the results. Some also identify problem areas and suggest remedies."*

It can be deduced from the definition by Jain, that the activities related to monitoring may also incorporate the presentation of results, the detection of problems, as well as the proposal of appropriate countermeasures. An even broader definition is given by Brown [24] in the context of business process monitoring in SOAs. Brown considers the following three activities as essential when it comes to monitoring in general: gathering data, identifying deviations from benchmark standards, and initiating a response in case of a deviation. When comparing the aforementioned definitions against the SLA lifecycle model (cf. Section 2.2), the term *monitoring* corresponds to at least the service level measurement and reporting phase and also incorporates the phase of corrective management actions in the definitions presented by Jain and Brown. However, while the former phase focuses on observing and assessing service levels, the latter already considers control actions and is therefore not addressed by several definitions. In the present work, we also concentrate on monitoring activities related to the first phase and follow the definition by Molina-Jimenez et al. [135]:

> *"Monitoring of contractual SLAs involves collection of statistical metrics about the performance of a service to evaluate whether the provider is delivering the level of QoS stipulated in a contract signed between the provider and the consumer."*

The definition by Molina-Jimenez et al. specifies the data to be collected in more detail as *"statistical metrics about the performance of a service"*. These metrics typically correspond to certain QoS parameters of a given service. In general, the QoS parameters to be monitored differ depending on the application area and the object under investigation as outlined in the next section.

2.4.2 Monitoring Objectives in Cloud Computing

As already mentioned in the previous section, monitoring activities provide particular information about certain activities in a system and, thus, are a prerequisite for certain management tasks. In cloud computing, monitoring is conducted for several reasons in different areas as outlined in the following [1, 60]:

Capacity and resource management   Cloud services require at least a certain amount of resources in order to work properly. Moreover, in order to provide some guarantees on the performance of services in terms of SLAs, appropriate capacity and resource planning is required [91, 180]. In this regard, monitoring the relevant parameters at runtime enables prediction of the need for additional resources or to determine wasted resources [60]. Metrics relevant in this area may incorporate the current utilization of memory, CPU, and storage.

SLA management Measuring QoS parameters during the lifecycle of an SLA is necessary for a cloud provider in order to assure compliance with the negotiated thresholds (cf. Sections 2.2.1 and 2.4.1). Furthermore, QoS assurance is essential for customer satisfaction and business continuity [60]. QoS parameters of cloud services are listed in Section 2.2.3.

Accounting and billing Measured service as one of the essential characteristics of cloud-based services (cf. Section 2.1.1) already indicates the need for metering capabilities that allow to track cloud usage and to design specific pricing models [1, 60]. In this regard, monitoring provides the means to capture the resource consumption of virtual resources and to measure specific properties of an application, such as used bandwidth and compute hours [49].

Fault and performance management Due to the high complexity of a cloud infrastructure comprising several layers and components, the detection of faults or performance issues and their root cause is a big issue [1]. A reliable and timely monitoring system not only enables cloud providers to locate faults and performance issues inside their infrastructure, but also allows customers to determine whether a failure or performance concern is caused by the cloud provider, the network, or the application itself [162]. Common metrics comprise the current load of a system and the availability of its components.

Security management Security is still considered to be one of the major obstacles in cloud adoption (cf. Section 2.2.3, [1]). Therefore, monitoring is required in order to support cloud security management by, e.g., detecting security breaches [60].

2.4.3 General Monitoring Principles

Besides the requirements derived from the application area, the design of monitoring systems also depends on the object under investigation. Based on the characteristics of the object to be observed, the following questions have to be answered in general [135]:

1. Should the collection of metrics happen in an active or passive manner?

2. From what points in the system should the metrics be collected?

3. Who should collect the metrics?

4. What information should be gained based on the collected metrics?

Concerning the first question, an active collection of metrics implies intrusive monitoring, while a passive collection allows for non-intrusive monitoring (cf., e.g. [140]).

This is due to the fact that active measurements are conducted by, e.g., actively sending synthetic requests to a component in order to gather information (also denoted as probing), and passive measurements are performed by, e.g., observing already existing messages exchanged in a system (cf., [135]).

The second question deals with monitor placement, i.e., the number of monitors to be used as well as their location. Basically, the monitor location is closely related to the location where the object under investigation resides, e.g., whether a monitor should be placed within the network in order to conduct network monitoring, and the perspective from which the object should be observed, e.g., from the provider's or the consumer's side. Regarding the number of utilized monitors, three approaches can be distinguished in general [24]: Monitoring can be either conducted at one point or at multiple points with or without correlation. While more information may be gathered when monitoring at multiple points, the monitoring tasks must be synchronized in order to achieve a reference to time.

The third question depends on who is interested in, or responsible for collecting the data and who has the expertise in collecting the data or access to the observed objects. Furthermore, for the case that data collection is performed by a third-party, the third question also depends on whether to trust that party or not.

Finally, concerning the fourth question, the information that can be obtained based on the collected data mainly results from the design of the monitoring system itself and from an appropriate elicitation of the relationships between collected metrics.

3 Related Work

As already mentioned in Section 1.3, the research goals of this work comprise a negotiation mechanism that allows achieving Pareto-efficient outcomes in concurrent multiple-issue negotiations despite incomplete knowledge (*CSLAB-Neg.KOM*), an approach for reliable consumer side availability monitoring (*CSLAB-Mon.KOM*), and different strategies for reliable monitor placement (*CSLAB-Loc.KOM*). This chapter presents and discusses related work and points out the drawbacks and differences to the contributions of the present work.

3.1 Pareto-Efficient Negotiations

This section describes approaches related to our contribution *CSLAB-Neg.KOM*. In general, different approaches concerning concurrent negotiations with multiple providers or negotiations over multiple issues have been proposed so far in different fields of research, such as multi-agent systems, internet-based services and cloud computing, and are discussed in the following. Furthermore, we provide an overview on related negotiation approaches, which aim to improve the negotiation outcome.

Concurrent and Multiple-Issue Negotiations   Several related approaches exist dealing with concurrent negotiations, in which one agent negotiates in parallel with multiple other agents. For example, Aknine et al. [3] and Dang and Huhns [43] present approaches for concurrent negotiations based on extensions of the contract net protocol (cf. Section 2.3.1). However, they are focusing only on protocol design in their approach. Concerning negotiation strategies, different approaches mostly based on time-dependent strategies (cf. Section 2.3.1) have been proposed so far. Wu et al. [216], for example, present a negotiation framework for one-to-many negotiations of SaaS services and apply time-dependent strategies. A SaaS broker negotiates concurrently with multiple providers considering time and market constraints. The authors propose two broker heuristics: either they minimize costs or maximize QoS values in terms of a customer satisfaction level. Hence, no total utility is considered. In [190], Sim proposes an agent-based economic model for resource sharing among different clouds. Concerning consumer-to-cloud interactions, he introduces a novel time-dependent negotiation strategy with adaptive concession rates and minimally sufficient concessions. Price proposals are exchanged in an alternate manner. In contrast to the present work, other non-functional parameters are not considered.

Mediator-based approaches   Since it is very challenging for the negotiating participants to reach an agreement when negotiating in a distributed manner without
knowing the opponents' preferences, some approaches introduce a so-called mediator,
which guides the process of decision making. The major drawback of mediator-based
approaches is that private information is (partly) disclosed to the mediator. In their
work in [143], Di Nitto et al. make use of such a mediator. The mediator issues proposals to the negotiating participants based on an optimization algorithm in order to
support the convergence of the offers. However, no protocol is specified for message
exchange. Chalamish and Kraus [30] also propose an automated mediator that elicits
the preferences of the negotiating parties and tries to determine the fairest agreement
among the set of proposed offers. However, the mediator component only attempts
to propose Pareto-optimal agreements based on its estimations, since it has no exact
numerical valuation of possible outcomes. Lai et al. [117, 118] propose a mediating
procedure, in which a mediator decomposes the negotiation space into a set of negotiation baselines. During each iteration, the mediator then explores the preferences of
the negotiating parties in order to find Pareto-optimal enhancements. Again, private
information is disclosed to a third party.

Trade-Offs using Similarity Criteria   When negotiating over multiple issues,
trade-offs are possible. Basically, a trade-off means that the values of two issues are
changed in such a way that the corresponding utility value of one issue is decreased
while the utility value of another issue is increased. In doing so, the total utility obtained
by that offer should not change compared to that obtained by the previous offer from a
proposer's point of view, but should increase for the opponent (cf. [59, 224]). Faratin
et al. [59] propose a meta-strategy to make issue trade-offs using similarity criteria.
Following the trade-off strategy, an agent selects that proposal as the next offer
from its indifference curve (cf. Section 2.3.2) that maximizes the similarity to the
opponent's last proposal. The algorithm is based on assumptions about the weights of
the opponent, hence assumes partial knowledge regarding the opponent's preferences.
Yan et al. [217] propose a trade-off algorithm for negotiating individual SLAs for
the services in a service composition. The authors also apply the concept of fuzzy
similarity [59] in order to increase the chance that a proposal gets accepted. They
make use of a combined concession and trade-off strategy. Pareto-efficient solutions
are not considered. In [195], Son and Sim propose an adaptive trade-off algorithm,
in which agents can propose a set of proposals concurrently exhibiting different
parameters while providing the same total utility. The number of concurrent proposals
is determined according to the difference between the current expected utility and the
utility obtained from the opponent's current best offer. Trade-offs are generated by
applying the concept of fuzzy similarity to time slot values and by randomly generating
the remaining attribute values. Again, Pareto-efficient outcomes are not considered.
In [224] and [225], Zheng et al. also propose a trade-off approach for cloud service

negotiation and compare it with a concession-based approach. The results of their evaluation show that concession-based approaches outperform trade-off approaches in terms of success rate, but that trade-off approaches outperform concession-based approaches in terms of individual utility. For their trade-off approach, they also assume knowledge regarding the opponent's preferences. A two-phase negotiation approach is proposed by Lang [121]. In the first phase, agents alternate in making proposals in order to obtain a preliminary contract, while the second phase aims at finding trade-offs that lead to joint utility gains. For this purpose, the agents randomly modify the contract using a Gaussian distribution. Hence, no guided trade-off generation occurs, in contrast to the approach proposed in this thesis.

Shortest Distance Some approaches also propose shortest-distance mechanisms, in which agents make their next proposal based on that offer on their current utility curve that has the shortest distance (in terms of Euclidean distance) to the opponent's best offer in the previous round. In contrast to similarity-based measures, these approaches do not require any private information from the negotiating parties. For example, Somefun et al. [46, 194] apply a short-distance-based measure in a specific bargaining scenario over a two-part tariff comprising a fixed and a variable component. They propose two Pareto-search mechanisms, the orthogonal and the orthogonal-DF strategy, combined with a concession strategy to approximate Pareto-efficient outcomes. For the second strategy, they additionally use a local search algorithm, the derivative follower with adaptive step size, to speed up the convergence process. However, the authors only consider two issues in their approach. Lai et al. [117, 118] propose a mechanism, in which agents also choose the offer with the shortest distance as seed offer and concurrently propose a certain number of additional proposals from their utility curve that reside in the neighborhood of their seed offer. However, the authors state that choosing the shortest distance proposal may not necessarily lead to a Pareto-optimal solution. In [223], Zheng et al. explore the alternating projection method, in which agents alternate in choosing the shortest-distance proposal in conjunction with concession strategies (as proposed in, e.g., [117]) in bilateral negotiations and extend their approach for multilateral negotiations in [222]. They prove that by using such a strategy, convergence to an agreement in finite time is guaranteed and a result close to the Nash bargaining solution can be obtained [138]. However, although the solution is close the Nash bargaining solution, it could still be improved. The authors themselves raise the question, whether a better agreement could be obtained by incorporating learning strategies. Furthermore, the authors consider bilateral negotiations and a number of 200 rounds as deadline for every agent in each experiment of their simulation. In contrast, we are investigating one-to-many negotiations and harder negotiation deadlines differing for each agent.

MRS-based Multiple-issue negotiation in general is also addressed by Saha in [168], who proposes a two-phase negotiation protocol for bilateral negotiations. The protocol consists of an allocation and a reallocation phase. In the allocation phase, the agents propose concurrently their desired share for a specific issue, i.e., an issue-by-issue negotiation is conducted. If they propose on different issues, they receive the whole share on that issue, otherwise, the total share will be proportionally divided according to the agent's proposed share. Negotiated issues will be removed. In the reallocation phase, shares of an issue are exchanged in order to improve both agent's utility. An exchange offer contains the amount of share an agent is willing to exchange for one unit of another issue as well as the maximum amount that an agent is willing to share. Thus, an agent directly reveals its MRS (cf. Section 2.3.2) and volume preferences. However, the author does not consider corresponding strategies that can be used in conjunction with the protocol. Furthermore, the strategic behavior of agents is very limited in the allocation phase due to the case of direct assignments of shares. In their extend work in [169], Saha and Sen propose three protocols based on their former work. Concerning the first protocol, agents reach Pareto-optimal solutions if they have identical ordinal preferences and reveal their partial cardinal preferences. Using the second protocol, agents obtain near Pareto-optimal agreements while revealing ordinal preferences. The third protocol combines both protocols. Again, agents have to disclose private information.

Table 3.1 summarizes the related approaches as discussed before. In the table, the following columns represent the criteria used to compare the related work against our proposed approach CSLAB-Neg.KOM.

- *Multiple Issues:* specifies whether the considered approach is able to cope with multiple issues that are negotiated concurrently

- *Concurrency:* indicates whether an approach is able to negotiate concurrently with multiple providers

- *Privacy:* states whether negotiations are conducted without disclosing private information

- *Pareto-Efficiency:* points out whether a related work aims at achieving Pareto-efficient outcomes

- *Trade-Off-Method:* describes whether trade-offs between multiple issues are considered and which method is used to determine the attribute values

- *Protocol:* specifies the protocol(s) that are applied in the related work

- *Strategies:* states which sorts of strategies are utilized by an approach

Table 3.1: Overview of related negotiation approaches

Publication	Multiple Issues	Concurrency	Privacy	Pareto-Efficiency	Trade-Off-Method	Protocol	Strategies
CSLAB-Neg.KOM	×	×	×	×	MRS-based	Extended Alternate Offers	Concessions + Trade-offs
Aknine et al. [3]	–	×	×	–		Extended CNP	–
Dang & Huhns [43]	×	×	×	–		Extended CNP	–
Sim [190]	–	×	×	–		Alternate Offers	Minimum Concessions
Wu et al. [216]	×	×	×	–		Alternate Offers	Concessions
Di Nitto et al. [143]	×	–	–	–		–	Optimization
Chalamish & Kraus [30]	×	–	–	×		Mediated Exchange	Issue and Value Ranking
Lai et al. [117, 118]	×	–	×	×	–	Mediated Exchange	Negotiation Baselines
Faratin et al. [59]	×	–	–	–	Similarity Criteria + Local Search	–	Trade-offs *vs.* Concessions
Son & Sim [195]	×	–	×	–	Similarity Criteria	Alternate Offers	Concessions + Trade-offs
Yan et al. [217]	×	×	×	–	Similarity Criteria	Iterated CNP	Concessions + Trade-offs
X. Zheng et al. [224, 225]	×	–	–	–	Predefined Factor	Alternate Offers	Trade-offs *vs.* Concessions
Lang [121]	×	–	×	×	Random	Alternate Offers	Concessions + Trade-offs
Lai et al. [117]	×	–	×	×	Shortest Distance + Random	Alternate Offers	Concessions + Trade-offs
Somefun et al. [46, 194]	×	–	×	×	Shortest Distance + Local Search	Alternate Offers	Concessions + Trade-offs
R. Zheng et al. [222, 223]	×	–	×	×	Shortest Distance	Alternate Offers	Concessions + Trade-offs
Saha et al. [168, 169]	×	–	–	×	MRS-based	POSE, EA, E-POSE	Issue Shares + Trade-offs

CSLAB-Neg.KOM It can be deduced from Table 3.1 that most of the related approaches solely focus on protocol design for negotiating concurrently with multiple opponents (e.g., [3, 43]). Other approaches solely propose new negotiation strategies for multiple-issue negotiations under, e.g., time and market constraints, while aiming to minimize cost, concession amounts or the distance to the desired quality values (e.g., [190, 216]). However, rational agents in a business context will strive for Pareto-efficient (cf. Section 1.3). However, existing approaches aiming to achieve Pareto-efficient outcomes either represent mediator-based approaches, in which the negotiating parties (partially) have to disclose private information to this entity (e.g., [30, 117, 118, 143]) or constitute bilateral negotiations based on shortest distance-based mechanisms, in which the strategic behavior of the negotiating parties is very limited (e.g., [46, 117, 194, 224, 225]). The limited strategic behavior refers to the drawback that the composition of a proposal of a negotiating party depends on the values proposed by the opponent in his/her former proposal. No strategic behavior at all is feasible in case of a random-based proposal generation (e.g., [121]). In contrast to the existing approaches, our approach enables a customer to negotiate concurrently with multiple providers over multiple issues and to approach Pareto-optimal solutions despite incomplete information while maintaining the strategic behavior of the negotiating parties. For this purpose, we make use of a new negotiation protocol that follows a new two-phase meta-strategy and apply existing time-dependent strategies and a new GRiP-based strategy during the first and second phase, respectively.

3.2 Reliable Monitoring

In this section, related approaches concerning our contribution *CSLAB-Mon.KOM* are discussed. Basically, several monitoring approaches have been proposed so far in the field of cloud computing and related research areas. However, only a few of them address the problem of monitoring SLA compliance from a consumer's perspective or that deal with application level monitoring or availability monitoring and its accuracy in general.

Generic Approaches for SLA and Application Level Monitoring The issue of monitoring and verifying SLA compliance in a cloud computing context is addressed by Chazalet in [31, 32]. In his work, he presents a generic layered architecture, that does not depend on a specific cloud service model or quality parameters. At the lowest layer, service components can be monitored using a push or pull model. The resulting monitoring data is then passed to the next higher layer, which collects, processes, and aggregates all the monitoring data from different components. Finally, the aggregated data is passed to the highest layer, which is responsible for conducting the actual verification against SLAs. Two different prototypes of the framework have been implemented. Both differ with respect to the monitoring techniques applied within the lowest layer. The first prototype monitors the latency times of the client side requests and responses passing an enterprise service bus by intercepting messages at different points in time and the second prototype monitors resource metrics (e.g., Central Processing Unit (CPU) time) of a Java-based application server using predefined probes provided by the server. Although the client side monitoring does not cause additional traffic, intercepting the existing client side messages only provides a restricted view, if transferred to availability monitoring of a cloud-based service. Furthermore, the author does not address interdependencies between consumer and provider side monitoring nor between application and VM level monitoring. In [129], Mastelic et al. present a generic approach for classifying and monitoring application level metrics in resource-shared cloud environments. As a prerequisite for deriving the required monitoring tasks, the authors present a model-driven approach, which allows the classification of metrics on the application level according to four different models. In detail, the models define, for which applications a metric is measured, how the metric is mathematically defined, how the metric is measured, and whether the metric refers to a qualitative or quantitative parameter. For the actual monitoring, the authors make use of agents that monitor the specified metrics in application-specific time intervals using the Java-based system information interface Sigar API[1]. However, the authors state that additional mechanisms have to be implemented by cloud providers for the monitoring of application-specific metrics. The agents are run as lightweight components on each VM in the cloud and transmit their measured data to a central server. Mastelic et al. only mention that each application has its own monitoring interval and refer to the work by Emeakaroha et al. [52] for more details on how to determine such an interval (cf. paragraph on efficient monitoring intervals below). Furthermore, uptime is only mentioned as one metric that can be monitored and client side monitoring is not considered by the authors.

Proxy-based SLA Monitoring In [158, 159], Repp et al. present an approach for SLA monitoring of business processes that are composed of several distributed Web services from a user's perspective. Basically, monitoring agents are created for each Web service of a given business process and afterwards, distributed within the service-oriented infrastructure in order to collect monitoring data. For the actual monitoring, Web service calls initiated during business process execution are forwarded to a proxy, which redirects them to a central monitoring component. The central monitoring component is responsible for managing monitoring agents and for further redirecting Web service calls to them. Monitoring agents perform the actual Web service invocations and deliver the results directly back to the proxy which, in turn, forwards them to the corresponding business process engine. Collected monitoring data is stored

---

[1]   https://support.hyperic.com/display/SIGAR/Home

in a repository managed by the central monitoring component for further analysis. Although availability is mentioned as one parameter that can be monitored, no details on the procedure of availability monitoring are given. Furthermore, besides network topology information as input for monitor placement, other network properties are not considered.

Availability Monitoring and its Accuracy   Haberkorn and Trivedi [86] present a generic approach for monitoring high-availability systems that consist of several different components (hardware and software). For this purpose, not only a real-time monitoring system is required but also establishing an overall availability model that covers all relevant subsystems. Since continuous monitoring of the entire system would highly affect the performance, the authors propose an approach, in which the availability is calculated separately for each component by measuring the Mean Time To Failure (MTTF) as well as the Mean Time To Repair (MTTR). The overall availability is then derived from these results by a central availability monitor. The actual monitoring at component-level is conducted by agents using a periodical pull model and an event-based approach is used in order to send the availability data to the central availability monitor. This is only done when the availability status of a component changes. The work by Haberkorn and Trivedi assumes access to all components to be monitored. Concerning the accuracy of their measurements, the authors determine a confidence interval based on their computed point estimates of availability. Client side monitoring and network conditions are not considered in their work. Another approach to guarantee the performance of cloud applications based on monitoring is suggested by Shao et al. [180, 181]. The authors make use of a combined server and client side monitoring approach. Monitoring agents are deployed on virtual machines on the server side to collect resource metrics and http detections are used to simulate end user requests on the client side. All monitoring data is sent to a central monitoring entity for further analysis. In order to obtain resource metrics (e.g., CPU, memory), several different techniques and libraries (e.g., Sigar API) are used by the agents. Concerning measurements from the client side, availability is calculated as the ratio of successful requests, i.e., http detections, and the total number of requests. Although the authors state that the accuracy increases with an increasing monitoring frequency, the authors do not further address this issue. Michlmayr et al. [133] propose an event-based approach for SLA violation detection of Web services. For this purpose, the authors apply client side and server side monitoring. The client side monitor periodically sends probe requests to the service to be monitored and the server side monitor performs continuous monitoring on the server where the monitored service is located. In addition, the client side monitor makes use of TCP packet sniffing in order to determine attributes of the server side, such as execution time (cf. [163]). However, the server side approach requires access to the Web service implementation and is restricted to .Net[2]-based Web services. Results from both monitors are sent to a central entity that allows the subscription for notifications in order to get informed whenever an SLA violation is detected. As part of the evaluation, Michlmayr et al. compare the results from the measurements on the client and the server side against each other and against the simulated availability in order to analyze accuracy. They also point out that it is useful to combine both measurement methods in order to distinguish between the client and the server side perspective. However, the authors do not describe how to combine the results from both monitors and do not specify how accuracy can be expressed mathematically or improved by modifying the monitoring frequency. Again, availability is only calculated based on the number of successful requests.

SLA Violation Detection and Efficient Monitoring Intervals   In their work in [52], Emeakaroha et al. focus on the autonomic detection of SLA violations in cloud computing environments based on resource monitoring. In this regard, the authors address two challenges: First of all, they describe how to conduct a mapping of measured low-level metrics to SLA parameters on the application-level. Second, they elaborate on how to determine monitoring intervals in such a manner that they do not interfere with the overall system performance but still allow for an accurate detection of SLA violations. As solution, Emeakaroha et al. present an architecture that makes use of the LoM2HiS framework [50] for monitoring purposes, which has been proposed by the authors in one of their earlier works. The LoM2HiS framework utilizes two core components: The host monitor makes use of monitoring agents that are placed on each node in order to monitor resource metrics continuously. In addition, the runtime monitor determines SLA violations on the application level based on mapping rules created by the service provider and predicts future SLA violations based on predefined thresholds and by analyzing historical resource usage information. Monitoring agents broadcast their data to other agents so that the current status is available on each agent in a certain resource pool. Concerning the second challenge, the authors propose a cost function as a foundation for determining an appropriate monitoring interval. The function expresses the trade-off between the measurement costs and the costs for missing SLA violations, which depend on the penalty costs specified within an SLA. All in all, the authors only focus on resource monitoring and derive application-level metrics from their collected data. However, solely focusing on resource monitoring cannot be perceived as sufficient. Concerning availability monitoring, certain services provided by an application may still be offline, although the underlying resources, such as a VM, are available. Regarding interval determination, the authors only consider the number and costs for missed SLA violations, but do not address the amount of missed downtime explicitly. In one of their subsequent works [51], Emeakaroha et al. focus

---

2   https://www.microsoft.com/net

on the design of techniques for cloud application monitoring. The authors propose a monitoring framework based on the Simple Network Management Protocol (SNMP), in which a central manager node periodically polls the distributed monitoring agents for monitoring information. For reasons of scalability, asynchronous communication is used between the manager and the agents. According to the authors, the retrieval of monitoring data can be done by analyzing log files of the application or operating system. For the determination of the effective monitoring interval, Emeakaroha et al. present an algorithm that iteratively explores each candidate interval for a specified amount of time. At the end of each iteration, the algorithm determines whether the net utility obtained from the current interval exceeds the maximum net utility determined so far. Finally, the measurement interval with the highest net utility represents the most effective one. The net utility is computed based on a utility function expressed as the difference between provider profit and the cost function proposed in their aforementioned work in [52]. Their proposed approach is not applicable in our considered scenario. Since information about SLA violations should be provided to consumers in a timely manner, asynchronous communication as well as the retrieval of monitoring data from log files increases the delay between SLA violation detection and notification. Again, the authors only consider the number and costs for missed SLA violations, but do not consider the accuracy of their measurements explicitly for the determination of measurement intervals.

Event-based Monitoring   Comuzzi et al. [37] propose an event-based approach for SLA monitoring from a service provider's perspective in complex service-based systems, such as cloud computing, where services at different levels (e.g., infrastructure, business software) are composed in order to provide complex services. In their monitoring framework, event captors located inside or outside a service capture runtime information from the different services and the collected information is published in the form of events to an event bus. Monitors can then subscribe to specific types of events in order to monitor the compliance with particular SLAs and can be coordinated in different formations (e.g., hierarchical) as required. Collected monitoring information is stored in a database, which serves as an additional basis for decision-making in subsequent SLA negotiations. Comuzzi et al. state that data collection routines of the event captors depend on the entity to be monitored. Hence, the authors do not propose a particular design for such routines. Furthermore, availability monitoring is mentioned but not considered explicitly in their approach. Smit et al. [192] also propose a publish/subscribe-based approach for application-level monitoring as a service across several heterogeneous clouds. The monitoring infrastructure is build on a stream processing framework, which emulates the scalable and distributed processing capabilities of MapReduce[3]. Monitoring data is collected from existing sensors

---

[3]   http://research.google.com/archive/mapreduce.html

acting as publishers, such as applications publishing their metrics or by using existing technologies, such as log files, to gather metrics from resources. The collected data is then pushed to the monitoring system in order to be transformed into a unified format and afterwards, to be converted into a series of streams. The resulting streams can then be processed by different subscribers. The monitoring infrastructure is managed by a broker, which performs transformations on streams, thus acting as an intermediary between publishers and subscribers. In comparison with CSLAB-Mon.KOM, publish/subscribe-based approaches decouple event detection and consumption in terms of time and depend on a specific middleware. Thus, message delivery depends highly on the availability and performance of that middleware, which may introduce additional delay in message delivery. Another approach for application-level monitoring of cloud services using Complex Event Processing (CEP) is proposed by Leitner et al. [122]. Their approach addresses application developers and enables them to define and monitor corresponding performance metrics. For this purpose, developers define event emitters within the source code of an application and the resulting events are later on processed into aggregated metrics using CEP. However, the approach proposed by Leitner et al. requires access to the source code of an application, an assumption that cannot be made for consumers in our considered scenario.

Peer-to-Peer-based Monitoring König et al. [113] propose a pure peer-to-peer-based monitoring framework for cloud environments in order to avoid a central point of failure and to allow for elastic monitoring by dynamically allocating additional resources for monitoring purposes. Their monitoring architecture is composed of three layers. The data layer comprises several adaptors responsible for collecting monitoring information from all layers of the cloud stack and can be implemented depending on the entity to be monitored using either a push or a pull-based approach. The processing layer provides means for describing complex queries over the collected data and final queries are then parsed in order to generate an operator tree for query execution. The distribution layer is responsible for creating the peer-to-peer overlay network, i.e., for deploying adaptors and operator trees across the cloud infrastructure. At runtime, the query evaluation follows a push-based approach, according to which data source operators process their data and forward the results to their parent in the query operator tree. The authors state that monitoring reliability depends on the fault tolerance of the VM responsible for query deployment and execution. In contrast, our approach explicitly incorporates the deployment of redundant monitor units in order to increase reliability. Furthermore, a pure peer-to-beer-based approach leads to increased (self-)management costs and distributed query evaluation introduces an additional delay in the delivery of monitoring results.

The following Table 3.2 summarizes the related approaches as discussed before. In the table, the following columns represent the criteria used to compare the related work against our monitoring approach CSLAB-Mon.KOM. Data in brackets indicates that the aspect has been mentioned in the related work, but has not been considered in detail, i.e., no model or mathematical expression has been provided.

- *Location-awareness:* states whether consumer side (C) and/or provider side (P) monitoring are considered

- *Resource-awareness:* specifies whether data is collected from the application-level (A) and/or system-level (S)

- *Network-awareness:* indicates whether information from the underlying network is taken into account

- *Availability Monitoring:* states whether availability monitoring is considered in a related work

- *Redundancy:* indicates whether redundant monitor data is created to establish reliability by, e.g., using redundant monitor units or by broadcasting measured data

- *Frequency:* points out whether a related work explores the determination of efficient monitoring intervals

- *Accuracy:* specifies whether the accuracy of the monitoring results is considered and whether mathematical expressions or algorithms are stated for calculating the accuracy

- *Availability Metric:* states the metric of availability used in a related approach

- *Area:* describes the field where a proposed approach is intended to be applied, i.e., cloud computing (CC), Web service-based systems (WS), high-availability systems (HA), or complex service-based systems (CS)

- *Approach:* describes the method that is applied for monitoring

- *Data Collection:* specifies whether monitoring data is collected using a pull- or a push-based approach. Data collection focuses only on how monitoring data can be obtained from the entity under consideration, i.e., does not incorporate result dissemination to higher-level components for further analysis.

Table 3.2: Overview of related monitoring approaches

Publication	Location-awareness	Resource-awareness	Network-awareness	Availability Monitoring	Redundancy	Frequency	Accuracy	Availability Metric	Area	Approach	Data Collection
CSLAB-Mon.KOM	C + P	A + S	×	×	×	×	×	$\frac{MTTF}{MTTF+MTTR}$	CC	probing	pull
Chazalet [31, 32]	C | P	A | S	–	–	×	–	–	–	CC	message interception, probing	push | pull
Mastelic et al. [129]	P	A + S	–	(×)	–	–	–	–	CC	agents, system API	pull
Repp et al. [158, 159]	C	A	×	×	–	(×)	–	$\frac{MTTF}{MTTF+MTTR}$	WS	message interception	pull
Haberkorn & Trivedi [86]	P	A + S	–	×	–	–	×	$\frac{MTTF}{MTTF+MTTR}$	HA	probing	pull
Shao and Wang [180, 181]	C + P	A + S	–	×	–	(×)	(×)	$\frac{\text{no. of successful requests}}{\text{no. of total requests}}$	CC	probing, system API	pull
Michlmayr et al. [133]	C + P	A + S	×	×	–	(×)	(×)	$\frac{\text{no. of successful requests}}{\text{no. of total requests}}$	WS	probing	pull
Emeakaroha et al. [50, 52]	P	(A) + S	–	×	×	×	(×)	$\left(1 - \frac{\text{downtime}}{\text{total time}}\right) \times 100$	CC	agents	pull
Emeakaroha et al. [51]	P	A	–	–	–	–	(×)	–	CC	retrieval from log files	pull
Comuzzi et al. [37]	P	A + S	–	×	–	×	–	$\frac{\text{uptime}}{\text{total time}}$	CS	publish/subscribe	push
Smit et al. [192]	P	A + S	–	–	–	–	–	–	CC	stream processing	push | pull
Leitner et al. [122]	P	A	–	–	–	–	–	–	CC	complex event processing	push
König et al. [113]	P	A + S	–	–	–	–	–	–	CC	adaptors in a P2P overlay	push | pull

CSLAB-Mon.KOM   As it can be deduced from Table 3.2, several approaches only consider provider side monitoring (e.g., [37, 51, 52, 86, 113, 122, 129, 192]). However, in order to obtain a reliable evidence base for verifying the compliance with the negotiated SLAs at runtime from a consumer's perspective, provider-independent monitoring solutions are required (cf. Section 1.3). Since cloud consumers only have restricted access to the provided cloud resources, measurements can only be conducted from remote locations over a network by sending monitoring requests to the observed cloud resources. Hence, the accuracy of the measurements depends highly on the monitoring frequency. Furthermore, monitoring messages may be subject to a varying latency, e.g., due to packet loss. Concerning existing approaches, only a few of them focus on application-level monitoring from a consumer's perspective (e.g., [32, 133, 158, 180]) and/or address availability monitoring and its accuracy (e.g., [51, 86, 133, 180]). Moreover, none of the related approaches considers the accuracy of measured availability explicitly in conjunction with the monitoring frequency and current network conditions. In contrast to related work, our approach CSLAB-Mon.KOM allows monitoring of the availability of cloud-based services from a consumer's perspective in a provider-independent manner and explicitly addresses the reliability of the monitoring results. For this purpose, the monitoring approach is provided by our envisaged broker acting as a trusted third-party and exhibits the following properties. First of all, our approach is *location-aware*. That is, we combine consumer and provider side monitoring in order to achieve visibility of the entire cloud service delivery chain. In doing so, issues on the provider side can be distinguished from other performance issues originating from, e.g., the ISP network. This is required since only issues on the provider side may constitute violations of cloud provider SLAs. In addition, CSLAB-Mon.KOM is *resource-aware*, which means that we combine application- and system-level monitoring for separating application-level violations from system-level issues. This permits the determination of the violated SLA clause. Furthermore, our approach accounts for the influence of the monitoring frequency and network impairments on the accuracy of the monitoring results, which allows the achievement of *accurate* monitoring information.

3.3 Robust Monitor Placement

This section discusses approaches related to our monitor placement strategies *CSLAB-Loc.KOM* as a third major contribution of the present work. The discussion focuses on monitor placement approaches that deal with active monitoring, i.e., actively sending synthetic requests, so-called probes, to distinct destinations. An explicit distinction is drawn between other placement approaches focusing on passive monitoring and the scenario considered in this thesis. Furthermore, besides robust monitor placement, also cost-efficient approaches are discussed, since they also consider relationships between monitor units and the locations to be monitored. Finally, we also consider approaches that address related location selection problems, such as resilient VM placement, and solutions based on the related facility location placement problem.

Robust Service and Probe Station Placement   Several works are based on a notion of resiliency, according to which network is considered to be resilient, if it continues to function correctly under a maximum number of k node and/or edge failures, also denoted as *k-node/edge-failure-resilience* (cf., e.g., [164]). These approaches only account for the existence of connections between communicating nodes or the existence of remaining monitoring nodes in the presence of node/edge failures, but do not consider the particular quality, i.e., reliability of nodes and edges.

In [164], for instance, Rosenkrantz et al. propose an approach for an optimal placement of services in a given service-oriented network, so that the placement costs are minimized while achieving at least a specified level of resilience. Basically, such a service-oriented network, usually implemented as overlay, comprises a set of nodes, which either provide certain services on their own or utilize services offered by other nodes. As input for their placement problem, the set of services required at each node is given. Rosenkrantz et al. only consider a resilience level of $k = 1$ and propose two separate polynomial algorithms for 1-edge and 1-node resiliency based on determining the set of bridgeless components and the set of cut points in a graph, respectively. In contrast to CSLAB-Loc.KOM, services can be placed on the same node where they are required. Furthermore, the authors only consider a fixed maximum number of unreliable nodes or edges and only total node/edge outages. In contrast, our placement strategies are based on probabilistic reliability values for all nodes and edges.

In [140], Natu and Sethi present approaches for selecting a minimum number of probe station locations across a network so that all nodes are covered, while being resilient in the presence of a maximum number of k node failures, including probe station failures. The authors consider static single-path routing, i.e., packets from a particular source to a particular destination are always routed along the same, single path. Besides an exhaustive search, the authors propose heuristic approaches based on determining a minimum placement that guarantees k independent probe paths from each probe station to each non-probe station node. An extension of this work is presented by Jeswani et al. in [106], in which the authors propose an approach based on a greedy algorithm for the minimum hitting set problem. They focus on node failures first and later show how their approach can be modified to account for link failures. In another related approach, Pan et al. [148] deal with probe station placement in dynamic, i.e., non-deterministic virtual networks. Probe stations can be deployed on a subset of the physical nodes hosting virtual nodes. The authors adapt the notion of resiliency as proposed by Natu and Sethi in [140], according to which there must be at least k independent probe-paths in a network in the presence of a maximum number of k failures of non-probe station nodes. Their approaches are based on a probabilistic dependency model that represents the different probabilities for the probes from a given probe station to a certain destination node. Due to these uncertainties in routing probes, the independence of two given paths can only be determined with a certain probability. The goal of their algorithm is to minimize the set of probe stations while covering all nodes in the network, even in the presence of at most k link failures. The algorithm iteratively adds new probe station locations until all nodes in the network are covered. In each step, that node is selected as probe station that maximizes node coverage at a maximum of k link failures. In order to determine whether two paths are independent, their corresponding probability must exceed a given threshold. In addition, the authors propose an algorithm for adapting the probe station placement in case of adding or deleting virtual nodes. In their work in [153], Patil et al. also aim to determine a minimal set of probe station locations that cover all the nodes in a network with a limit of k node failures while reducing the size of the resulting probe set. For this purpose, they also determine probe station locations in such a way, that these locations exhibit k unique paths to all nodes in the network. Their algorithm incrementally selects probe stations that have the highest depth in the spanning tree in order to reduce the final size of the probe set. The authors further make use of the algorithm for probe set selection as proposed by Natu and Sethi in [139] in order to show the reduction of the probe set size. Similar to the work by Rosenkrantz et al. [164], all aforementioned probe station placement approaches place a limit on the total number of faulty nodes and/or edges and do not consider probabilistic reliability values for all nodes and edges as it is the case in our proposed approach.

Cost-Efficient Monitor Placement   In [170], Salhi et al. propose an approach for joint optimization of monitor placement and monitor path selection while minimizing the total monitoring cost. The resulting path selection must cover all the links in the network and redundant link measurements should be minimized. The total monitoring costs comprise monitor deployment costs at nodes, communication costs between the monitors and a central network operations center as well as link measurement costs due to injected monitoring flows. The authors present two so-called Integer Linear Program (ILP) optimization problems and corresponding optimization models. Basically, an ILP problem (cf., e.g., [95]) constitutes an optimization problem with a linear objective function to be either minimized or maximized that incorporates so-called decision variables, which can only take integer values. The first ILP-based model of the authors assumes that the set of network paths is given in advance as input and the second model overcomes this limitation by directly considering the links carrying monitoring flows and introducing additional criteria for flow conservation at nodes. Their ILP models can be mapped to the uncapacitated facility location problem. Since this problem is NP-hard, the authors developed two heuristic approaches in their subsequent work in [171]. The first heuristic is an exhaustive search that iteratively selects additional monitor locations. In each iteration, the algorithm analyzes the set of all candidate paths between the new monitor and the previously added monitors in order to select additional monitoring paths that cover yet uncovered nodes. The second heuristic performs an in depth-first order search between two monitor locations selected in the first step in order to determine non-overlapping paths while maximizing link coverage. The second step aims at covering the remaining links by choosing path segments that maximize the number of uncovered links while minimizing redundant measurements. In contrast, our placement strategies focus on maximizing the reliability of the monitoring infrastructure while placing a predefined number of redundant monitor units at different locations in multiple data centers. Furthermore, we assume that the costs for each monitor unit to be placed are location-agnostic and can be determined in advance based on the consumers' requirements and the underlying cost model of the cloud broker.

In another related approach, Li et al. [124] explore the optimization of a distributed polling system. The authors aim to minimize the number of SNMP managers (pollers) to be placed on network nodes in order to reduce the deployment costs while taking bandwidth constraints on the links into account. In conjunction with the poller placement, the set of network nodes to be polled by each poller is also determined. The resulting optimization problem corresponds to the multi-processor scheduling problem (cf. [124]) and the authors propose three greedy algorithms for solving the problem. Basically, all of their greedy algorithms iteratively follow three steps: firstly, an additional poller is selected, then, the maximum possible number of nodes not yet being polled is assigned to that poller, and finally, reassignments of pollees from other pollers to that new poller are explored with the aim to reduce the overall bandwidth usage. The three algorithms differ in their first phase and select the next poller to be included in the poller set based on the highest polling demand, on the maximum possible number of additional pollees, or on random selection as a baseline. In contrast to the work by Li et al., our approach neglects bandwidth constraints due to the high bandwidth capacities of modern data centers and the lean design of the monitor units. The monitor units are intended to send solely simple requests that do not constitute a substantial burden for the overall bandwidth. In addition, we do not consider deployment costs. We rather focus on maximizing the reliability of the monitoring infrastructure independent of cost considerations and assume that the SLM broker is able to pass on the costs incurred to his/her customers.

Repp et al. [158, 159] address monitor placement in a distributed service-oriented infrastructure with the aim to minimize the total cost, comprising setup and communication costs, while considering so-called alignment demands of service providers and capacity restrictions of candidate nodes for monitor placement. The concept of alignment demands indicates how often a monitor unit will likely have to perform corrective actions for a corresponding service and node capacities restrict the number of monitor units with their corrective actions that can be placed on a certain node. In order to solve the corresponding monitor unit location problem, the authors propose an optimal solution approach based on a mapping to the (capacitated) warehouse (facility) location problem, a greedy heuristic based on a depth-first search as well as an improvement procedure based on simulated annealing (cf., e.g., [95]). In comparison with our approach, Repp et al. also consider capacity constraints of the target nodes. Furthermore, the authors state that although the distribution of monitor units within a service-oriented infrastructure contributes to the overall robustness compared to a centralized solution, the possibilities for improving the overall robustness by distributing additional monitor units are very limited. Hence, we consider probabilistic reliability values of all nodes and edges in our approach in order to maximize the overall reliability while placing a predefined number of monitor units.

Cost-Efficient and Robust Facility Location Selection   A fault tolerant version of the uncapacitated facility location problem is introduced by Jain and Vazirani in [102]. While the uncapacitated facility location problem aims at minimizing the total costs for opening facilities and connecting cities to these facilities, each city must be connected to a specified number of facilities as additional constraint in the fault-tolerant version. Furthermore, the authors address the metric version of this problem, which means that the costs for connecting cities to open facilities satisfy the triangle inequality. They propose an approximation algorithm that iteratively determines facilities to be opened and assigns them to cities. In doing so, the overall maximum number of residual required facilities decreases in each iteration. Similar to our approach, redundant placements are considered in order to account for fault-tolerance. However, the authors aim to minimize the total costs and do not consider node or edge reliabilities.

Resilient Virtual Machine Placement   In [16], Bin et al. introduce the Resilient VM Placement Problem. While the original VM placement problem aims to find an optimal placement with respect to, e.g., performance or energy, so that constraints such as resource demands, isolation policies, and location restrictions of the VMs are met, the resilient version additionally aims to guarantee the relocation of VMs in case of (predicted) host failures. In detail, Bin et al. denote a VM as k-resilient if it can be relocated to another host in the presence of (k-1) host failures in addition to the failure of the current host of the VM. The authors consider a placement to be resilient if k-resiliency (with a different value k for each VM) can be guaranteed for all VMs. Their solution is based on the introduction of so-called shadow VMs that represent place-holders for VMs in terms of extra resource space for relocation purposes in case of host failures. Shadow spaces of different VMs can overlap if it is guaranteed that, in each scenario of k host failures, only one of the VMs assigned to the same shadow space is relocated to that space at the same time (anti-colocation constraint). As solution, the authors define several corresponding constraints and utilize a constraint programming engine to determine a feasible, resilient placement. Hence, they do not consider to optimize VM placement.

Fault-tolerant VM placement is also addressed by Machida et al. [127]. The authors consider a scenario, in which applications need to be run on at least a certain number of redundant VMs or CPUs in order to satisfy given performance constraints in terms of maximum average response times. In their work, the authors aim to determine a VM placement with the minimum number of hosts required to run the VMs of a given set of applications with specified response time requirements so that the resulting placement is k-fault-tolerant. K-fault-tolerant means that the applications continue working correctly even in the presence of at most k host failures. The authors propose methods to estimate the minimum number of redundant VMs required for each application in order to satisfy the performance requirements as well as the fault-tolerance level. In this regard, they also determine the minimum number of servers required to host the VMs. Based on the estimated values, an algorithm then determines a corresponding VM placement. While placing VMs, redundant VMs of the same application should be placed on different hosts in order to account for host failures. Similar to aforementioned related approaches dealing with robust probe station placement (cf., e.g., [140]), Bin et al. and Machida et al. both utilize the notion of k-resiliency, i.e., only account for a maximum of k node failures. Although both works incorporate resource and location constraints, similar to our approach, they do not consider network properties or probabilistic reliability values.

Network Tomography Although utilizing active monitoring, other works focusing on so-called network tomography (cf., e.g., [97, 115, 141]) must also be distinguished from our considered scenario. According to Horton et al. [97], network tomography aims at gathering (Internet) topology information, such as connectivity and latency characteristics, by distributing measurement points (also denoted as beacons) across a network, since standard routing protocols only provide that kind of information in an aggregate form. In this regard, the problem of determining a placement of beacons across the network emerged that minimizes the number of beacons while covering all links in the network and being robust to routing dynamics (cf., e.g., [115]). As solution, Horton et al. [97] present a heuristic according to which beacons should be placed at higher arity nodes in the Internet. A node is considered to be a higher arity node if there exist multiple disjoint paths to other nodes in the network. The authors assume two BGP-like routing models: routing based on local preferences and routing based on link distance minimization. Kumar and Kaur [115] first propose a graph-theoretic algorithm to compute the monitorable edge set for each candidate beacon while considering all possible routing states. The authors then apply a heuristic of the corresponding minimum set cover problem in order to minimize the number of beacons so that the union of their corresponding monitorable edge sets covers all links in the network. In order to further reduce the final beacon set, the authors reduce the set of candidate beacons in the first step to high arity nodes.

In contrast, other works (e.g., [13, 14, 141]) consider network tomography in the presence of link failures. Nguyen et al. [141], for example, aim to detect and locate multiple simultaneous link failures in IP networks. For this purpose, they propose a two-phase approach that first minimizes the number of probes by applying max-plus algebra theory and subsequently minimize the number of beacons using a greedy approximation algorithm based on their results obtained in the first step. In [13, 14], Bejerano and Rastogi apply network tomography in order to address monitoring of link latencies and faults in the presence of at most k network failures. They propose a two-phase approach. In the first phase, a minimal set of monitoring stations is determined, so that all links in the network are covered, even in the presence of at most k link failures. The authors consider a network to be k-fault-resilient if there exist at least k disjoint routing paths from the monitoring stations to each link in the network. In the second phase, the authors determine a minimal set of probe messages, so that the latency and failure of each link can be determined at minimal cost. The problem of selecting monitoring stations considered in the first phase can be mapped to a variant of the set cover problem, whereas the problem of probe assignment can be mapped to a variant of the vertex cover problem. For solving both problems, the authors propose a greedy algorithm for each phase. In contrast to this thesis, the related approaches mentioned before focusing on network tomography either deal with routing dynamics or multiple link failures and aim to observe link characteristics in a network.

Differentiation from Passive Monitor Placement Problems Similar to the present work, the aforementioned approaches address active monitoring. In contrast, several other approaches exist that also deal with monitor placement but consider passive monitoring (cf., e.g., [28, 201]). When using passive monitoring, monitor stations are placed on links at several locations within a network in order to monitor Internet Protocol (IP) flows by sampling packets carried by these links [201]. Constraints to be considered are the deployment costs for monitors as well as their operating costs determined by their sampling rates [201]. By way of contrast, our scenario as well as related approaches consider actively sending probes to particular locations in the network, thereby passing several links.

Table 3.3 summarizes the related approaches as discussed before. In the table, the following columns represent the criteria used to compare the related work against our proposed placement strategies CSLAB-Loc.KOM.

- *Reliability:* states whether only failures of nodes (N) or edges (E) are considered or both types of failures are considered simultaneously

- *Redundancy:* indicates whether redundant nodes or paths are used to establish reliability

- *Location Constraints:* specifies whether location constraints, such as anti-colocation constraints, or other placement restrictions are considered

- *Resource Constraints:* indicates whether resource constraints of nodes, such as capacity limits of VMs, or of links, such as available link bandwidth, are taken into account

- *Resiliency despite:* defines the notion of resiliency used in the related approach, i.e., whether total node and/or link failures are considered or whether probabilistic values are used to express their reliability

- *Path Consideration:* points out how connections between nodes are taken into account, e.g., whether static paths are given or whether dynamic routing or an end-to-end perspective is considered

- *Area:* describes the field where the proposed approach is intended to be applied, i.e., cloud monitoring (CM), service placement (SP), network monitoring (NM), virtual network monitoring (VNM), service monitoring (SM), facility placement (FP), VM placement (VMP), network tomography (NT)

- *Objective:* states the objective, i.e., the optimization goal of the approach such as, e.g., minimizing the total cost or the number of locations

- *Approach:* describes the method that is applied as solution approach, e.g., whether an exact optimization approach such as an ILP and/or a heuristic solution is proposed

CSLAB-Loc.KOM Table 3.3 shows that most of the related approaches focus on a maximum number of simultaneous node and/or link failures in order to consider a network to be resilient while placing monitoring units (e.g., [106, 140, 148, 153, 164]). However, setting upper bounds on the number of failures is not sufficient in order to maximize the reliability of the whole monitoring infrastructure. In addition, monitoring units are tied to certain resource demands depending on their monitoring tasks to be fulfilled and the candidate locations for monitor placement in terms of, e.g., certain VMs, only offer a limited resource supply. Regarding existing approaches, only a few of them take resource constraints into account (cf., e.g., [16, 124, 127, 158]). Moreover, in contrast to this thesis, none of the related approaches considers probabilistic reliability values of all the nodes and edges that are involved in the monitoring process.

Table 3.3: Overview of related placement approaches

Publication	Reliability	Redundancy	Location Constraints	Resource Constraints	Resiliency despite	Path Consideration	Area	Objective (minimize...)	Approach
CSLAB-Loc.KOM	N + E	×	×	×	probabilistic node + link unreliability	end-to-end	CM	unreliability of mon. infrastructure	MILP + heuristics
Rosenkrantz et al. [164]	N|E	–	–	–	1 node/edge failure	static connections	SP	placement costs	polyn. algorithms
Natu & Sethi [140]	N	×	–	–	k node failures	static single-path	NM	no. of locations	exhaustive + heuristics
Jeswani et al. [106]	N|E	×	–	–	k node/link failures	static single-path	NM	no. of locations	greedy heuristic
Pan et al. [148]	E	×	–	–	k link failures, add/delete virt. nodes	probabilities for routing paths	VNM	no. of locations	heuristic + extensions
Patil et al. [153]	N	×	–	–	k node failures	static single-path	NM	no. of locations	heuristic
Salhi et al. [170, 171]	–	–	–	–	–	path selection	NM	total mon. cost	ILPs + heuristics
Li et al. [124]	–	–	–	×	–	fixed paths	NM	no. of pollers	greedy heuristics
Repp et al. [158, 159]	–	–	×	×	–	fixed paths	SM	total mon. cost	ILP + heuristics
Jain & Vazirani [102]	N + E	×	–	–	faulty facilities	static connections	FP	total cost	approx. algorithm
Bin et al. [16]	N	×	×	×	k host failures	–	VMP	(feasible placement)	constraint programming
Machida et al. [127]	N	×	×	×	k host failures	–	VMP	no. of hosts	estimations + algorithm
Horton et al. [97]	–	×	–	–	routing dynamics	BGP-like routing	NT	no. of beacons	heuristic
Kumar & Kaur [115]	–	×	–	–	routing dynamics	possible routes	NT	no. of beacons	graph algo. + heuristic
Nguyen et al. [141]	E	×	–	–	link failures	fixed paths	NT	no. of probes, no. of beacons	max-plus algebra + algo.
Bejerano & Rastogi [13, 14]	E	×	–	–	k-1 link failures	IP forwarding	NM	no. of locations, probe set size	two-phase greedy algo.

In this thesis, we propose different placement strategies that aim to maximize the overall reliability of the monitoring infrastructure while placing monitor units at different locations in multiple data centers on the broker and the provider side and considering resource and location constraints. In addition, we incorporate a predefined number of redundant monitor units to be placed for each application, which further increases the reliability. According to our monitoring approach, at least one monitoring unit has to be placed on both, the broker and the provider side for each cloud application in order to achieve location-awareness (cf. Section 4.3.4). In this regard, we assume that a corresponding redundancy factor is specified by the enterprise cloud consumer in advance according to the level of importance of each application. Note that we do not consider placing monitoring units on every VM in each data center since each additional monitoring unit results in higher deployment and communication costs of the whole monitoring infrastructure. Furthermore, we do not consider the problem of achieving a certain level of reliability of the monitoring infrastructure while minimizing the number of monitoring units to be placed. This is due to the fact that such an approach may result in a placement, in which some applications of minor importance are observed by a large number of monitoring units while some business critical applications are only observed by a small number of monitoring units.

Concerning our strategies for robust monitor placement, reliability is expressed as the probability that at least one monitor unit is working for each cloud application and is computed based on probabilistic reliability values of the nodes and links that are involved in monitoring. We present an exact solution approach in terms of a mathematical optimization model that corresponds to a so-called Mixed-Integer Linear Program (MILP), which can be solved using off-the-shelf methods such as, e.g., the branch-and-bound algorithm (cf., e.g., [95]). Similar to an ILP problem, a MILP problem is an optimization problem that exhibits a linear objective function, but in contrast to an ILP, only some of the decision variables have to take integer values while other decision variables can take real values (cf., e.g., [95]). Since the exact approach exhibits exponential time complexity (cf. Sections 7.3.2 and 8.4.3) we propose two heuristic approaches that exhibit polynomial time complexity (cf. Section 8.4.3) and, thus, are applicable for solving large-scale problem instances in practice.

4 Basic System Design – CSLAB.KOM

Having presented existing approaches related to the scenario considered in this thesis in the previous Chapter 3, this chapter now presents the basic system design of the envisaged SLM broker CSLAB.KOM [96, 183, 185, 188] in Section 4.1. Afterwards, the conceptual design of the two major tasks the SLM broker is responsible for, namely, the negotiation of SLAs and the subsequent monitoring of the adherence of a cloud provider to the negotiated guarantees is presented. In this regard, Section 4.2 outlines our basic negotiation design [96, 185] and Section 4.3 describes our basic monitoring design [186, 187, 188].

4.1 Service Level Management Broker

Basically, our scenario focuses on a cloud market model, in which brokers act as mediators between consumers and providers [25]. The general interaction between a customer, a broker, and providers is depicted in Figure 4.1 and explained in detail in the following.

   Initially, cloud providers have to announce their services to the public, so that they can be found by customers. For this purpose, cloud providers publish descriptions of the services they offer in a public database, e.g., a service registry (cf. Section 2.1.3), that is managed by a broker residing in the market. In order to discover appropriate cloud services, consumers submit their functional and non-functional requirements for a desired cloud service to the broker, which then queries a database (or service registry) to determine the most suitable cloud providers matching the consumers' functional requirements. Subsequently, the broker acting on behalf of the cloud consumer can negotiate over the non-functional requirements with the most suitable cloud providers determined in the preceding step using our negotiation approach *CSLAB-Neg.KOM* (presented in Chapter 5), which is based on our negotiation model described in Section 4.2. In case of a successful negotiation, the broker agrees on individual quality guarantees, i.e., closes a contract in terms of SLAs with a specific provider. In order to enable customers to verify compliance with the negotiated SLAs from their perspective and independent of the respective cloud provider later on, the broker also provides monitoring services to consumers. For this purpose, the information contained within a negotiated SLA is passed to the monitor component of the broker

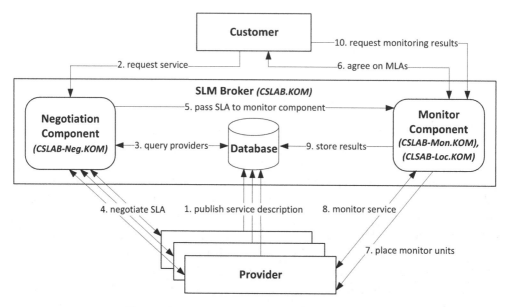

Figure 4.1: Scenario considered in this thesis

after a successful negotiation and serves as input to configure the monitoring tasks for the corresponding cloud service. In addition, we propose the concept of an *Monitoring Level Agreement (MLA)* upon which a customer and a broker agree on. Basically, the idea behind MLAs is that customers can also request specific properties to be guaranteed for the monitoring tasks conducted by the broker. MLAs will be elaborated on in more detail in Section 4.3.5. Having agreed on MLAs, the monitoring component of the broker configures monitor units accordingly and utilizes our monitor placement strategies *CSLAB-Loc.KOM* (presented in Chapter 6) in order to determine appropriate locations for the monitor units. Subsequently, the monitor component verifies at runtime, whether the respective cloud service complies with the negotiated SLAs or not. For this purpose, the broker applies our reliable consumer side monitoring approach *CSLAB-Mon.KOM* described in Chapter 6, which is based on our basic monitoring design described in Section 4.3. The current monitoring results can be directly accessed by consumers and are stored in the database maintained by the broker, so that customers can also retrieve historical monitoring results later on.

The advantage of such a broker-based approach is the exploitation of global knowledge. Since a broker is aware of the functional and monitored non-functional properties of several cloud providers, a broker is able to recommend the most suitable cloud providers and to initiate SLA re-negotiations or recommend alternative cloud providers in case of SLA violations. In order to be able to switch seamlessly between different cloud providers, interoperability between cloud providers is a prerequisite, which is currently addressed by several activities (cf. Section 2.2.3).

4.2 Negotiation Design

As already mentioned in the previous section, we envision a scenario in the present work, in which consumers approach a cloud broker residing in the market in order to obtain individual guarantees on the non-functional properties of a particular cloud service. Basically, cloud services of public cloud providers are provided over the Internet and network services are predominantly delivered on a best effort basis (cf. Section 2.2.3) by an Internet Service Provider (ISP). Hence, no quality guarantees on the network connections from a consumer to a cloud provider will be commonly given by an ISP, unless an ISP supports dedicated network access, usually at very high cost. Cloud providers, in turn, can only offer quality guarantees with respect to their own infrastructure. Therefore, SLAs are mostly only defined for the control sphere of a cloud provider. The requirements for negotiation of such cloud provider SLAs are described in the following in Section 4.2.1. Moreover, a generic model of negotiation performance is presented in Section 4.2.2. The model encompasses influencing factors on negotiation performance and common metrics to express the performance of a negotiation. Thus, the model can be considered to be a foundation for negotiation design and for comparing different negotiation mechanisms against each other. Based on our findings, we describe the basic model of our negotiation mechanism in Section 4.2.3.

4.2.1 Negotiation Requirements

In order to enable the provisioning of SLAs according to the specific business constraints of cloud consumers on-demand, automated SLA negotiation mechanisms are required (cf. Section 1.1). Furthermore, multiple competing providers may exist in the market offering similar services with different QoS values (cf., e.g., [114, 204]). Hence, cloud consumers require appropriate means that allow to compare these different cloud providers against each other with respect to their offered quality levels before establishing a contract with the most suitable one [185]. The requirements for a negotiation mechanism in our broker-based scenario are described in the following.

1. **Multiple Issues:** The negotiation mechanism should be able to cope with multiple issues that are negotiated in parallel. Since we assume that the negotiating parties specify different levels of importance for each issue, trade-offs are possible. When making trade-offs, the value of one issue is increased by a certain amount while the value of another issue is decreased to a certain extent, so that the overall benefit for one or both negotiating parties increases [59]. Hence, several proposals exist that, although exhibiting different values for each issue, provide the same benefit to one negotiating party, but vary in the benefit for the opponent. This raises the question, which trade-off to make at a given point in time during negotiation.

2. **Concurrency:** In our scenario, a broker must be able to negotiate concurrently with multiple providers. This bears the challenge to compare the offers from multiple providers against each other and to decide, which proposals to announce next.

3. **Privacy:** The negotiating parties should be supported in finding an efficient agreement while protecting each party's privacy (cf. Section 1.1).

4. **Pareto-Efficiency:** When negotiating with multiple providers over multiple issues in a business scenario, in which trade-offs are possible and the negotiating parties want to protect their private information, the resulting decision process is quite complex. Nonetheless, if the negotiating parties act in a rational manner, they will strive for Pareto-optimal solutions (cf. Section 1.1).

5. **Time Limits:** Since a broker cannot negotiate over an infinite amount of time [38], we assume that each negotiating party has an individual time limit in order to complete a negotiation.

4.2.2 Generic Model of Negotiation Performance

The automation of negotiations is realized by the use of computer systems and several negotiation mechanisms of different complexity have been proposed for that purpose (cf. Section 3.1) resulting in different outcomes. Therefore, the design space of negotiation mechanisms is analyzed in the following in order to identify relevant parameters influencing their performance. The resulting performance model as depicted in Figure 4.2 constitutes a further contribution of the present work and is described in detail in the following.

Basically, the performance of a negotiation mechanism is mainly influenced by the negotiation protocol and the negotiation strategies of the negotiating parties applied during negotiation. The aspects of negotiation design have already been described in Section 2.3.1 and have been summarized in Figure 2.8. All these aspects can have an influence on particular negotiation performance metrics. These metrics are described in the following and can address either computational performance or contractual aspects. The former characterizes the effort to find an agreement in terms of, e.g., time and communication costs, and the latter focuses on the quality of the contract. We distinguish two groups of computational performance aspects that either concern the overall interaction between the negotiating parties or single-sided actions conducted by the negotiators on their own. Performance metrics resulting from the overall interaction are scalability, execution time, the total number of rounds (e.g., [216], [223]), and the total number of exchanged messages (e.g., [195]). Scalability, in computer systems, means that the efficiency of a system can be maintained at a desired level, if the machine and problem size are increased proportionally [98] (cf. Section 2.2.3). Thereby, efficiency can be expressed in terms of, e.g., execution time. Hence, an algorithm can be denoted as scalable if the execution time grows proportionally, i.e., linearly, to the problem size, holding other resources, such as memory and CPU, constant [36]. Transferred to negotiations, the scalability of a mechanism can be determined by analyzing the ratio of a growing number of participants or negotiated issues on the total execution time or the number of exchanged messages. Concerning single-sided actions, the time to create an own proposal and the time to valuate an opponents (counter-)offer can also be considered to be performance metrics. In contrast, contractual performance indicates how well the interests of the parties involved in a negotiation have been met in the end represented by contract value and contract coverage. The value of a contract can be expressed in terms of the achieved (individual) utility of the negotiating parties (e.g., [190], [224]), social welfare (e.g., [224]) or Pareto-efficiency (e.g., [118], [223], [194]) of an agreement. Contract coverage corresponds to the fact whether a negotiation design has led to (all-embracing) agreements or not. This comprises the number or percentage of successful negotiations (e.g., [216], [190]) and the number of negotiated issues covered by a contract.

Summarizing the attributes of the negotiations considered in our scenario according to the model of negotiation performance, the present work focuses on one-to-many negotiations conducted concurrently in a bilateral manner concerning multiple issues that are proposed simultaneously in the context of incomplete information and time limits. Since these attributes are already given by the considered scenario, only the remaining attributes can be modified in order to improve negotiation performance. That is, the negotiation protocol and the strategies applied during negotiation. Concerning computational performance, the present work neglects single-sided actions since they are already included in the total execution time. Furthermore, as part of our requirements, the negotiating parties should aim to achieve Pareto-efficient solutions, since they should not miss the opportunity to achieve a better solution without making the opponent worse off (cf. Section 4.2.1). Hence, concerning contractual performance, this work addresses the Pareto-efficiency of a negotiation mechanism in our considered scenario and the individual gains in utility of the negotiating parties. Since we focus on all-embracing agreements, we only measure the success rate regarding the conclusion of contracts besides the Pareto-efficiency in the evaluation of our negotiation approach in Chapter 8.

4.2.3 Basic Negotiation Model

The scenario considered in the present work explores one-to-many negotiations, in which a broker concurrently negotiates with multiple providers on behalf of a consumer over the non-functional parameters of a particular cloud service. Based on the requirements presented in Section 4.2.1, the underlying negotiation model of our negotiation mechanism (introduced in Chapter 5) is described in the following.

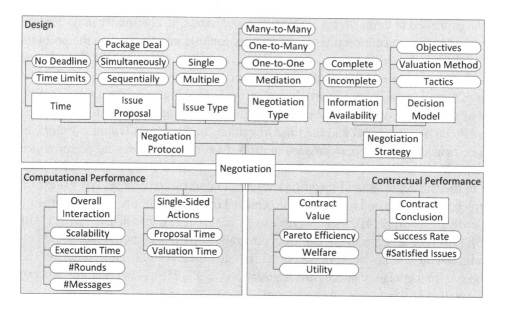

Figure 4.2: Model of negotiation performance

As a prerequisite for our negotiation model, we assume that the non-functional parameters of each service can be modified resulting in different priced configurations for each service, similar to, e.g., approaches proposed in the field of Web service research [227]. The non-functional requirements of a consumer or provider on a service are expressed in terms of constraint intervals based on the proposal by Sierra et al. [189]. Each interval reflects the lower and upper bounds, i.e., the acceptance range for a given parameter (e.g., execution time between 5 ms and 10 ms). Usually, a negotiating party either proposes the lower or upper bound for each issue as initial proposal, so that the remaining minimum or maximum values represent a party's reserve values. Hence, a proposal can be defined as follows:

Definition 1. (Proposal)
Given a set $X = \{x_1,...,x_n\}$ of values for n issues, in which each issue represents a parameter under negotiation. A message sent from a negotiating party a to a negotiating party b that contains such a set X of values proposed by a is denoted as proposal. A proposal is considered to be valid, if each value x_i for a given issue in the proposal is within the constraint intervals for that issue defined by a and b, i.e., $x_i \in [min_i^a, max_i^a]$ and $x_i \in [min_i^b, max_i^b]$.

In order to assess the benefit obtained from a given proposal, a negotiating party p must assign a certain utility to the value of each issue x_i being part of the proposal.

For this purpose, the following scoring function is used, which maps each constraint interval to a utility range from 0 to 1 in order to make different proposals comparable (e.g., [59, 227]):

$$
U_i(x_i) = \begin{cases} \dfrac{max_i^p - x_i}{max_i^p - min_i^p} & \text{if } U_i(x_i) \uparrow \text{ as } x_i \downarrow & (4.1a) \\[3mm] \dfrac{x_i - min_i^p}{max_i^p - min_i^p} & \text{if } U_i(x_i) \uparrow \text{ as } x_i \uparrow & (4.1b) \end{cases}
$$

Since a negotiating party may consider some of the issues as being more important than others, we assume that the parties specify weights W for all n issues representing their levels of importance for each issue.

$$
W = \{w_1, ..., w_n\} \quad \text{with } \sum_{i=1}^{n} w_i = 1 \tag{4.2}
$$

Furthermore, we assume that the parties alternate in making proposals while trying to achieve an agreement. Hence, negotiations are conducted over several rounds. In each of these rounds, decisions have to be made on both sides. That is, one party has to compose an initial offer or appropriate counter-offer for the case that the former offer turns out not to be acceptable and the other party has to determine the benefit of that offer and to decide whether it is acceptable or not. Basically, a negotiating party can determine the benefit obtained from a given offer based on a utility function (cf. Section 2.3.2). In this regard, we follow other research works and consider linear, additive utility functions in our negotiation model for reasons of computational simplicity[1](cf., e.g., [59, 62, 217, 224]). Hence, in our negotiation model, the total utility U for a given offer is calculated as follows, where $U_i(x_i)$ represents the utility of issue x_i.

$$
U = \sum_{i=1}^{m} U_i(x_i) * w_i \tag{4.3}
$$

The parties joining a negotiation have conflicting interests and aim to achieve a mutual agreement through negotiation. Hence, concessions have to be made by the parties during each round. In doing so, the negotiating parties apply individual negotiation strategies resulting in different concession amounts. Further, during each round, the parties further have to decide whether a proposal is acceptable to them or not. In this regard, it is intuitive that a party considers a proposal to be acceptable, if the utility obtained from that proposal is at least as high as the utility gained from the proposal the party will announce in the following round. However, in our considered

---

[1]   Note that the underlying concept of our negotiation mechanism CSLAB-Neg.KOM presented in Chapter 5 is also applicable when using other types of utility functions. Solely the negotiation algorithm has to be slightly adapted in this case.

scenario, more than a single acceptable proposal may exist, since a broker concurrently negotiates with multiple providers. Since each party wants to maximize its total utility, a party will choose that offer among all the acceptable proposals providing the highest utility. The resulting acceptance condition can be expressed mathematically, as follows ([189], [43]):

Definition 2. (Acceptance Condition)
Let a be a consumer who concurrently negotiates with a set of providers $B = \{b_1, ..., b_m\}$ and let $O^t_{b_i \to a}$ be an offer sent from provider b_i to consumer a in round t of a negotiation. Further, let $O^{t+1}_{a \to b_i}$ be the offer consumer a is going to send in the next round to provider b_i. Then, the offer $O^t_{b_i \to a}$ is acceptable to consumer a, if $U(O^{t+1}_{a \to b_i}) \leq U(O^t_{b \to a})$ and $U(O^t_{b \to a}) = max(U(O^t_{b_i \to a})) \forall b_i \in B$.

From a business perspective, the negotiating parties do not only aim to reach a mutual agreement. They rather have specific demands on the performance of a negotiation and want to obtain the best result that is achievable. Therefore, we introduce a new negotiation mechanism CSLAB-Neg.KOM in Chapter 5, based on our negotiation model, which allows approaching a Pareto-efficient solution despite incomplete knowledge.

4.3 Monitoring Design

Besides the demand for more specific SLAs and the design of appropriate, corresponding negotiation mechanisms, cloud consumers must also be able to verify that they are receiving the quality of service for which they are paying for. This is especially of interest to consumers, when they are running business critical tasks in the cloud. Hence, also means for monitoring the negotiated SLAs later on at runtime are required. In our considered scenario, such monitoring services are also provided by the envisaged SLM broker, since monitoring solutions offered by cloud providers cannot be considered to be an independent and reliable evidence base for SLA violation detection from a consumer's point of view. In this thesis, we focus on availability monitoring, since an uptime guarantee is one of the very few performance guarantees that are currently offered by today's cloud providers (cf. Section 1.1).

4.3.1 Availability of Cloud Services

In general, availability is not only business-critical, but also essential for service provisioning. Amazon [5], for example, guarantees an availability - expressed by the percentage of service uptime to total time - for EC2 of at least 99.95% over a year, which equals a downtime of approximately not more than 5 minutes per week. Although availability is a well-known quality parameter of IT systems in general, new issues arise with respect to availability in the field of cloud computing. Due to the different service models and the utilization of virtualization as one of the enabling technologies of cloud computing (cf. Section 2.1), new interdependent layers are introduced that must be taken into account for monitoring. The complexity further increases, since cloud applications on the SaaS level comprise a broad range of different functions. Besides this additional complexity, the high level of flexibility concerning cloud-based resources also bears new risks with respect to availability. Cloud computing leverages the benefits of virtualization by co-locating different virtual resources on the same physical machine. However, the co-located resources can interfere with each other, e.g., when workload changes. Furthermore, virtualized resources can be easily migrated to other physical machines, so that surrounding conditions change in the background without being noticed by consumers. Finally, consumers face a loss of control when utilizing services from a public cloud, since the insights are invisible to them. Hence, adequate means for monitoring the availability of a cloud-based service from a consumer's perspective are required.

Although availability is often considered to be a security aspect, we follow the definition of Jain [103] and consider availability as an inherent condition for service performance. According to Jain, the availability of a system can be expressed as *"the fraction of the time the system is available to service users' requests"*. This translates into the following formula:

$$availability = \frac{uptime}{uptime + downtime} \tag{4.4}$$

Availability can also be expressed in terms of the mean uptime, also denoted as Mean Time To Failure (MTTF), and the mean downtime, also referred to as Mean Time To Repair (MTTR) as stated below in Equation 4.5. This formula is valid for renewal processes. A renewal process exists, if the process restarts when a considered event occurs for the first time and the probability for the second occurrence of that event is the same as before [125]. Since we assume in this thesis that the individual Time To Failure (TTF) and Time To Repair (TTR) intervals are independent of each other, we utilize Equation 4.5 in order to measure availability in our monitoring approach.

$$availability = \frac{MTTF}{MTTF + MTTR} \tag{4.5}$$

Besides the metric, also different types of outages must be distinguished depending on the system for which to measure availability. For example, when determining network availability, only connectivity issues must be considered. In contrast, cloud service SLAs deal with the availability of a cloud service itself, which is also influenced by the level of availability of several other components in a cloud environment. Hence, we analyze the reasons for downtimes of cloud applications in the next section, in order to derive the requirements for a corresponding monitoring approach.

4.3.2 Reasons for Downtimes

In cloud computing, cloud applications are provided and consumed remotely over the Internet. Typically, a cloud application is deployed on a VM, which in turn is hosted on a physical machine within a cloud provider's data center. In order to be able to invoke a certain functionality of a cloud application without a failure, consumer's not only require working IT systems on-premise, but also a proper network connectivity of their own IT systems to the cloud provider's infrastructure. Furthermore, cloud applications often comprise several different components, so that also other resources (e.g., a database) connected to the cloud application can indirectly affect its functioning. Since cloud service delivery spans a variety of resources, downtimes of cloud applications can have several different root causes. Therefore, we have compiled a taxonomy for downtimes of cloud applications, which incorporates the most common types of incidents. The taxonomy is depicted in Figure 8.17 and explained in detail in the following.

First of all, whenever a service becomes unavailable or is perceived to be unavailable from a consumer's perspective, the cause may lie outside a cloud provider's sphere of control. In this case, issues on the consumer side may prevent a consumer from accessing a certain application or network connectivity problems within an ISP may exist (cf., e.g., [144]). Therefore, we distinguish downtimes based on the *location*, where an incident has happened that caused a downtime. In addition, such an incident may concern different types of resources, which have an influence on the availability of a cloud service. For example, software failures, outages of VMs, an overload of physical machines, VM migration, or maintenance may prevent a cloud service from serving requests (cf., e.g., [137, 144, 208]). Since several types of incidents relate to multiple types of resources, and vice versa, two additional categories, namely *resource* and *incident*, have been added to our taxonomy. Besides the actual occurrence of downtimes, which can be described by the three aforementioned categories, also the

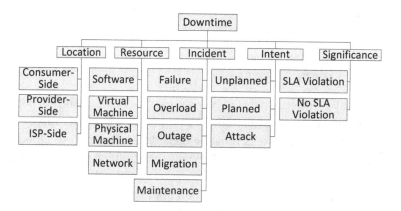

Figure 4.3: Taxonomy for downtimes of cloud applications

conditions (denoted as *intent* in the taxonomy) under which a downtime happens must be considered in order to be able to distinguish downtimes covered by an SLA from other downtimes. Basically, the set of potential downtimes does not only comprise unplanned downtimes that happen by accident. However, scheduled maintenance, for example, represents planned downtime and is therefore usually excluded from the set of possible SLA violations within an SLA (cf., e.g., [11]). Furthermore, downtimes can also happen with criminal intent for the case that a system is attacked by a hacker. However, depending on the terms and conditions of a certain SLA, downtimes related to each type of intent can either represent an SLA violation or not. Concerning planned downtimes, a maximum length, for example, can be specified within an SLA for scheduled maintenance (cf., e.g., [11]). Hence, downtimes are only considered to be an SLA violation if they are covered by an SLA. But also unplanned downtimes can be included or excluded in the set of possible SLA violations. For instance, a provider usually assumes no liability for emergency maintenance (cf., e.g., [172]), but may be responsible in case of a failure of a physical machine. And even in the case of an attack, SLAs may not be violated due to negligence of consumers or may represent an SLA violation since a provider should have taken more care by implementing according security mechanisms that are covered by an SLA (cf., e.g., [44]). For all the above reasons, similar types of downtimes can either represent SLA violations or not. Therefore, not only the type of downtime, but also the terms and conditions within the corresponding SLAs must be taken into account. Furthermore, cloud providers can only make guarantees in the form of SLAs with respect to their own IT systems and cloud consumers have only direct control of their own IT systems. Due to the current best-effort service model of the Internet (cf. Section 2.2.3), consumers usually cannot obtain any guarantees with respect to availability or network performance from ISPs. However, causes for downtimes perceived by consumers can lie within all spheres of control. Therefore, our availability monitoring solution must be able to assess the *significance* of a downtime in order to distinguish perceived downtimes due to incidents on the consumer or the ISP side from real SLA violations on the cloud provider side.

4.3.3 Monitoring Requirements

Based on the analysis of reasons for downtimes in the last section, we will now elaborate on the requirements for developing an approach for reliable consumer side availability monitoring of cloud applications. Concerning the *intent* of a downtime, the present work focuses on unplanned downtimes. This is due to the fact that cloud providers usually announce planned downtimes in advance, so that consumers are aware of such downtimes. Moreover, detecting attacks on cloud systems is beyond the scope of this thesis.

From a cloud provider's perspective, availability monitoring faces lower barriers in contrast to a consumer side approach because of the direct access to the own infrastructure. However, from a consumer's perspective, it is very difficult to assess if the promised level of availability is really maintained, since the insights of a cloud environment are invisible to consumers and access to cloud services and resources is provided over interconnected third-party networks, such as the Internet. If a VM, where a cloud application to be monitored is hosted, crashes, the responsible cloud provider could claim that the cloud application is still up and running and that a failure must have occurred outside the provider's sphere of control. Therefore, a consumer needs appropriate means to monitor the status of a cloud application in order to be able to provide evidence that an SLA violation has happened. The corresponding requirements are listed in detail in the following (cf. [1]):

1. **Reliable SLA violation detection**

    a) **Location-awareness:** Distinction of downtimes according to the control sphere (cf. Section 4.3.2) where the incident causing the downtime occurred

    b) **Resource-awareness:** Determining the resources that are directly and indirectly affected by a downtime

    c) **Accuracy:** Calculation of availability with the required precision

2. **Robustness:** Demand for a reliable, i.e., correctly working, underlying monitoring infrastructure, even in the presence of unforeseen failures

3. **Timeliness:** Measurements concerning the current status of a cloud application should be available on time in order to be able to react timely to incidents

4. **Agility**

    a) **Scalability:** Easily adapt to an increased number of users and components, i.e., to a large number of probes

    b) **Elasticity:** Ability to cope with the dynamic nature of cloud-based systems, i.e., dynamic assignment of cloud resources to consumers

    c) **Adaptability:** Easily adapt to varying workloads in order not to interfere with service and network performance

    d) **Autonomicity:** Ability to self-manage the distributed monitoring resources and to react automatically to unforeseen changes

5. **Functional flexibility**

    a) **Comprehensiveness:** Support for monitoring various types of cloud resources and corresponding metrics from multiple consumers

b) **Extensibility:** Easily enhance the functional capabilities of the monitoring system

c) **Non-Intrusiveness:** Adoption without requiring significant modifications of the cloud environment

Regarding our envisaged approach for consumer side availability monitoring, requirements no. 1-3 are the focus of the present work, while requirements no. 4 and no. 5 are considered rudimentally in monitor system design. The requirements above are based on the following considerations. Despite the restricted access of consumers to the cloud provider's infrastructure, our approach should be able to detect SLA violations reliably. For this purpose, the envisaged monitoring approach must be *location-aware*. That is, it must be able to determine whether a downtime occurred within the control sphere of a cloud provider or not, since a cloud provider can only offer SLAs with regard to its own resources. In addition, the monitoring approach must be *resource-aware*. Since a variety of resources is involved in cloud service delivery, downtimes may directly or indirectly affect a cloud application. While the former comprises downtimes that directly originate from the cloud application, the latter incorporates downtimes, which originate from other resources and, thus, may indirectly prevent a cloud application from delivering its services. By identifying the resource where a downtime originated from, it can be determined whether a corresponding SLA clause has been violated or not. Finally, reliable monitoring results should represent as closely as required the real state of the object under investigation. By adjusting the monitoring frequency, for instance, the minimum length of a downtime that can be detected is determined. Hence, monitoring has to be performed with a certain *accuracy*. As a prerequisite for providing reliable monitoring results, the monitoring system itself must also work correctly. However, since some monitoring components may fail, the envisaged monitoring approach requires a *robust* underlying monitoring infrastructure. Such a robust infrastructure enables a monitoring system to continue working correctly even in the presence of failures. Another important requirement concerns the *timeliness* of monitoring results. Customers should receive up-to-date information about the current state of a cloud application in order to initiate an appropriate response, such as an alert message or service migration [1]. In general, the timely delivery of monitoring results depends on the sampling interval, the analysis delay, and the communication delay [1]. The sampling interval thereby influences the delay until an incident is detected. The analysis delay comprises the time until all required input parameters have been delivered and the subsequent computation time of an aggregate result. The communication delay incorporates the transmission of all the monitoring information to its final processing node. It should be noted that not all the aforementioned requirements are independent of each other. Although a shorter sampling interval, for instance, implies a higher accuracy as well as an increased timeliness, a higher monitoring frequency leads to a higher resource consumption.

Thus, there is a trade-off between accuracy and monitoring frequency [1]. Besides the major requirements discussed so far, further requirements concerning the *agility* and *functional flexibility* of the envisaged monitoring approach have to be considered in monitoring design. Since cloud environments are very dynamic, the monitoring approach should exhibit an agile behavior. Such a behavior comprises the abilities to react to a changing number of users and components as well as to varying resource assignments and workloads and to adapt the monitoring resources accordingly. The present work lays the foundation for the monitoring system to act in an agile manner. However, agility is not the focus of the present work. The same applies for functional flexibility. As already mentioned in Section 1.2, we focus on the SaaS level of cloud-based services and availability monitoring. But our monitoring approach can be slightly adapted for monitoring other types of cloud resources and corresponding metrics. Nonetheless, the envisaged monitoring approach should be *non-intrusive*, so that it is applicable without greater modifications to the existing cloud resources. This is especially of major importance, given the restricted access of cloud consumers to a provider's cloud environment.

4.3.4 Basic Monitoring Approach

Given the aforementioned requirements, an intuitive solution would be to allow a consumer to access the monitoring data of a cloud provider. Unfortunately, in doing so, cloud providers could introduce false information or restrict the consumer's access to a subset of the data, so that not all SLA violations can be detected. Furthermore, consumers would not be able to determine the cause of a downtime easily during a downtime of a cloud provider. In this case, they could not decide if the downtime results from an outage of the cloud provider's infrastructure or if network impairments only prevent them from reaching the cloud provider's infrastructure.

However, consumers need monitoring results they can trust. Therefore, a cloud consumer not only requires means to assess the status of a cloud application independent of a cloud provider, but also requires visibility of the entire cloud service delivery chain in order to be able to attribute downtimes to their correct root cause. This can be realized by combining appropriate availability checking functions for the different components involved in cloud application delivery and by providing a holistic view of the end-to-end performance of a cloud-based service to consumers. For this purpose, we suggest a hybrid monitoring approach with regard to the location of the monitoring entities and the monitored resources. Hence, we combine monitoring on the broker and the cloud side as well as on the application and the VM level. Basically, our design consists of three different types of entities (cf. Figure 4.4): broker side monitors, cloud side monitors, and a Monitoring Data Aggregator (MDA). In this regard, the MDA represents a coordinating entity that is responsible for aggregating data monitored by the monitoring entities to complex final results. The broker side and cloud side entities both monitor the cloud application and the VM, where the cloud application is hosted. While cloud side monitors are placed inside the cloud, the other entities are located within the control sphere of the broker, i.e., outside the cloud. A precondition for cloud side monitoring is that a consumer has some access to a cloud provider's infrastructure. Usually, consumers are able to start and access own VMs within a cloud provider's data center, where cloud side monitors can be placed. Cloud side monitors will not be co-located with a cloud application on the same VM. This is due to the fact that a cloud-monitor would not be able to report any downtime when that VM goes down. Therefore, we make use of additional VMs within a cloud provider's data center for placing cloud side monitors.

Admittedly, in order to separate the VM where a certain cloud application is hosted fully from the VM where a corresponding monitoring unit is placed, also the underlying physical machines should be different for the same reason as stated above. However, cloud consumers are not able to control the VM placement with regard to the utilized physical machines, since this would interfere with the existing load-balancing mechanisms implemented on the provider side. Nevertheless, cloud providers could provide a unique Identification Number (ID) for each physical machine and information about the respective ID that is currently associated with each VM in the future. This would enable the specification of advanced anti-co-location constraints with regard to the monitor placement by the envisaged broker and further enhance the reliability of our approach. Cloud providers could benefit from supporting our monitoring approach in the sense that data obtained in a provider-independent manner showing their adherence to the offered SLAs would increase their reputation. In case of such advanced anti-co-location constraints, a replacement of certain VMs with regard to the physical machines conducted by the implemented load-balancing mechanisms at runtime violating any of the constraints would raise the need for adapting the placement of the monitoring units accordingly. The development of such adaptation mechanisms could be of interest for future research.

Another benefit that can be obtained from using a separate VM to place a cloud side monitor is that it can be used for collecting monitoring data from multiple applications. Usually, enterprise customers utilize several different cloud applications. Hence, it is reasonable to establish a central monitoring entity with multiple monitoring tasks in order to reduce the effort for maintenance and coordination. In contrast to broker side monitors, the monitoring frequency of a cloud side monitor can be much higher. However, a cloud side monitor alone cannot provide visibility of the whole service delivery chain. That means, from a consumer's perspective, it cannot detect all incidents that cause a downtime perceived by consumers. Figure 4.4 shows the basic design of the monitoring architecture.

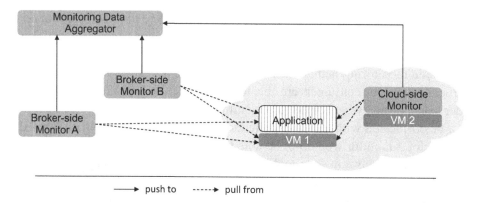

push to   pull from

Figure 4.4: Overview of the monitoring architecture

Application-level Monitoring   As the name already indicates, the objective of application-level monitoring is to assess the state of a cloud application. In order to reduce the impact of our monitoring approach on system performance, only prede- fined services are tested that are considered to be essential for a correctly working cloud application from a consumer's point of view. Of course, the set of essential services of a cloud application must be defined in advance, e.g., as part of MLAs (cf. Section 4.3.5). For the actual invocation of these services, we make use of a periodical pull model, i.e., active probing. In doing so, the required precision, i.e., the desired accuracy regarding the measured availability of a cloud application can be achieved by adjusting the monitoring (i.e., invocation) frequency accordingly. Note, that we do not conduct passive measurements, since we would obtain a very limited view of the cloud application's availability, when the corresponding services are only invoked from time to time (cf. Section 2.4.3). As soon as responses arrive at a monitoring entity, they are checked for correctness in order to derive the current status of a cloud application. From a consumer's perspective, we consider a cloud application to be unavailable, if one of the essential services fails, i.e., no (correct) response is received within a given time period. For the actual invocation of services, a monitoring entity can directly use the API of a cloud application without modification. Most cloud applications provide their services using Web service technologies, i.e., services can usually be invoked using REST or SOAP (cf. Section 2.1.2). The overall availability is determined by the MDA. For this purpose, monitoring entities push their monitored data to the MDA. Basically, three different types of messages are exchanged between a monitoring entity and the MDA:

- **Registration:** Once a monitoring entity is started, it registers at the MDA by stating its ID, its sphere of control (e.g., broker side network domain), the name of the cloud application, the essential service(s) to be observed, and the starting time of monitoring that application.

- **Uptime:** Whenever a monitoring entity receives a correct response from a cloud application, a notification is sent to the MDA indicating the time period of the corresponding service invocation.

- **Downtime:** If a cloud application does not seem to be available from the perspective of a monitoring entity, a notification is also sent to the MDA indicating a perceived downtime during the respective measurement interval.

Depending on the desired resolution of the measured availability, the monitoring frequency can be increased in order to gain a higher precision. Theoretically, any downtime of a cloud application can be detected in this way (cf. Section 6.2.1). However, besides a too low monitoring frequency, also failures within the network between a monitoring entity and a cloud application could prevent a monitoring entity from accessing an essential service causing a perceived downtime. In this case, our monitoring approach should not only retry sending requests, but also conduct availability checking from a different location. In this regard, we assume that the broker, similar to a cloud provider, is running several data centers at different locations worldwide. Thus, we add at least two independent broker side monitors located at different network domains to our design. All entities monitoring the same application must be either synchronized or at least the offset between the monitoring entities must be known in order to be able to compare their monitoring results with regard to the observed state at simultaneous time intervals.

Although performing application-level monitoring will be sufficient to detect a downtime of a cloud application, such a solution is not able to determine the root cause and, thus, which SLA clause has been violated. A VM failure, for instance, may cause a downtime of an application or a cloud application may go down, while the underlying VM continues working correctly. While the former represents a violation of a VM-related uptime guarantee, the latter concerns the availability of the application. This raises the need for additional VM-level monitoring.

VM-level Monitoring   The objective of VM-level monitoring is to check the status of the VM where a cloud application is hosted. If that VM goes down, the cloud application will also fail. A basic availability checking function on VM-level is to send an Internet Control Message Protocol (ICMP) echo request to the IP address of the VM. If the VM answers by sending an ICMP echo response, the VM is up and running. Otherwise, an error message is sent by, e.g., an intermediate router indicating that the VM is not reachable. Besides sending ICMP echo requests, a more detailed root cause analysis can be conducted, if a consumer has access to the VM where a cloud application is running on. In this case, the monitoring capabilities can be expanded to check the status of the processes on VM-level that are essential for running a cloud application by installing a lightweight software component (denoted as VM monitor) on the VM. This may be reasonable whenever the VM is up, but no response is received from the application. Again, these processes have to be specified in advance, e.g., as part of MLAs. In doing so, VM-level monitoring proceeds similar to application-level monitoring. A periodical pull model is applied for data collection, i.e., for sending ICMP echo requests or invoking the VM monitor in order to retrieve information about the processes on VM-level. A push-based model is used for sending data to the MDA. In this regard, the same three message types apply that are exchanged for application-level monitoring. However, additional information is added to registration messages, namely, the VM-level process(es) to be observed. Uptime and downtime messages are sent by a monitoring entity according to the current state of a VM-level process or response to an ICMP echo request. A separate VM monitor component is required since no Web service-based interfaces usually exist on system-level in order to gather knowledge regarding VM-level processes.

In addition to the actual monitoring tasks described above, the monitored data is also stored locally on each level for backup purposes. This may be beneficial for later analysis in case of disputes due to, e.g., network outages. Furthermore, it is important to mention that our solution constitutes a generic monitoring approach. On the one hand, the fact of being a generic approach may reduce its accuracy in some cases, in which specific properties of a certain cloud service, which are not considered by the generic approach, have an influence on the monitoring results. However, on the other hand, our generic monitoring approach bears the advantage that it is applicable for monitoring all cloud services in general, which exhibit functionalities that can be invoked from remote locations using, e.g., Web service technologies such as REST or SOAP. In addition, the monitoring approach can also be easily extended to consider further QoS parameters such as response time. Finally, concerning a real implementation of our monitoring approach, we have validated the feasibility of a remote deployment of monitoring units in terms of autonomous agents on Amazon EC2 in a related research work (cf. [142]).

4.3.5 Monitoring Level Agreements

As already mentioned in Section 4.1, we also propose the concept of MLAs representing agreements between the broker and a customer with regard to the monitoring tasks to be conducted by the broker. As a prerequisite for applying our hybrid monitoring approach, a consumer has to specify the set of essential services to be invoked for monitoring a certain cloud application and, optionally, the set of processes to be observed on VM-level. In this regard, MLAs can specify the consumer's requirements concerning all the cloud applications to be monitored, such as the monitoring frequencies for the monitoring entities on both sides. However, these frequencies depend on the availability guarantees agreed upon in the SLAs. Therefore, lower bounds for these frequencies should be determined automatically based on the negotiated SLAs in order to obtain a minimal resolution required to assess the negotiated level of availability. Besides the monitoring frequencies, the number of redundant monitoring entities to be utilized for each cloud application can also be specified as part of the MLAs. This is especially reasonable, if enterprise customers are running business critical applications in the cloud. In this case, a higher number of redundant monitoring entities increases the robustness of the monitoring system, i.e., decreases the probability that all monitoring entities fail concurrently. Basically, MLAs can be defined in a similar manner as the definition of SLAs. MLA negotiations can be conducted over the different parameters, such as the monitoring frequency, the number of redundant monitoring entities, and the monitoring fees. Intuitively, providers will associate a higher fee with a higher monitoring frequency, since the resource consumption increases. The same applies for utilizing a higher number of monitoring entities resulting in higher deployment and maintenance costs.

4.4 Summary

Having presented the basic design of our envisaged SLM broker CSLAB.KOM and its two major tasks SLA negotiation and monitoring, the details of these tasks will be described in the next chapters. While Chapter 5 presents our negotiation mechanism CSLAB-Neg.KOM that allows approaching Pareto-efficient outcomes, Chapter 6 describes the details of our reliable consumer side monitoring approach CSLAB-Mon.KOM. In this regard, Chapter 6 also elaborates on how to determine the monitoring frequency in order to obtain a certain level of accuracy. Following the assumption that the robustness of the monitoring system can be increased by utilizing redundant monitoring entities, we propose strategies for robust monitor placement CSLAB-Loc.KOM in Chapter 7.

5 Pareto-Efficient Negotiations - CSLAB-Neg.KOM

Based on our basic negotiation model introduced in the previous Chapter 4, this chapter proposes a corresponding negotiation mechanism. In order to address the drawbacks of related approaches, the proposed negotiation mechanism - denoted as CSLAB-Neg.KOM - allows approaching Pareto-efficient outcomes despite incomplete information and permits the strategic behavior of the negotiating parties to be maintained when negotiating with multiple providers over multiple issues. This chapter is structured as follows. Section 5.1 provides a detailed problem statement. Subsequently, Section 5.2 introduces how Pareto-efficiency of a negotiation mechanism is determined in the considered scenario resulting in an ex post Pareto-efficiency reference model that serves as a baseline for our negotiation mechanism. The model allows the computation of a representation of the space of Pareto-efficient solutions for a given negotiation setting by utilizing information gained from simulating that negotiation. In Section 5.3, we describe our negotiation mechanism CSLAB-Neg.KOM [96, 185], which comprises a negotiation protocol, negotiation strategies, and a negotiation algorithm. The chapter closes with a summary in Section 5.4.

5.1 Problem Statement

As cloud service consumption will further grow in the next years (cf. Chapter 1), the number of cloud providers will also increase. Hence, the cloud market will become more competitive among the providers offering similar services and the non-functional properties, i.e., QoS of the services will gain more importance [225]. The present work is based on a global cloud marketplace following the vision of the IoS, in which consumers entrust a broker residing in the marketplace with the negotiation of SLAs. As a prerequisite for SLA negotiation, we assume that a set of functionally equivalent services meeting the functional requirements of a consumer can be determined by the broker in advance by, e.g., querying a global registry (cf. Section 4.1). The resulting functionally equivalent services only differ in terms of QoS and cost, so that the subsequent SLA negotiations conducted by the broker with the corresponding providers only concern the non-functional properties of these services. In order to determine the most suitable service during SLA negotiation and to reach an agreement, the negotiating parties exchange proposals following a common negotiation protocol.

Admittedly, parties that are willing to participate in a negotiation in general have to agree on a common protocol in advance before entering a certain negotiation. For this purpose, so-called meta-negotiations are usually conducted (e.g., [21]). However, in the present work, we focus on a scenario with particular requirements. Therefore, we assume that the negotiating parties apply a specific negotiation protocol preset by the SLM broker, which has been designed for this specific scenario (cf. Section 5.3.2). Following our basic negotiation model, we further assume that each negotiating party has individual preferences that are expressed as follows.

For each issue, the parties specify constraint intervals representing the lower and upper bounds as well as weights indicating their personal level of importance with regard to each issue. Furthermore, each party has a private utility function that permits the determination of the level of utility that a party would obtain by accepting a given proposal. Proposals comprise the desired values for each QoS issue and the price of a service a party would be willing to pay if the provider guarantees the specified QoS levels. In order to reach an agreement, the negotiating parties have to make concessions during negotiation due to conflicting interests and apply individual negotiation strategies. Since the negotiating parties do not have an infinite amount of time to negotiate, we further assume that each party has an individual deadline. If the deadline of a party is reached before an agreement could be achieved, the party opts out of the negotiation. We already argued that the negotiating parties will strive for a Pareto-efficient agreement, so that no free gains will be lost. Given the envisaged scenario, the following challenges arise.

First of all, a negotiating party has to decide when and how to make concessions, since the parties have conflicting interests and want to achieve an agreement. The negotiations are conducted over multiple issues. This is in contrast to a single issue negotiation, in which the preferences of the negotiating parties are perfectly negatively correlated, so that all possible agreements are Pareto-efficient [59]. However, in multiple issue negotiations, trade-offs can be made between the different issues. Hence, multiple proposals exist, which provide the same level of utility to a proposing party, but different levels of utility to each of the opponents. Proposals exhibiting the same level of utility are located on the same indifference curve (cf. Section 2.3.2). As already mentioned, we focus on an incomplete information setting in the present work, so that none of the negotiating parties is aware of the preferences of the other parties. Hence, a proposing party does not know, which of the offers on a certain indifference curve, i.e., which trade-off provides a higher benefit to the opponent(s) or represents a Pareto-efficient solution.

The overall goal is to achieve a (near) Pareto-efficient solution when negotiating with multiple providers over multiple issues without knowing the preferences of the opponents. To the best of our knowledge, none of the related approaches has addressed Pareto-efficient outcomes given the conditions of the envisaged scenario while maintaining the strategic behavior of the negotiating parties. As already stated in

Chapter 3, the strategic behavior is limited when the composition of the next proposal of a party depends on the content of the opponent's last offer.

5.2 Ex Post Pareto-Efficiency Reference Model

The present work focuses on concurrent one-to-many negotiations, in which multiple conflicting objectives of the negotiating parties exist simultaneously. Such problems are denoted as *multiobjective optimization problems*. Multiobjective optimization problems have the following characteristics [134]: First of all, no explicit set of feasible solutions is given in advance, but restrictions in the form of constraint functions exist. Furthermore, no unique solution exists, but a set of Pareto-optimal solutions can be determined, which are equally good from a mathematical point of view. Usually an infinite set of Pareto-optimal solutions exists, so that only a representation of this set can be generated. However, the generation process typically involves expensive computations and is sometimes difficult.

In general, different approaches exist in order to generate such a representation of the set of Pareto-optimal solutions, also denoted as *Pareto frontier*. In the present work, the *adaptive weighted sum method* as proposed by Kim and de Weck [99] is used in order to compute the Pareto frontier. Other methods typically determine, a priori, the set of solutions that are considered by predefining weights, whereas the method by Kim and de Weck explores the Pareto frontier iteratively until a certain level of resolution is reached. The idea behind their approach is to compute a rough representation of the Pareto frontier in the first step using the weighted sum method and in the second step, to conduct further refinements iteratively in some of the regions determined so far. Thereby, a region represents the area between two adjacent solutions.

For the computation of the Pareto frontier in the considered scenario, an ex post evaluation is conducted. This means that each negotiation is simulated first in order to determine the properties of the final outcome. More specifically, the simulation aims at determining the provider among all the participating providers who concludes the final agreement with the broker acting on behalf of a certain consumer. An ex post evaluation is performed for the sake of simplicity. The computational complexity to determine the best provider in advance is huge when a broker negotiates on behalf of a consumer with multiple providers simultaneously. The preferences of the best provider resulting from the simulation and the consumer's preferences, both can then be used as input for the computation of the Pareto frontier. Otherwise, conducting an analysis over all providers' preferences in advance would permit to explore, whether a consumer has reached an agreement with the theoretically best provider without incorporating drawbacks resulting from bad strategic behavior. However, in line with the work in [121], this thesis aims at the development of a supportive negotiation mechanism that allows reaching Pareto-efficient agreements while preserving advantages the negotiating parties gain from their applied strategies.

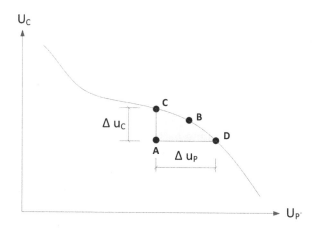

Figure 5.1: Pareto-efficient frontier and efficiency-measures

By applying the method of Kim and de Weck to the considered scenario, a representation of the Pareto frontier for a given negotiation result can be obtained, as illustrated in Figure 5.1. The Pareto frontier typically has a convex and a concave region [99]. Let U_C be the consumer's total utility and U_P the provider's total utility. Further, let the solution point A be the final result obtained from a negotiation. Now, in order to determine the Pareto-efficiency of such a given solution, we measure the maximum amount in utility that a consumer or provider could additionally achieve without making the other party worse off (cf. [46]). In doing so, Δu_c and Δu_p represent the consumer's and provider's maximum utility gain, if solution point C and D would have been reached, respectively. In contrast, solution point B would represent a result where the share in additionally utility is divided among consumer and provider.

The representation of the Pareto frontier obtained in this way serves as a baseline for our negotiation approach. In doing so, the goal to achieve a (near) Pareto-efficient solution can be expressed in a more operational manner. Concerning a final agreement, the difference of each party's total utility obtained from that agreement to the maximum amount in utility that a party could have additionally achieved in a certain negotiation without making the opponent worse off should be minimized. Consequently, a solution is considered to be efficient if no additional utility could have been achieved from both, a consumer's and provider's point of view. Thus, the goal is to reach one of the agreements that are located on the Pareto frontier. It must be noted that our negotiation approach does not explicitly aim for a specific agreement from the set of agreements on the Pareto frontier. We rather aim to provide a non-biased approach to consumers and providers from a broker's perspective. That is to provide a negotiation framework, in which the negotiating parties may act according to their individual strategic preferences, so that different final outcomes can be obtained depending on their strategic behavior.

5.3 Pareto-Efficient Negotiation Mechanism

This section presents our negotiation mechanism CSLAB-Neg.KOM, which constitutes one of the major contributions of this thesis. The proposed negotiation mechanism allows approaching Pareto-efficient agreements in concurrent multiple-issue negotiations without disclosing private information to an opposing party and to preserve the strategic behavior of the negotiators. Based on the considerations while designing our ex post Pareto-efficiency reference model, Section 5.3.1 presents the underlying concept of the negotiation mechanism expressed in the form of a two-phase meta-strategy. Following that meta-strategy, a corresponding negotiation protocol is described in Section 5.3.2. Subsequently, Section 5.3.3 introduces the negotiation strategies that are applied by the negotiating parties during each of the two phases of a negotiation according to the meta-strategy. Note that although being strategies, they still represent generic procedures that have to be parameterized by the negotiating parties in order to define their specific strategic behavior during a negotiation according to their individual strategic preferences. Furthermore, in order to enable to approach Pareto-efficient outcomes, the negotiating parties have to stick to these negotiation strategies. A detailed negotiation algorithm that defines the details of the negotiation strategy applied in the second phase is provided in Section 5.3.4.

5.3.1 Meta-Strategy

Based on our findings from the analysis of related work (cf. Chapter 3) and the design of our ex post Pareto-efficiency reference model (cf. Section 5.2), our negotiation approach follows a two-phase meta-strategy. An overview of the different phases is provided in Figure 5.2. In line with related approaches (e.g., [121, 168]), the first phase, denoted as *Agreement Phase*, aims at determining a first allocation, i.e., initial agreement, while the second phase, denoted as *Trade-Off Phase*, serves to improve that initial agreement. As illustrated in conjunction with our ex post Pareto-efficiency reference model, there is still room for improving each party's utility starting from a non Pareto-efficient agreement without making the opposing party worse off. Hence, the second phase strives to maximize each party's utility increase. The details of both phases are described in the following.

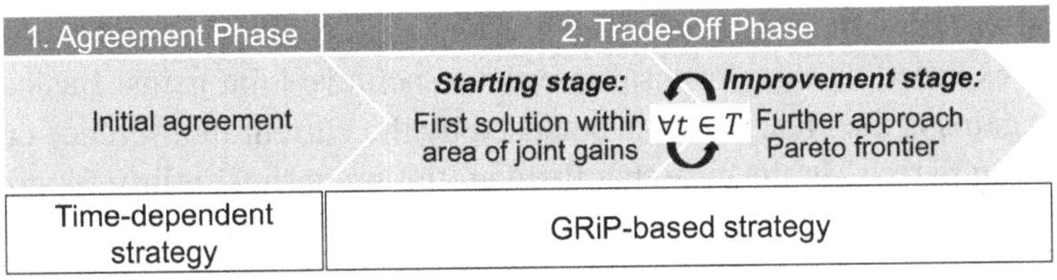

1. Agreement Phase	2. Trade-Off Phase	
Initial agreement	*Starting stage:* First solution within area of joint gains	$\forall t \in T$ *Improvement stage:* Further approach Pareto frontier
Time-dependent strategy	GRiP-based strategy	

Figure 5.2: Overview of our meta-strategy

In the Agreement Phase, the negotiating parties exchange proposals over several rounds, thereby exploring their mutual interests. A concession-based approach is employed, meaning that concessions are made in each round if no agreement can be achieved. A concession-based approach has been chosen due to the fact that, as stated by Zheng et al. [224], these kinds of approaches will eventually achieve an agreement, i.e., they exhibit a success rate of 100%. This statement holds for negotiations without any time restrictions, i.e., if negotiations are conducted over a sufficient amount of time, given that the negotiating parties' preferences overlap to a certain extent. In case of individual negotiation deadlines as considered in our envisaged scenario, an agreement may not be guaranteed in every negotiation. Nevertheless, we do not want to limit a party's scope of action, but keep the option to withdraw from a negotiation without an agreement. In this case, negotiating parties can enter new negotiations with different opponents, whose proposals may possibly better fit their preferences. In order to realize a concession-based approach, we apply time-dependent strategies (cf. Section 5.3.3.1), which are based on the individual deadlines of the negotiating parties.

Having achieved a preliminary agreement with a specific provider after a certain number of rounds, the negotiating parties may enter the Trade-Off Phase. As already mentioned above, the goal of this second phase is further to improve a preliminary agreement. For this purpose, improvement proposals are exchanged. In this regard, we assume that an improvement proposal is only considered to be acceptable, if it represents an improvement for both negotiating parties, i.e., leads to joint gains. This assumption can be considered to be reasonable, especially in a business scenario. A negotiating party would not be willing to proceed to the Trade-Off Phase, if there is the risk that this phase only yields single-sided gains in favor of the opponent. While exchanging improvement proposals, a preliminary agreement is successively improved, thereby approaching a Pareto-efficient solution.

Recalling Figure 2.9 in Section 2.3.2, the negotiation mechanism determines an initial agreement in the first phase, such as solution point A or B. In the second phase, the mechanism tries further to improve that solution towards a Pareto-efficient outcome, i.e., to reach a tangent point within the dark gray area such as solution point C. For the generation of an improvement proposal, we propose a new negotiation strategy considering *Greed*, *Risk*, and *Patience* levels of the negotiating parties (in the following denoted as *GRiP-based strategy*, cf. Section 5.3.3.2). The idea behind that strategy is to use the current agreement as a reference proposal and to conduct trade-offs between different issues based on that proposal in order to achieve joint gains. Basically, the area of joint gains is the area, which is enclosed by the current indifference curves of two negotiating parties. In the case that the negotiating parties' utility functions are non-linear, the area of joint gains is represented by the dark gray area in Figure 2.9. As already mentioned, we consider linear utility functions in the present work. This is because they are the most common in the field of utility theory concerning multiple

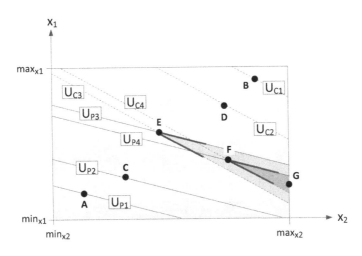

Figure 5.3: Pareto-efficient search in case of linear utility functions

issues and computing trade-offs becomes tractable [62]. Nevertheless, our approach can also be adapted to suit other types of utility functions (cf. Section 4.2.3). In case of linear utility functions, the indifference curves are also linear, as depicted in Figure 5.3. In that case, the area of joint gains is not fully enclosed by the indifference curves, but also limited by the borders of the overlap of the negotiating parties' constraint intervals defined for each issue. Hence, the negotiating parties can continue searching for improvements with regard to a certain QoS parameter until the proposed value for that QoS parameter exceeds the overlap of the negotiating parties' constraint intervals. Concerning Figure 5.3, two parties negotiating over the two issues x_1 and x_2 alternate in making the proposals A, B, C, and D, until an initial agreement is obtained in solution point E. Now, since their utility functions are linear, the negotiating parties can continue in making improvements, such as solution point F, until they reach a final agreement in solution point G.

In the present work, we focus on multiple-issue negotiations concerning availability, execution time, and price, for the sake of simplicity. However, this does not limit the general applicability of our negotiation mechanism. Concerning trade-offs, we assume that an increased quality will usually come at a higher price. Therefore, negotiating parties using our negotiation mechanism can conduct trade-offs between a certain QoS parameter and the price. In this regard, a lower price in conjunction with a lower quality level may be also beneficial for some of the consumers, if the utility gain resulting from the lower price exceeds the loss in utility resulting from the lower quality level. At the same time, the provisioning of that lower quality level has to provide a higher utility gain from a provider's perspective than the decrease in utility resulting from the lower profit in order to permit joint gains. Hence, two different directions of trade-offs are feasible, which may result in joint gains. Considering

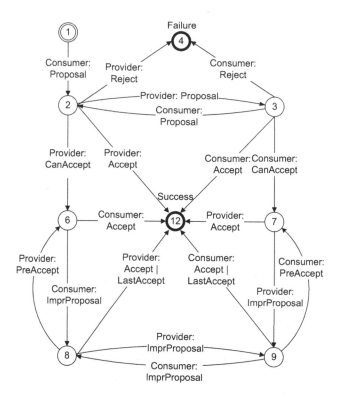

Figure 5.4: Extended alternate offers negotiation protocol

the three issues mentioned above, the values proposed for availability or execution time can be either increased or decreased in conjunction with a change in price, so that four different types t of trade-offs can be considered. Each type t from the set T of available trade-offs is explored within two different stages during the Trade-Off phase (cf. Figure 5.2). In detail, an iterative search for joint gains is accomplished for each type t of trade-off over a *Starting Stage* followed by an *Improvement Stage*. Thereby, the Starting Stage aims at determining an initial solution residing in the area of joint gains, while the Improvement Stage serves further to improve that initial solution towards a Pareto-efficient agreement. The corresponding negotiation protocol is described in the next section.

5.3.2 Negotiation Protocol

The negotiation protocol follows our two-phase meta-strategy as described in the previous section and, thus, also comprises two different phases. Basically, it represents an extension of the alternate offers negotiation protocol (cf. Section 2.3.1). Our resulting negotiation protocol is depicted in Figure 5.4. An overview of the corresponding message types is provided in Table 5.1.

In the Agreement Phase, a broker initiates a negotiation on behalf of a consumer by sending an initial proposal to multiple providers. The proposal is then evaluated by the providers and they reply according to their own preferences. Subsequently, proposals are exchanged for a certain number of rounds. As a result, the broker acting on behalf of a consumer tries to reach a preliminary agreement with one of the providers during that first phase. In this regard, a received proposal can either comply with a negotiating party's acceptance condition or not. In the latter case, a negotiating party can either make a counter-proposal or withdraw from the negotiation by sending a *Reject* message. In the former case, a negotiating party can either send an *Accept* message resulting in a final agreement or a *CanAccept* message resulting in a preliminary agreement. If the broker receives a set of counter-proposals from the providers, their proposals are also evaluated according to the consumer's preferences. If at least one of their proposals is acceptable to the broker, that proposal providing the highest utility to the consumer is accepted by the broker. Otherwise, the broker compiles another counter-proposal, which is again sent to all the remaining providers that did not withdraw from the negotiation in the previous round(s). By sending a *CanAccept* message, a negotiating party signals its willingness further to improve that initial agreement. If the other party is also willing further to improve that agreement, both parties enter the Trade-Off Phase of the negotiation protocol. Otherwise, the other party can reject this *CanAccept* message by sending a final *Accept* message. In this case, the negotiation ends without improving the initial agreement.

During the Trade-Off Phase, improvement proposals are exchanged with the aim to achieve joint gains. Upon receipt of such an improvement proposal, a party has to choose one option out of the following available message types. By sending an *Accept* message, a party agrees with the opponent on the current improvement proposal and the negotiation ends with a final SLA. A second option is to send a *PreAccept* message. In doing so, the current improvement proposal is also considered to be acceptable by the party who's turn it is. In addition, that party is still willing to continue in making improvements and signals that willingness to the opponent. Having agreed upon an improvement proposal, a new (preliminary) agreement is achieved. Similar to the case, in which an improvement proposal is acceptable to a party, there are also two options for the case that an improvement proposal is considered to be not acceptable. One option is to reject that current proposal and to continue by sending a counter improvement proposal. Another option is to send a *LastAccept* message, which terminates the negotiation and the last accepted preliminary agreement becomes the final agreement.

5.3.3 Negotiation Strategies

In conjunction with the negotiation protocol presented before, the negotiation strategies described in this section build a complete negotiation mechanism that allows

Table 5.1: Overview of the different message types

Message	Description
Proposal	a party makes a proposal to reach an initial agreement
Accept	a party accepts a proposal as final agreement
Reject	a party withdraws from the negotiation
CanAccept	a party signals its willingness to improve an agreement
ImprProposal	a party makes an improvement proposal
PreAccept	a party accepts an improvement proposal
LastAccept	a party accepts the previous agreement as final agreement

approaching Pareto-efficient outcomes in concurrent multiple-issue negotiations. In line with our meta-strategy (cf. Section 5.3.1), a concession-based approach has been chosen for the first phase of our negotiation mechanism. In doing so, the negotiating parties can explore mutual interests and eventually achieve an initial agreement. As already mentioned, we apply time-dependent strategies for this purpose in order to account for the individual deadlines of the negotiating parties. This first Agreement Phase is followed by a trade-off-based approach in the Trade-Off Phase. This second phase is based on an exchange of improvement proposals with the aim further to improve the initial agreement towards a Pareto-efficient solution. As already stated, we propose a new GRiP-based negotiation strategy to be applied during this second phase. Starting from the current preliminary agreement, the GRiP-based strategy supports the negotiating parties in searching for beneficial trade-offs between different issues that lead to joint gains. The individual preferences concerning greed, risk, and patience of a negotiating party are thereby considered to be parameters for configuring the GRiP-based strategy according to a negotiating party's needs. The details of the strategies applied in both phases are described in detail in the following.

5.3.3.1 Agreement Phase

In order to generate proposals during this first phase, time-dependent strategies are applied as proposed by Sierra et al. [189]. Time is crucial in a business scenario, especially when negotiating simultaneously with multiple providers. Hence, a consumer should soon achieve an initial agreement with a certain provider. However, other strategies are also applicable in general, if they are suitable to achieve an initial agreement in a certain amount of time. As already mentioned, a negotiation is initiated by the broker. In this regard, the broker generates a first proposal comprising the values that are the most preferred ones from a consumer's perspective. In the likely case, that this initial proposal is not acceptable to any of the multiple providers, they generate their first counter-proposals in a similar manner. That is these proposals also specify the most preferred values from their perspective. If still no agreement can be achieved, concessions have to be made from that point on. Thus, both sides continue to alternate in making proposals and make concessions in each round until an agreement is reached. In this regard, a (counter-)proposal, i.e., the value for an issue x_i at round t with $t \leq t_{max}^P$ and t_{max}^P representing the individual negotiation deadline of a certain negotiating party p is determined as follows [189]:

$$x_i = \begin{cases} min_i^P + \alpha_i(t)(max_i^P - min_i^P) & \text{if } U_i(x_i) \downarrow \qquad (5.1a) \\ min_i^P + (1 - \alpha_i(t))(max_i^P - min_i^P) & \text{if } U_i(x_i) \uparrow \qquad (5.1b) \end{cases}$$

The amount of concession is thereby determined using the descending function $\alpha_i(t)$. Two families of this function are typically distinguished: exponential and polynomial [189]. In our approach, we use the exponential function, since it concedes slower at the beginning preserving a higher utility level during the first rounds. The exponential function is defined as follows, where β determines the amount of concession in each round and k_i represents a constant that can be set based on experience [189]:

$$\alpha_i(t) = exp\left((1 - \frac{t}{t_{max}^P})^\beta \ln k_i\right) \qquad (5.2)$$

Depending on the value of β, the literature usually distinguishes the following three types of time-dependent strategies [189]:

- Conceder ($\beta > 1$): great concessions already after start

- Linear ($\beta = 1$): equal[1] concessions in each round

- Boulware ($\beta < 1$): great concessions near the end

When using time-dependent strategies, the negotiating parties have to specify their individual preferences for concessions in terms of a value for β as input parameter, amongst others, for the negotiation mechanism. In order to provide intuitive means to consumers for specifying these preferences, we assume that the broker in our envisaged scenario provides a corresponding input form in the user interface of each consumer showing different sliders. These sliders represent the ranges of the different parameters that have to be specified in order to parameterize the strategies applied during a negotiation. In order to provide an intuitive slider for concessions to be made during a negotiation, the three types of time-dependent strategies can be considered from a business perspective. Basically, the strategies reflect the willingness of a negotiating party to assume a risk. In this regard, a risk-seeking party will probably choose a boulware strategy in contrast to a risk-averse party preferring a conceder strategy.

---

[1] Note that near constant concessions are made in case of the exponential variant of the $\alpha_i(t)$ function.

While the former is seeking to maintain a very high level of utility, for as long as possible, such a strategy exhibits a higher risk to end up with no agreement. In contrast, a risk-averse strategy resulting in higher concessions permits a faster convergence to an opposing party's interests and, thus, to a mutual agreement. Unfortunately, such a risk-averse strategy will more likely yield a lower utility in the end due to high concessions. As a third type of strategy, linear strategies reflect risk neutrality. Admittedly, such a linear strategy can be easily recognized and an opponent could exploit that knowledge to his/her own advantage. However, as already stated, the negotiation mechanism is configured once in advance and no modifications can be made anymore during a negotiation. Based on this risk perspective, the slider expressing the concessions can show different intuitive risk levels ranging from "low risk" over "moderate risk" up to "high risk", which can be mapped to the following values for the input parameter β in our approach. In case of low risk, values can be selected in the range $(0.0, 1.0)$, a moderate risk level equals 1.0, and the values are in the range $(1.0, 5.0]$ in case of a high risk level. The specific ranges for β are based on the work by Patel et al. [151]. Similar to the slider for the concessions, sliders for the individual weights of each QoS parameter under negotiation can be provided. Each of these sliders can also show intuitive weights ranging from "less important" over "important" up to "very important", which can be mapped to the numerical range of $(0.0, 1.0)$. The specified weights of the parameters can be normalized afterwards by the negotiation mechanism so that they add up to 1.

5.3.3.2 Trade-Off Phase

Having determined an initial agreement in the first phase, a search for improvements is conducted in the subsequent Trade-Off Phase. For this purpose, the current (preliminary) agreement is used as a starting point and trade-offs between different issues are proposed in order to detect joint gains. The search for improvements is based on the following considerations. Recalling Section 2.3.2, proposals that provide the same level of utility to a negotiating party can be represented by an indifference curve. Furthermore, the absolute value of the slope at a given point of an indifference curve expresses the exchange ratio of the issues, i.e., the MRS, in order to maintain the same level of utility. Hence, a negotiating party can use her\his own current MRS as a reference. By deviating from the own current MRS, improvements are feasible. Of course, a deviation from the own MRS must be conducted in such a manner that it leads to an increase in utility of a negotiating party. Basically, when making trade-offs between two issues, a certain QoS parameter and the price, for instance, two directions can be considered. Either a decrease or an increase in price and quality may provide a higher utility to a negotiating party. From a consumer's perspective, for instance, an improvement can be achieved if the increase in utility caused by a higher quality of a certain attribute is larger than the corresponding decrease in utility caused by a higher price. In a similar manner, if a decrease in utility caused by a lower quality is compensated by a very large reduction in price, an overall higher utility is achievable. However, such an increase in utility of one party does not necessarily also lead to an increase in utility for the opponent and, thus, to joint gains. Whether joint gains can be achieved or not, depends on how both MRS relate to each other. Concerning our envisaged scenario, we aim to approach a Pareto-efficient solution. As already mentioned in Section 2.3.2, Pareto-efficient solutions are represented by tangent points of the negotiating parties' indifference curves. Since the slopes of both indifference curves are equal at these points, both corresponding MRS are also equal in case of a Pareto-efficient solution. Consequently, joint gains are only feasible as long as the provider's MRS_{prov} and the consumer's MRS_{cons} differ. The conditions for joint gains can be formally expressed as follows:

- $MRS_{prov} > MRS_{cons}$: a decrease in price and quality is required
  - the deviation from MRS_{cons} is positive
  - the deviation from MRS_{prov} is negative

- $MRS_{prov} < MRS_{cons}$: an increase in price and quality is required
  - the deviation from MRS_{cons} is negative
  - the deviation from MRS_{prov} is positive

To put it another way, assuming that a trade-off in the form of an increase in quality and price is proposed by a consumer resulting in a new proposal that constitutes an improvement from the consumer's perspective. Furthermore, let us assume that $MRS_{prov} < MRS_{cons}$. If at the same time from a provider's perspective, the increase in utility caused by a higher price is larger than the corresponding decrease in utility caused by a higher quality of a certain attribute, a joint improvement is made. Therefore, in order to achieve joint gains, deviations from the own MRS must be conducted in such a way that the own and the opponent's utility is increased simultaneously. However, in our considered scenario, we assume incomplete knowledge so that the negotiating parties are only aware of their own MRS. Since a negotiating party won't be willing to disclose that information to the opponent, trade-offs in the form of improvement proposals can only be made in favor of the proposing party in the first instance. Hence, some feedback is required from the opponent in order to determine whether that proposal also constitutes an improvement for the opponent or not.

Following our negotiation protocol, the Trade-Off Phase consists of an exchange of improvement proposals between the negotiating parties. In this regard, the basic idea behind that phase is to conduct an iterative, distributed search for improvements. That is, each of the n QoS parameters under negotiation is explored in one of n different iterations. In each of these iterations, all types of available trade-offs concerning a specific QoS parameter in conjunction with the price are tested with regard to joint gains. Since we assume that the negotiating parties do not want to reveal their private information, the search for joint gains can only be performed in a distributed manner, i.e., by incorporating the knowledge of both negotiating parties. The distributed search for joint gains proceeds as follows.

Distributed Search for Joint Gains   Starting from a current preliminary agreement, the negotiating party, who's turn it is, determines a trade-off using his/her own current MRS as a reference resulting in a new improvement proposal. This proposal is sent to the opponent in order to acquire feedback on its ability for also improving the opponent's utility. For the case that the improvement proposal is successful, i.e., results in joint gains, the opponent replies with a positive feedback. Subsequently, if both negotiating parties are willing to continue to negotiate, that improvement proposal is set as new preliminary agreement. Based on that agreement, the search for joint gains continues. Otherwise, if the proposal does not provide an increased utility to the opponent, we assume that the opponent directly replies with an own improvement proposal in the next step, thereby indicating, that the previous proposal of the proposing party has not been successful.

For the generation of improvement proposals in general, the level of greed and risk of a negotiating party is considered, in addition to the own MRS. As already mentioned, we propose a GRiP-based strategy to be applied during the Trade-Off Phase, that considers the preferences of the negotiating parties in terms of greed, risk, and patience. The notion of patience will be elaborated on in the next section. For proposal generation, we assume that a negotiating party starts with a very large deviation from the own MRS in the first step at the beginning of each iteration. This assumption is intuitive, since a higher deviation yields a larger gain in utility, given that an improvement proposal is successful. However, the higher the deviation, the higher is the risk to exceed the limit of deviating from the own MRS represented by the opponent's MRS, i.e., for an improvement proposal to be unsuccessful. Therefore, we assume that each negotiating party specifies a risk factor for each of the n QoS parameters under negotiation. This is formally defined as follows for some negotiating party a:

- *risk factor* $R = \{\rho_1^a, ..., \rho_n^a\}$: initial amount of deviating from the own MRS in percent for each QoS parameter

Besides the risk factor, also the desired additional or subtractive units for a certain QoS parameter must be specified. For this purpose, a greed factor is defined for each QoS parameter by a negotiating party a. This results in the following formal expression:

- *greed factor* $G = \{\gamma_1^a, ..., \gamma_n^a\}$: units to be added (or removed) in percent for each QoS parameter

In order to conduct a trade-off between a specific QoS parameter and the price resulting in a new improvement proposal, new values must be calculated for the QoS parameter and the price. In this regard, the greed factor γ_i^a of a negotiating party a is used in order to determine the new value x_i' for the considered QoS parameter i. Recall that trade-offs can be conducted in two different directions, which leads to an increase or decrease of the current value x_i as follows:

$$x_i' = x_i \left(1 \pm \gamma_i^a\right) \tag{5.3}$$

For the computation of the new $price'$ resulting from a certain trade-off, the amount of deviating from the own MRS_i must be taken into account resulting in a new MRS_i' for a given QoS parameter i. Using the corresponding risk factor ρ_i^a, the calculation of the new MRS_i' can be formally specified as:

$$MRS_i' = |MRS_i| \pm |MRS_i| \times \rho_i^a \tag{5.4}$$

Based on the increase or decrease of a QoS parameter i involved in a trade-off as well as the new MRS_i', the new $price'$ can then be calculated using the following formula:

$$price' = price \pm \Delta price = price \pm \left(x_i \times \gamma_i^a \times MRS_i'\right) \tag{5.5}$$

Besides the value of a QoS parameter i considered in a certain trade-off and the price, other values concerning further QoS parameters are not modified when composing an improvement proposal. Considering our meta-strategy, the composition and exchange of improvement proposals during the iterative, distributed search for improvements is conducted over two different stages, a *Starting Stage* and an *Improvement Stage*. Both stages will be described in detail in the next section.

5.3.4 Negotiation Algorithm

Over the two aforementioned stages of the Trade-Off Phase, the negotiating parties apply a GRiP-based strategy in order to search for improvements. In this section, we present a negotiation algorithm that describes the behavior, i.e., actions and decisions, of a negotiating party a following a GRiP-based strategy during the Trade-Off Phase. The main negotiation algorithm is provided in Algorithm 1.

As a preparatory step, several global auxiliary variables are defined at the beginning (lines 1-4). The purpose of each of these variables will be described in the context of their first occurrence within the algorithm. These variables are defined as *global*, since all *subroutines* must be able to access and modify their values. The main procedure starts in line 5 and receives the following input parameters: a reference to the opposing party b, the initial agreement O^* that should be improved, the set Pr of preferences of negotiating party a and his/her configuration parameters for the GRiP-based strategy.

According to our basic negotiation model (cf. Section 4.2.3), the set Pr is formally defined as follows:

- *preferences* $Pr = \{Pr_1^a, ..., Pr_n^a\}$: each subset Pr_i^a specifies the preferences of a certain negotiating party a for a given issue i in terms of a weight w_i^a, a lower bound min_i^a, and an upper bound max_i^a, i.e., $Pr_i^a = \{w_i^a, min_i^a, max_i^a\}$

The configuration parameters for the GRiP-based strategy incorporate a set R of risk factors and a set G of greed factors, which have already been defined in a formal manner in the previous section. In addition, the configuration parameters comprise a set P of patience levels and two sets C_1 and C_2 of cooling factors. A formal definition for the set P of patience levels is provided in the following. The notion of a cooling factor is explained in the context of Algorithm 3.

- *patience* $P = \{\pi_1^a, ..., \pi_n^a\}$: defines an upper bound for the number of own trials to search for an improvement in one direction for each QoS parameter

In line with our meta-strategy, the Trade-Off Phase first enters the Starting Stage. Therefore, the variable *start* indicating the current stage is set to *start* in line 6. Recall that the goal of the Starting Stage is to achieve a first solution within the area of joint gains. Since the QoS parameters are considered issue-by-issue during the Trade-Off Phase, the counter i indicating the currently considered issue is set to 1 in line 7. Subsequently, the auxiliary function GETNEXTPARAM is called in order to determine, which of the QoS parameters should be the first (i.e., i-th) issue to be considered from the perspective of negotiating party a. As a result, the auxiliary function GETNEXTPARAM returns the index j of the entry in the set of preferences Pr that corresponds to the currently considered issue i (line 8). In this regard, we make the intuitive assumption that the issues are explored in descending order of their weights. Hence, the most important issue is considered at the beginning. Furthermore, we assume, for the sake of simplicity, that the index j of an entry in all other sets (i.e., R, G, P, C_1, C_2) of a negotiating party a also corresponds to the currently considered issue i. The just determined index j is then added to the set A of already considered issues (in terms of indices j) and the risk factor ρ^a is set to the risk factor ρ_j^a of the current issue (lines 9+10). Now, starting from the initial agreement O^*, which has been obtained in the Agreement Phase, the auxiliary function CREATEMSG is called in order to compose a first improvement proposal as described in the previous section based on the current risk factor ρ^a and the specified greed factor γ_j^a (line 11). For the sake of readability, we have refrained from adding further lines of code at this point dealing with constraint checking functions and assume that the first improvement proposal stated in the Algorithm is created without violating any constraints, e.g., upper or lower bounds, and that the negotiating party would directly proceed to the next type of trade-off otherwise. For a real implementation, according constraint

---

Algorithm 1 Negotiation algorithm during Trade-Off Phase

---

input: agent b, initial agreement to be improved O^*, parameters as described in Sections
    5.3.3.2 and 5.3.4

output: final agreement O^*

  1: $i \leftarrow 0, A \leftarrow \emptyset, j \leftarrow 0$ ▷ initialize global auxiliary variables

  2: $t \leftarrow 0, f \leftarrow 0, dir \leftarrow 1, keepdir \leftarrow false$

  3: $\rho^a \leftarrow 0, \rho^a_{min} \leftarrow 0, \rho^a_{max} \leftarrow 0, \rho^a_{last} \leftarrow 0$

  4: $ownprop \leftarrow false, out \leftarrow false$

  5: **procedure** IMPROVEAGREEMENT($b, O^*, Pr, R, G, P, C_1, C_2$)

  6:       $state \leftarrow start$

  7:       $i \leftarrow 1$

  8:       $j \leftarrow$ GETNEXTPARAM(Pr)

  9:       $A \leftarrow A \cup \{j\}$

10:       $\rho^a \leftarrow \rho^a_j$

11:       $M_{a \rightarrow b} \leftarrow$ CREATEMSG(*"ImprProposal"*, O^*, γ^a_j)

12:       SENDMSG($M_{a \rightarrow b}$)

13:       $ownprop \leftarrow true$

14:       $t \leftarrow 1$

15:       **while** ($state \neq success$) **do**

16:           $M_{b \rightarrow a} \leftarrow$ RECEIVEMSG()

17:           **switch** EVALUATEMSG($M_{b \rightarrow a}$) **do**

18:               **case** *PREACCEPT*

19:                   $O^* \leftarrow (M_{b \rightarrow a} \rightarrow O_{b \rightarrow a})$

20:                   $keepdir \leftarrow true$

21:                   $state \leftarrow$ PROCESSPREACCEPT($state, b, O^*, Pr, R, G, P, C_1, C_2$)

22:               **case** *ACCEPT*

23:                   $O^* \leftarrow (M_{b \rightarrow a} \rightarrow O_{b \rightarrow a})$

24:                   $state \leftarrow success$

25:               **case** *LASTACCEPT*

26:                   $state \leftarrow success$

27:               **case** *IMPRPROPOSAL*

28:                   $state \leftarrow$ PROCESSPROPOSAL($state, M_{b \rightarrow a}, b, O^*, Pr, R, G, P, C_1, C_2$)

29:           **end switch**

30:       **end while**

31: **end procedure**

---

checking functions similar to the constraint checking functions in the COMPOSEREPLY
procedure (cf. Algorithm 4) would have to be added at the beginning with regard to the
first improvement proposal. The improvement proposal is then sent to the opponent
b, a flag is set that an own proposal has been sent, and the counter t of trials for
sending improvement proposals is updated (lines 12-14). In the remaining steps, the
negotiating parties continue exchanging messages over several iterations until they
reach a final agreement (lines 15-31). In this case, the variable *state* is set to *success*
(line 15). In each iteration, the negotiating party a waits for a reply from the opponent

(line 16) and proceeds according to the received message type. The two auxiliary functions RECEIVEMSG and EVALUATEMSG are used in this regard to manage the receipt of a message and to determine its type, respectively. Following our negotiation protocol, a negotiation ends when receiving an "Accept" or a "LastAccept" message from the opponent. In the former case, the current proposal is set as final agreement. In contrast, the current proposal is discarded in the latter case and the last preliminary agreement is set as final agreement. When receiving a "PreAccept" message, the current proposal is set as preliminary agreement and a flag is set to maintain that promising search direction for the currently considered QoS parameter (lines 19+20). Similar to the receipt of a "PreAccept" message, further actions taken upon receiving an "ImprProposal" message are executed by a separate subroutine. Both subroutines will be elaborated on in detail in the following.

Having received an improvement proposal from the opponent, a response is generated in the subroutine PROCESSPROPOSAL based on the following conditions:

$$SendMsg = \begin{cases} Accept & \text{if acceptable \& max. no. of trials reached} \\ PreAccept & \text{if acceptable \& not max. no. of trials reached} \\ LastAccept & \text{if acceptable \& max. no. of trials reached} \\ & \text{OR bounds violated \& last QoS parameter} \\ ImprProposal & \text{if not acceptable \& not max. no. of trials reached} \end{cases}$$

In short, the corresponding subroutine PROCESSPROPOSAL has to determine, whether a proposal is acceptable or not, whether the maximum number of own trials has been reached for each QoS parameter, or whether composing a new improvement proposal would violate the specified bounds and the last QoS parameter is currently considered. The decisions and actions taken by a negotiating party a upon receiving an improvement proposal are described in detail in the Algorithms 2 and 3.

As it can be seen from Algorithm 2, the subroutine PROCESSPROPOSAL receives the following input parameters: the current stage, the opponent's improvement proposal, a reference to the opponent, the current preliminary agreement, as well as the configuration parameters for the GRiP-based strategy (line 1). The improvement proposal just received from the opponent is then analyzed with respect to the considered QoS parameter. Specifically, the auxiliary function GETPARAM is called in order to determine whether the opponent has switched to proposing trade-offs for the next QoS parameter or not (line 2). In the former case, the index of the QoS parameter addressed in the received improvement proposal differs from the index j of the QoS parameter considered so far. Hence, the algorithm proceeds with the first iteration of a new Starting Stage concerning the "new" QoS parameter by setting the variable $state$ to $start$ (line 3). In addition, several auxiliary variables are reset or updated with regard to that "new" QoS parameter (lines 4-9). For the case that the currently considered QoS parameter has not changed, an update of some variables is only required if an own

---

Algorithm 2 Procedure PROCESSPROPOSAL for processing a received proposal

---

input: current stage *state*, received proposal $M_{b \to a}$, agent b, preliminary agreement O^*,
    parameters as described in Sections 5.3.3.2 and 5.3.4

output: current stage *state*

  1: **procedure** PROCESSPROPOSAL($state, M_{b \to a}, b, O^*, Pr, R, G, P, C_1, C_2$)

  2:    **if** ($j \neq$ GETPARAM($M_{b \to a}, Pr$)) **then**

  3:        $state \gets start$

  4:        $t \gets 0, f \gets 0, dir \gets 1, keepdir \gets false$ $\triangleright$ reset auxiliary variables

  5:        $j \gets$ GETPARAM($M_{b \to a}, Pr$)

  6:        $A \gets A \cup \{j\}$

  7:        $\rho^a \gets \rho_j^a$

  8:        $i \gets i + 1$

  9:        $ownprop \gets false$

 10:    **else**

 11:        **if** ($ownprop$) **then**

 12:           $f \gets f + 1$

 13:           $\rho_{last}^a \gets \rho^a$

 14:        **end if**

 15:    **end if**

---

improvement proposal has been sent before (line 11). Recalling Section 5.3.3.2, we assume that an opponent replies with an own improvement proposal if the previously received improvement proposal is not acceptable to him\her. Therefore, we make use of an auxiliary variable f indicating the number of failed improvement proposals for a certain QoS parameter and direction (line 12). Furthermore, the value of the risk factor ρ^a, which has been applied for composing the previously failed improvement proposal is stored in variable ρ_{last}^a (line 13). In doing so, ρ_{last}^a can serve as a reference for creating a new improvement proposal in the next iteration.

Having conducted the aforementioned preparatory steps, Algorithm 3 further evaluates whether the improvement proposal received from the opponent is acceptable or not (line 16). In this regard, the auxiliary function ISACCEPTABLE checks whether a certain improvement proposal leads to an improvement in utility for a negotiating party a and whether the proposal adheres to all specified constraints, such as not violating any lower or upper bounds. If a given improvement proposal turns out to be acceptable, it is stored as preliminary agreement (line 17). Subsequently, the algorithm checks whether the end of the negotiation has been reached or not (line 18). A negotiation ends, if the current number of own trials t equals the maximum number of own trials for the currently considered QoS parameter π_j^a in both directions and if the number of considered QoS parameters equals the number of QoS parameters under negotiation. For the latter, the auxiliary function GETLENGTH is used. If the end of the negotiation has been reached, an "Accept" message is sent to the opponent and the overall *state* is set to *success* (lines 19-21). Otherwise, a PreAccept message is sent to the opponent and a flag is set that no own improvement proposal has been sent (lines 23-25). In addition, the auxiliary function GETDIR is invoked in order to retrieve the direction considered in the received improvement proposal and to potentially update the variable *dir* indicating the current direction (lines 27+28). If the direction has changed recently, corresponding auxiliary variables are updated (lines 29+30). Finally, the *keepdir* flag is set in line 32 to maintain the current direction, since that direction has led to an improvement. For the case that the received improvement proposal is not acceptable, the algorithm also checks whether the end of the negotiation has been reached or not (line 35). If the end has been reached, a LASTACCEPT message is sent to the opponent, thereby accepting the last preliminary agreement and discarding the received improvement proposal (lines 36+37). In addition, the overall *state* is set to *success* (line 38). If the negotiation has not yet come to an end, the negotiating party *a* aims to compose a (counter) improvement proposal. As a preparatory step, corresponding variables must be updated. In this regard, Algorithm 3 only performs an update in the first instance, if the maximum number of own trials for the currently considered QoS parameter has not been reached, yet (line 8). Otherwise, further actions are taken by the auxiliary function COMPOSEREPLY later on, such as to choose the next QoS parameter or to terminate the negotiation. Before invoking the auxiliary function COMPOSEREPLY, the algorithm may have to change the current direction, if the maximum number of own trials in that direction has been reached without having found an improvement (lines 43+44). In this case, the counter for the number of failed improvement proposals and the risk factor are reset and the algorithm enters the Starting Stage with regard to that new direction. If the search direction is not changed, the risk factor is not reset, but has to be adapted based on the following considerations.

Recalling our meta-strategy, the objective of the *Starting Stage* is to achieve a first improvement with regard to a certain QoS parameter *i* and search direction. As already mentioned, a negotiating party *a* can make use of his\her own current MRS as a reference. By deviating from the current MRS to a certain amount, which depends on a negotiating party's current risk factor ρ^a, a joint improvement might be achieved. At the beginning of a negotiation, each negotiating party specifies an initial risk factor ρ_i^a for each QoS parameter *i* under negotiation. The more a negotiating party *a* deviates from his\her own current MRS in terms of a higher, initial risk factor ρ_i^a, the higher is a potential gain in utility and the lower is the opponent's gain in utility. However, with an increasing risk factor, also the risks increases for an improvement proposal to be unsuccessful. Therefore, the initial risk factor has to be adapted each time an improvement proposal fails. For the adaptation of the risk factor, we make use of an equation that is inspired from simulated annealing, which constitutes a heuristic search method for solving combinatorial optimization problems [48]. It was first introduced by Kirkpatrick et al. in 1983 and exploits an analogy to the annealing of solids in statistical mechanics [110].

Algorithm 3 Procedure PROCESSPROPOSAL (ctnd.)

16:     **if** ISACCEPTABLE($M_{b \to a} \to O_{b \to a}$) **then**

17:         $O^* \leftarrow (M_{b \to a} \to O_{b \to a})$

18:         **if** $\left(t = 2 * \pi_j^a \right)$ & ($i = $ GETLENGTH(Pr)) **then**

19:             $M_{a \to b} \leftarrow$ CREATEMSG("*Accept*")

20:             SENDMSG($M_{a \to b}$)

21:             *state* $\leftarrow$ *success*

22:         **else**

23:             $M_{a \to b} \leftarrow$ CREATEMSG("*PreAccept*")

24:             SENDMSG($M_{a \to b}$)

25:             *ownprop* $\leftarrow$ *false*

26:             *olddir* $\leftarrow$ *dir*

27:             *dir* $\leftarrow$ GETDIR($M_{b \to a} \to O_{b \to a}, O^*$)

28:             **if** (*olddir* $\neq$ *dir*) **then**

29:                 $\rho^a \leftarrow \rho_j^a, f \leftarrow 0$ ▷ reset auxiliary variables

30:                 *state* $\leftarrow$ *start*   ▷ start search in other direction

31:             **end if**

32:             *keepdir* $\leftarrow$ *true*

33:         **end if**

34:     **else**

35:         **if** $\left(t = 2 * \pi_j^a \right)$ & ($i = $ GETLENGTH(Pr)) **then**

36:             $M_{a \to b} \leftarrow$ CREATEMSG("*LastAccept*")

37:             SENDMSG($M_{a \to b}$)

38:             *state* $\leftarrow$ *success*

39:         **else**

40:             *out* $\leftarrow$ *false*

41:             **if** $\left(t \neq 2 * \pi_j^a \right)$ **then**

42:                 **if** *state* $\neq$ *impr* **then**

43:                     **if** $\left(t = \pi_j^a \right)$ & (*keepdir* $\neq$ *true*) **then**

44:                         *dir* $\leftarrow -dir, f \leftarrow 0, \rho^a \leftarrow \rho_j^a$ ▷ reset auxiliary variables

45:                         *state* $\leftarrow$ *start*   ▷ start search in other direction

46:                     **else**

47:                         $\rho^a \leftarrow \rho_j^a * exp\left(-\tau_j^{a1} * f \right)$

48:                     **end if**

49:                 **else**

50:                     $\rho^a \leftarrow \rho_{min}^a + (\rho_{max}^a - \rho_{min}^a) * exp\left(-\tau_j^{a2} * f \right)$

51:                 **end if**

52:                 *out* $\leftarrow$ ISOUTOFBOUNDS(γ_j^a, Pr, O^*)

53:             **end if**

54:             COMPOSEREPLY("*LastAccept*", *state*, b, O^*, Pr, R, G, P)

55:         **end if**

56:     **end if**

57:     **return** *state*

58: **end procedure**

Basically, the aim of simulated annealing is to overcome local optima while performing a local search as described in the following [48]. It utilizes an acceptance function, corresponding to a cooling schedule in its analogy with statistical mechanics. That acceptance function is originally set to $exp(-\delta/T)$, where δ represents the amount of deterioration with regard to the best solution found so far and T corresponds to the temperature in the analogy. The acceptance function constitutes the probability for temporarily accepting a deterioration in order to overcome a local optimum. As the temperature T is gradually decreased over time, worse solutions are accepted with a high probability at the beginning in contrast to later on. In doing so, simulated annealing approaches a global optimum.

Inspired from the function expressing the decreasing temperature in the simulated annealing-based negotiation approach proposed by Di Nitto et al. [143] (cf. Section 3.1), we make use of Equation 5.6 in order to model the adaptation of the risk factor ρ_i^a during the Starting Stage of our GRiP-based strategy. In detail, the risk factor is decreased to a certain amount according to the number f of (own) failed improvement proposals so far, thereby utilizing a predefined cooling factor τ_i^{a1}.

$$\rho^a = \rho_i^a \times exp\left(-\tau_i^{a1} \times f\right) \tag{5.6}$$

The set C_1 of cooling factors used during the Starting Stage is also part of the configuration parameters of the GRiP-based strategy specified by each negotiating party a and can be formally defined as follows:

- *cooling factor* $C_1 = \left\{\tau_1^{a1}, ..., \tau_n^{a1}\right\}$: each cooling factor affects the speed of convergence of the risk factor ρ^a to zero for a certain QoS parameter i during the Starting Stage

For the case that the Improvement Stage has not been reached, yet, the risk factor is adapted according to the aforementioned Equation 5.6 in Algorithm 3 (line 47). Having achieved a first improvement with regard to a certain QoS parameter i, the algorithm enters the *Improvement Stage*. In this stage, the adaptation of the risk factor is conducted according to Equation 5.7 (line 50).

$$\rho^a = \rho_{min}^a + (\rho_{max}^a - \rho_{min}^a) \times exp\left(-\tau_i^{a2} \times f\right) \tag{5.7}$$

When utilizing Equation 5.7, at least one "own failed improvement proposal" has been sent before. Otherwise, the opponent would directly reply with a "PreAccept" message, instead of sending a (counter) improvement proposal. Given these circumstances, Equation 5.7 is based on the following considerations. ρ_{min}^a represents the successful risk factor observed before entering the Improvement Stage and ρ_{max}^a represents the last unsuccessful risk factor observed during the Starting Stage. In doing so, ρ_{min}^a and

ρ_{max}^a indicate the lower and upper bound, respectively, between which the current MRS of the opponent lies. Recall that the MRS of the opponent constitutes the limit for deviating from the own MRS. Hence, there's still room for achieving higher gains in utility in the next iteration with a MRS higher than the lower bound ρ_{min}^a. Of course, these bounds have to be adapted each time a further improvement is achieved. The corresponding adaptations will be described in detail when elaborating on the processing of "PreAccept" messages. In Equation 5.7, we make use of a cooling factor τ_i^{a2}, which differs from the cooling factor used during the Starting Stage. This is due to the fact that a more fine-grained convergence of the risk factor is required during the Improvement Stage.

The set C_2 of cooling factors used during the Improvement Stage is also predefined by the negotiating parties in advance. A formal definition is given as follows:

- *cooling factor* $C_2 = \left\{ \tau_1^{a2}, ..., \tau_n^{a2} \right\}$: each cooling factor affects the speed of convergence of the risk factor ρ^a to the last successful risk factor observed prior to/during the Improvement Stage

Having finished the adaptation of the risk factor ρ^a at the end of Algorithm 3, the auxiliary function ISOUTOFBOUNDS is called (line 52). This function determines whether the creation of a new improvement proposal, given the current greed and risk factor, would violate the constraint intervals as specified in the set of preferences *Pr* of negotiating party *a*. The result of this invocation is then evaluated in the subroutine COMPOSEREPLY. Recall that the current risk factor ρ^a and the auxiliary variable *out* constitute global variables and are therefore accessible from all subroutines without further action. The pseudocode of the subroutine COMPOSEREPLY is provided in Algorithm 4.

As it can be seen from Algorithm 4, the following input parameters are passed to the subroutine COMPOSEREPLY: the message type to be used to terminate the negotiation, the current stage, a reference to the opponent, the current preliminary agreement, as well as the configuration parameters for the GRiP-based strategy (line 1). The main objective of this subroutine is to react to a message received from the opponent and to compose a reply, as the name of the subroutine already indicates. Basically, that reply either terminates the negotiation or constitutes a new improvement proposal. At the beginning of the subroutine COMPOSEREPLY, the algorithm checks if a new improvement proposal would violate the predefined bounds of negotiating party *a* and if, at the same time, the conditions for changing the current direction are satisfied (lines 2-6). If this is the case, the direction is changed and corresponding auxiliary variables are reset. In addition, the auxiliary function ISOUTOFBOUNDS is invoked again in order to check whether a new improvement proposal with regard to the other direction would violate any predefined constraints. If any constraints would be violated again and if, at the same time, the last QoS parameter is currently considered, a message is sent to the opponent in order to terminate the negotiation (lines 7-10).

Algorithm 4 Procedure COMPOSEREPLY for composing a reply

---

input: final message type *msgtype*, current stage *state*, agent b, preliminary agreement O^*,
    parameters as described in Sections 5.3.3.2 and 5.3.4

output: current stage *state*

 1: **procedure** COMPOSEREPLY(*msgtype*, *state*, b, O^*, Pr, R, G, P)
 2:     **if** $(out) \,\&\, \left(t < \pi_j^a\right) \,\&\, (keepdir \neq true)$ **then**
 3:         $dir \leftarrow -dir, f \leftarrow 0, \rho^a \leftarrow \rho_j^a$ ▷ reset auxiliary variables
 4:         $state \leftarrow start$ ▷ start search in other direction
 5:         $out \leftarrow$ ISOUTOFBOUNDS(γ_j^a, Pr, O^*)
 6:     **end if**
 7:     **if** $(out) \,\&\, (i = $ GETLENGTH$(Pr))$ **then**
 8:         $M_{a \rightarrow b} \leftarrow$ CREATEMSG$(msgtype)$
 9:         SENDMSG$(M_{a \rightarrow b})$
10:         $state \leftarrow success$
11:     **else**
12:         $next \leftarrow (out) \,\&\, (i \neq$ GETLENGTH$(Pr))$
13:         **while** $(next) \,|\, \left(t = 2 * \pi_j^a\right)$ **do**
14:             $state \leftarrow start$
15:             $t \leftarrow 0, f \leftarrow 0, dir \leftarrow 1, keepdir \leftarrow false$ ▷ reset auxiliary variables
16:             $i \leftarrow i + 1$
17:             $j \leftarrow$ GETNEXTPARAM(Pr)
18:             $A \leftarrow A \cup \{j\}$
19:             $\rho^a \leftarrow \rho_j^a$
20:             $out \leftarrow$ ISOUTOFBOUNDS(γ_j^a, Pr, O^*)
21:             $next \leftarrow (out) \,\&\, (i \neq$ GETLENGTH$(Pr))$
22:         **end while**
23:         **if** $(out) \,\&\, (i = $ GETLENGTH$(Pr))$ **then**
24:             $M_{a \rightarrow b} \leftarrow$ CREATEMSG$(msgtype)$
25:             SENDMSG$(M_{a \rightarrow b})$
26:             $state \leftarrow success$
27:         **else**
28:             $M_{a \rightarrow b} \leftarrow$ CREATEMSG$(``ImprProposal", O^*, \gamma_j^a)$
29:             SENDMSG$(M_{a \rightarrow b})$
30:             $ownprop \leftarrow true$
31:             $t \leftarrow t + 1$
32:         **end if**
33:     **end if**
34:     **return** *state*
35: **end procedure**

That message constitutes a "LastAccept" message, if the subroutine COMPOSEREPLY
is invoked from the procedure PROCESSPROPOSAL and an "Accept" message, if the
calling procedure is processing a PREACCEPT message. Otherwise, as long as some
constraints would still be violated, but the last QoS parameter is not considered, yet, or

the maximum number of own trials has been reached for the currently considered QoS parameter, the next QoS parameter is selected and corresponding auxiliary variables are updated accordingly (lines 13-22). For the case that no QoS parameter remains without violating any constraints, the negotiation is terminated (lines 23-26). In any other case, a new improvement proposal can be composed and the number of own trials is increased (lines 28-31). At the end of this procedure COMPOSEREPLY, the current state is returned to the calling procedure (line 34). Depending on the type of message that has been sent before, the negotiation will be in one of the following states:

- *success*: a message has been sent to terminate the negotiation

- *start*: any constraints would be violated with regard to the formerly considered QoS parameter, so that the algorithm starts considering a "new" QoS parameter

- *impr*: the currently considered QoS parameter can be further considered, so that the negotiation remains in the Improvement Stage

Instead of the receipt of an "ImprProposal" message in Algorithm 1, a negotiating party *a* may receive a "PreAccept" message from the opponent. In this case, the previously sent improvement proposal has been accepted by the opponent, so that the preliminary agreement is updated (line 18+19). Since a "PreAccept" message from the opponent reveals that the current search direction is promising, the corresponding flag *keepdir* is set in order to continue searching in this direction (line 20). Further actions that are performed upon receiving a "PreAccept" message are handled by the subroutine PROCESSPREACCEPT. The pseudocode of that subroutine is provided in Algorithm 5. In line 1, the subroutine PROCESSPREACCEPT receives the following input parameters: the current stage, a reference to the opponent, the current preliminary agreement, as well as the configuration parameters for the GRiP-based strategy. Subsequently, a response is generated based on the following conditions:

$$SendMsg = \begin{cases} Accept & \text{if max. no. of trials reached \& last QoS parameter} \\ ImprProposal & \text{otherwise} \end{cases}$$

In short, the subroutine PROCESSPREACCEPT has to check, if conditions apply for terminating the negotiation or if a new improvement proposal can be created. Basically, the subroutine starts similar to the processing of an "ImprProposal" message. At first, the algorithm checks if the maximum number of own trials has been reached and if, at the same time, the last QoS parameter is currently considered (line 2). If this is the case, an "Accept" message is composed and sent to the opponent in order to terminate the negotiation (lines 3-5). Otherwise, if the maximum number of own trials for the currently considered QoS parameter has not been reached, yet, the current risk factor has to be adapted as described in the following.

Algorithm 5 Procedure PROCESSPREACCEPT for processing a preaccept message

input: current stage $state$, agent b, preliminary agreement O^*, parameters as described in Sections 5.3.3.2 and 5.3.4

output: current stage $state$

 1: **procedure** PROCESSPREACCEPT($state$, b, O^*, Pr, R, G, P, C_1, C_2)
 2:     **if** $\left(t = 2 * \pi_j^a \right)$ & $(i = \text{GETLENGTH}(Pr))$ **then**
 3:         $M_{a \to b} \leftarrow \text{CREATEMSG}(\text{"Accept"})$
 4:         $\text{SENDMSG}(M_{a \to b})$
 5:         $state \leftarrow success$
 6:     **else**
 7:         $out \leftarrow false$
 8:         **if** $\left(t \neq 2 * \pi_j^a \right)$ **then**
 9:             $\rho_{min}^a \leftarrow \rho^a$
10:             $state \leftarrow impr$
11:             **if** $f = 0$ **then**
12:                 $\rho^a \leftarrow \rho_{min}^a * 2$
13:                 $\rho_{max}^a \leftarrow \rho^a$
14:             **else**
15:                 $f \leftarrow 1$
16:                 $\rho_{max}^a \leftarrow \rho_{last}^a$
17:                 $\rho^a \leftarrow \rho_{min}^a + (\rho_{max}^a - \rho_{min}^a) * exp\left(-\tau_j^{a2} * f \right)$
18:             **end if**
19:             $out \leftarrow \text{ISOUTOFBOUNDS}(\gamma_j^a, Pr, O^*)$
20:         **end if**
21:         COMPOSEREPLY($\text{"Accept"}, state, b, O^*, Pr, R, G, P$)
22:     **end if**
23:     **return** $state$
24: **end procedure**

First of all, since the last improvement proposal has been accepted by the opponent, the corresponding risk factor ρ^a is stored in variable ρ_{min}^a (line 9). The risk factor ρ_{min}^a indicates the lower bound for deviating from the own MRS when creating a new improvement proposal. In addition, the algorithm switches to/remains in the Improvement Stage, since an improvement has been found (line 10). If no own improvement proposal has failed before, i.e., $f = 0$, no upper limit concerning the risk factor ρ^a has been detected, yet. Therefore, the duplicated risk factor is explored with the next improvement proposal according to Equation 5.8a (line 12). For the case that the duplicated risk factor also leads to an improvement with $f = 0$, the risk factor is doubled again. Such a duplication of the risk factor is performed as long as an improvement can be achieved with $f = 0$. In the event that a first improvement proposal is unsuccessful, the current risk factor ρ^a constitutes an upper bound while the last successful risk factor represents a lower bound. In order to account for that event, variable ρ_{max}^a is already initialized with the value of the current risk factor in line 13 (cf. Equation 5.9a). From that point on, the current risk factor ρ^a is iteratively decreased towards the lower bound as described in the following in order to approach the highest successful risk factor, which results in the highest utility gain. The adaptation of the risk factor is inspired from the slow start phase of TCP in order to detect an upper bound for the risk factor in a small amount of time. During the slow start phase of TCP the sending rate is exponentially increased by doubling the congestion window until a loss is detected, after which the congestion window is decreased to the half of its size and only linearly increased from that point on (cf., e.g., [116]). In doing so, TCP can quickly determine the available bandwidth.

$$\rho^a = \begin{cases} \rho^a_{min} \times 2 & \text{if } f=0 \quad (5.8a) \\ \rho^a_{min} + (\rho^a_{max} - \rho^a_{min}) \times exp\left(-\tau_i^{a2} \times f\right) & \text{if } f \neq 0 \quad (5.8b) \end{cases}$$

Each time an own improvement proposal has failed, the value of the unsuccessful risk factor ρ^a is stored in the variable ρ^a_{last} (cf. line 13 in Algorithm 2). When receiving a "PreAccept" message from the opponent in a later iteration and an improvement proposal has failed before (i.e., $f \neq 0$), the value of the last unsuccessful risk factor ρ^a_{last} observed before is stored in the variable ρ^a_{max} as an upper bound (line 16 in Algorithm 5, cf. Equation 5.9b). Also in this case, the lower bound ρ^a_{min} is set to the value of the current successful risk factor ρ^a (line 9).

$$\rho^a_{max} = \begin{cases} \rho^a & \text{if } f=0 \quad (5.9a) \\ \rho^a_{last} & \text{if } f \neq 0 \quad (5.9b) \end{cases}$$

As already mentioned, $[\rho^a_{min}, \rho^a_{max}]$ constitutes an interval, in which the MRS of the opponent resides. Recall that the opponent's MRS represents an upper bound for the deviation from the own MRS. Therefore, the current risk factor ρ^a is iteratively decreased towards the lower bound ρ^a_{min} during the Improvement Stage based on the number f of own failed improvement proposals using cooling factor τ_i^{a2} (line 17, cf. Equation 5.8b). Whenever a "PreAccept" message is received from the opponent, the current risk factor ρ^a has been successful. Therefore, the lower bound ρ^a_{min} and the upper bound ρ^a_{max} are both adapted each time an own improvement proposal has been accepted by the opponent. In doing so, each negotiating party iteratively approaches the MRS of the opponent. Thus, the preliminary agreement incrementally converges to a Pareto-efficient solution. Having finished the adaptation of the current risk factor and other corresponding, auxiliary variables, the subroutine PROCESSPREACCEPT invokes the subroutine COMPOSEREPLY, which has already been described before (line 21). In contrast to an invocation from the subroutine PROCESSPROPOSAL, the message type "Accept" is passed to the subroutine COMPOSEREPLY as one of the input parameters. This message type is used within the subroutine in case that the negotiation should be terminated.

Concerning intuitive means for consumers in order to specify the input parameters for the GRiP-based strategy applied during the second phase, sliders can also be provided by the envisaged broker to consumers in a similar manner to the sliders for concessions and weights in the first phase (cf. Section 5.3.3.1). In this regard, sliders are required to specify the risk factor, the greed factor, and the patience for each QoS parameter considered in the negotiation. All other parameters can be determined by the broker. Regarding the weights, the values specified in the first phase can also be utilized in the second phase of the negotiation. Concerning the cooling factors, the broker can derive according values automatically based on the risk level specified by a consumer. Recall that the cooling factors define the decrease of the risk factor during the Trade-Off Phase. Similar to the input parameter β required to define the amount of concession of a time-dependent strategy applied during the Agreement Phase, the risk level specified by a consumer can be mapped to different ranges for the cooling factors. In this regard, a high cooling factor resulting in a fast decrease of the risk factor can be used in case of a low risk level and a small cooling factor leading to a slow decrease can be used in case of a high risk level. This is due to the fact that the probability of an unsuccessful proposal in subsequent rounds is higher in case of a high risk factor in contrast to a low risk factor.

5.4 Summary

In this chapter, we have presented CSLAB-Neg.KOM, which constitutes one of the major contributions of this thesis. It enables approaching Pareto-efficient outcomes while negotiating concurrently with multiple providers over multiple issues. In contrast to related approaches, negotiating parties do not have to disclose their private information to the opponent. Furthermore, our approach permits the maintenance of the strategic behavior of the negotiating parties, so that a proposal of a negotiating party does not depend on the former values proposed by the opponent. CSLAB-Neg.KOM is realized as a two-phase approach. In doing so, an initial agreement can be obtained in the first phase, which then serves as a reference in order to achieve joint improvements in the second phase. For this purpose, we apply time-dependent strategies in the first phase and propose a new GRiP-based strategy to be applied in the second phase. However, our approach is also applicable further to improve inefficient solutions that have been obtained by applying other types of strategies in the first phase. This is due to the fact that we only aim to achieve an initial solution in the first phase. Nevertheless, time-dependent strategies have been chosen since they are able to achieve a solution in a certain amount of time. Besides the total execution time of a negotiation, other parameters concerning the performance of our negotiation mechanism CSLAB-Neg.KOM are evaluated in Section 8.2.

6 Reliable Monitoring – CSLAB-Mon.KOM

This chapter describes the details of our approach for reliable consumer side availability monitoring CSLAB-Mon.KOM [186] based on the basic monitoring design already presented in Chapter 4. In contrast to related work, our approach not only allows monitoring of the availability of a cloud-based service from a consumer's perspective, but also considers the reliability of the monitoring results explicitly. In doing so, consumers become able to distinguish incidents outside the control sphere of a cloud provider from real SLA violations within a cloud provider's sphere of control as well as to identify the affected resources in order to determine the SLA clause that has been violated. Furthermore, in order to provide reliable monitoring results, CSLAB-Mon.KOM also addresses the obtained accuracy of the measurements, so that they represent the real state of the cloud-based service under investigation as closely as required. For this purpose, CSLAB-Mon.KOM provides decision support in two ways. First of all, it permits the determination of an adequate monitoring frequency in conjunction with the number of required samples in order to obtain measurements at a certain level of confidence. Secondly, it enables the determination of a minimum timeout period in order to account for network impairments in terms of packet loss. This chapter is structured as follows. In Section 6.1, a detailed problem statement is provided. The subsequent Section 6.2 elaborates on the details of our monitoring approach with respect to the collection and aggregation of monitoring data and with respect to the influence of the monitoring frequency and packet loss on the accuracy. Finally, this chapter concludes with a summary in Section 6.3.

6.1 Problem Statement

Having negotiated SLAs with a certain cloud provider, cloud consumers must also have means to verify whether the prior negotiated SLAs are maintained by the respective cloud provider at runtime or not. In the scenario considered in this thesis, we envision an SLM broker acting as a trusted third-party that provides according monitoring solutions to cloud consumers (cf. Section 1.2). An intermediary-based monitoring approach is proposed since existing monitoring solutions offered by cloud providers themselves cannot be considered to be an independent and reliable evidence base for detecting SLA violations from a consumer's point of view. However, in order to achieve reliable consumer side monitoring, our envisaged approach must be location-aware, resource-aware, and accurate (cf. Section 4.3.3). In this regard, location-awareness permits attributing a downtime to the control sphere where the incident, which caused that downtime, occurred. Hence, it enables consumers to distinguish downtimes just perceived due to incidents on the consumer side or ISP side from real SLA violations on the provider side. Furthermore, resource-awareness is required in order to trace back downtimes to their root cause in terms of the affected resources. Only by enabling resource-awareness can the corresponding SLA clause, which has been violated, be identified. Finally, the question whether a certain incident constitutes an SLA violation or not further depends on the extent of the incident. Thus, the monitored data must be provided with a certain accuracy that allows assessing the severity of an incident. The requirements mentioned before raise the questions on how to collect and aggregate monitoring data to enable location-awareness and resource-awareness and in doing so, how to achieve accurate results. There are several challenges that need to be addressed in order to meet these requirements.

First of all, due to the closed nature of cloud environments, consumers have only very limited access to a cloud provider's infrastructure. Therefore, they can only rely on monitoring data obtained within their admitted area of access. Hence, when monitoring from a consumer's perspective with no direct access to the inside of a cloud-based service or the VM where a cloud service is running, measurements can only be obtained by sending probe requests from remote locations. In doing so, failures in the network between such a remote location and the location of the cloud service to be monitored can prevent monitoring units from collecting or transmitting data. This raises the question how to deal with differing results from different monitoring units. Secondly, although sending probe requests at a very high frequency permits the achievement of a very high accuracy, the higher the frequency the more the probe requests may affect the system performance and network traffic. Therefore, appropriate methods are required in order to determine the minimum required monitoring frequency and number of samples in order to obtain estimates of the real availability at a certain confidence level. In addition, probe requests may also cause additional communication costs from, e.g., a data center of our SLM broker to a cloud provider's data center. Hence, it may be reasonable to perform monitoring tasks on the broker's side with a lower frequency in contrast to monitoring tasks conducted on the provider's side. In this regard, methods for data aggregation must also be able to cope with results at different levels of accuracy from different monitoring units. Third, when collecting monitoring data over a network, monitoring messages may be affected by a varying latency, e.g., due to packet loss. As a consequence, monitoring requests may reach a cloud service at a later point in time and may, thus, report an outdated state or monitoring data may not be available when expected. Hence, appropriate methods are required in order to account for these kinds of network impairments. Finally, the VMs where the monitoring units are running can also be subject to failure and only exhibit a certain level of reliability. This last issue will be explored in the context of the Robust Cloud Monitor Placement Problem presented in the next Chapter 7. It should be noted that we assume truthful monitoring units and do not consider compromised monitoring units sending false information.

6.2 Approach for Reliable Consumer Side Availability Monitoring

This section presents the details of our approach for reliable consumer side availability monitoring CSLAB-Mon.KOM as another major contribution of this thesis. In doing so, the issues outlined in the preceding problem statement are addressed in different subsections as follows. Section 6.2.1 describes the foundations of CSLAB-Mon.KOM in terms of where monitoring units are deployed, how monitoring data is collected, and under which conditions a single monitoring unit considers a service to be unavailable. Subsequently, Section 6.2.2 elaborates on how the monitoring data of the different monitoring units is aggregated by the monitoring data aggregator, referred to as MDA (cf. Section 4.3.4). In this regard, the section describes how location-awareness and resources-awareness is achieved and how to deal with differing results from different monitoring units in terms of the monitored state and the level of accuracy. As already mentioned before (cf. Section 4.3.3), there is a trade-off between the accuracy of the monitoring results and the monitoring frequency due to its impact on system performance and network traffic. Therefore, Section 6.2.3 presents a mathematical model and corresponding method for determining the minimum required monitoring frequency and sample size, so that the required accuracy is obtained at a certain level of confidence. Furthermore, the accuracy may also be affected by packet loss resulting in a higher latency, which may prevent to obtain monitoring data with respect to a certain time interval. Hence, Section 6.2.4 presents a mathematical model that allows the determination of an appropriate timeout at a certain level of packet loss.

6.2.1 Data Collection

Having presented our basic monitoring design in Section 4.3.4, we will now describe the collection of monitoring data in detail. As already mentioned, we apply a hybrid monitoring approach that combines monitoring on the broker and the cloud side. Each of the monitoring units either deployed on the broker or the cloud side further conducts application-level and VM-level monitoring. In doing so, a monitoring unit periodically invokes essential services using, e.g., REST or SOAP, on application-level at fixed time intervals and also checks the availability of the corresponding VM by sending ICMP echo requests. Essential processes can also be invoked on VM-level in order to get a more precise picture, if a consumer has direct access to the VM. However,

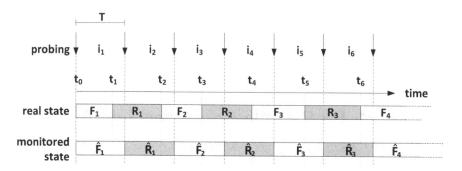

Figure 6.1: Basic data collection

since consumers usually have no direct access to the VM where a SaaS cloud service is running, we take a more restricted perspective in the following and only consider the possibility of sending ICMP echo requests for VM-level monitoring. The length of the fixed time intervals at which an essential service is invoked or an ICMP echo request is sent is defined by the monitoring frequency.

The generic procedure of data collection is depicted in Figure 6.1. Monitoring requests are actively send (i.e., probing is conducted) to the cloud service and the underlying VM at the beginning of each time interval i_x. The length T of these equidistant time intervals constitutes the reciprocal of the monitoring frequency, i.e., the period with $T = \frac{1}{f}$. Following other works (e.g., [191]), we assume that the times to failure F_i and the times to repair R_j are exponentially distributed with a failure rate of λ_F and a repair rate of λ_R, respectively. Whenever the real state of the object under investigation changes during a certain time interval i_x, this change in state is not recognized before the beginning of the next time interval i_{x+1}. Therefore, the monitored state at the beginning of a certain time interval approximates the state of the observed object during that time interval. Hence, the accuracy increases with an increasing monitoring frequency. However, the higher the monitoring frequency the higher is the impact of our monitoring approach on system performance. Furthermore, it is not reasonable to monitor at a monitoring frequency that achieves a higher accuracy than required. The monitoring frequency thus depends on the required accuracy of the monitoring results. The required accuracy in turn depends on the thresholds specified in the negotiated SLAs, the minimum length of a downtime that should be detectable, and the desired level of confidence of the estimated availability. A mathematical model and corresponding method on how to determine an appropriate monitoring frequency and sample size are presented in Section 6.2.3.

Basically, we consider a cloud service or the underlying VM to be available during a certain time interval i_x with respect to a corresponding request, which has been sent at the beginning of that time interval, if a response is received within a predefined timeout period. Details on how to determine an appropriate timeout period are presented in

Section 6.2.4. If no response is received within the given timeout period, we consider the cloud service or the VM to be unavailable with respect to the respective request. For example, an outage of the length R_1 occurs from t_1 until t_2 in Figure 6.1, which is detected at the beginning of time interval i_2, and the subsequent uptime F_2 is detected at the beginning of time interval i_3. Hence, the length of the observed downtime is represented by $\hat{R}_1$. All in all, we consider a cloud service to be unavailable at a certain time interval i_x from the perspective of a single monitoring unit, if one of the essential service invocations fails. The same applies to the state of the underlying VM at a certain time interval, if an ICMP echo request fails. A corresponding uptime or downtime message concerning the cloud service or the underlying VM is then forwarded to the MDA. How the monitoring data from different monitoring units is aggregated by the MDA is described in the next section.

6.2.2 Data Aggregation

As already stated before, CSLAB-Mon.KOM utilizes multiple monitoring units, which are deployed on the broker and the cloud side, in order to achieve location-awareness and to account for the possibility that (parts of) the monitoring infrastructure itself may fail. While the latter is addressed by developing according placement strategies (cf. Chapter 7), location-awareness is achieved by comparing the monitoring information from monitoring units located at different spheres of control (cf. Section 4.3.3). In doing so, location-awareness enables the MDA to determine the corresponding control sphere where an incident happened and to distinguish real SLA violations on the provider side from other incidents. In order for the MDA to be able to compare the monitoring information from different monitoring units with respect to time, the clocks of the different monitoring units have to be synchronized with, or compared to the clock of some reference Network Time Protocol (NTP) server at regular intervals (e.g., [37, 112]). In the former case, the monitoring units become able to generate timestamps directly according to the same reference clock. In the latter case, the monitoring units can compute the differences of their clocks to the same reference clock and transform their local timestamps into timestamps according to that reference clock.

Having collected monitoring information from the different monitoring units, the MDA derives the overall state, i.e., the availability of the cloud application. Based on the three different types of messages, which can be sent to the MDA as defined in Section 4.3.4, the MDA proceeds as follows. When receiving a new registration message, the MDA creates a new result list associated with the respective monitoring unit and the object to be monitored (i.e., the cloud application or the underlying VM). Now, whenever a monitoring unit has sent a request to the object to be monitored and locally evaluated its current state with respect to a certain time interval i_x, the monitoring unit either sends a corresponding uptime or downtime message to the

MDA. The details of such a message, i.e., the timestamps of the considered time interval and the current state, are then added to the respective result list. Based on the result lists of the different monitoring units, the MDA periodically computes and updates the overall state of a certain cloud service. Although multiple monitoring units are utilized to observe the same cloud service, their monitoring results may differ depending on, e.g., their current abilities to connect to the cloud service from their locations, their utilized monitoring frequencies, and their probing offsets. Hence, the question arises for the MDA how to aggregate the monitoring information from the different monitoring units. As a preparatory step, the following considerations are made.

Whenever at least a single uptime message is received from one of the monitoring units deployed within a certain control sphere, the corresponding cloud application or the underlying VM can be considered to be available from that control sphere during the respective time interval. If no monitoring information is received from a monitoring unit with respect to a certain time interval, network impairments on the provider side, for example, could prevent the monitoring unit from reporting any data or the monitoring unit itself may be down. Since no further information on the root cause is available, this case is treated similar to a downtime message. All in all, a cloud application or an underlying VM is only considered to be unavailable from a certain control sphere during a certain time period if all of the monitoring units in that control sphere report a downtime. However, the observed downtimes may differ in terms of their timestamps and duration. Therefore, downtimes that (partly) overlap in time for all of the monitoring units in a certain control sphere are considered to represent the same overall downtime. In order to determine the duration that best reflects the real downtime, the earliest timestamps indicating the start and the end of a downtime are selected among all the monitoring information received. Depending on the affected resource and control sphere, such a downtime may constitute an SLA violation or not. In this regard, a downtime can only be considered to be a potential SLA violation concerning the cloud application, if the underlying VM is still available. Otherwise, an SLA clause concerning the underlying VM may be violated. However, whether such a downtime really constitutes an SLA violation also depends on whether that downtime has been caused by an incident on the provider side or not. The possible outcomes resulting from the affected control sphere when aggregating the monitoring information from the different monitoring units are summarized in Table 6.1.

According to Table 6.1, the MDA proceeds in a two-step approach in order to aggregate monitoring information. In the first step, the MDA separately aggregates the monitoring information from the monitoring units on the broker side and the monitoring units on the provider side based on the considerations stated before. In doing so, the observed state on each side is obtained. In the second step, the MDA further aggregates the states on the broker and the provider side to the overall state of the cloud application. If an uptime is perceived on both sides, the cloud application can

Table 6.1: Overview of the possible outcomes of aggregated monitoring information

State on the Broker Side	State on the Provider Side	Overall State	SLA Violation
up	up	available	no
down	down	unavailable	yes
up	down	partly available	no
down	up	partly available	no

be considered to be available and no SLA violation has occurred. If the monitoring units on the broker and the provider side all report a downtime, the cloud application can be considered to be unavailable and an SLA violation has been detected. However, it may also be the case that the states on both sides differ. For example, the cloud application may be perceived to be unavailable from the provider side and available from the broker side. This may happen if only a certain section of the provider's data center is down or subject to failure, which prevents the monitoring unit placed on the provider side from accessing the other section of the provider's data center where the cloud application is located or from sending monitoring requests at all, so that the cloud application is only perceived to be available from the broker side. In that case, no SLA violation is detected. In other cases, both states also differ if the monitoring units on the broker side report a downtime in contrast to the monitoring units on the provider side. This also constitutes no SLA violation, since the monitoring units on the provider side are still able to reach the cloud application and to connect to the MDA on the broker side in order to report their results. Hence, an incident outside the provider's sphere of control must have been occurred that prevents the monitoring units on the broker side from collecting data. Summarizing, an SLA violation has only occurred, if a downtime is reported on both, the broker and the provider side.

The results obtained from aggregating monitoring information, i.e., the observed uptime and downtime periods, are stored in a final result list. Based on this result list, the MDA periodically calculates the overall availability of the cloud application. As already stated in Section 4.3, we express the availability in terms of the ratio of the MTTF to the sum of the MTTF and the MTTR. In order for the MDA to determine the overall availability at a certain point in time, we follow the approach proposed by Haberkorn and Trivedi [86]. According to the authors, the calculation depends on the current state of the cloud application as described in the following. Let $\hat{F}_i$ and $\hat{R}_j$ be the ith and j^{th} observed uptime and downtime period, respectively. Further, let n be the total number of (completely) observed uptime periods. Depending on whether the MDA is calculating the overall availability during an uptime or a downtime of a cloud application, this last uptime or downtime period is not finished, yet. Therefore, either

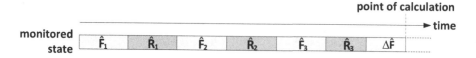

Figure 6.2: Calculation of the overall availability during an uptime

the duration of this unfinished uptime period ΔF or downtime period ΔR, which equals the difference from the current point in time to the end of the last completely observed downtime or uptime period must also be taken into account (cf. Figure 6.2). Now, let $\hat{m}(F)$ be the estimated MTTF and let $\hat{m}(R)$ be the estimated MTTR. The point estimate of the overall availability $\hat{A}$ of a cloud application can then be determined as follows.

$$\text{point estimate } \hat{A} = \frac{\hat{m}(F)}{\hat{m}(F) + \hat{m}(R)} \tag{6.1}$$

Using the variables introduced before, $\hat{m}(F)$ and $\hat{m}(R)$ are calculated during an uptime as follows:

$$\hat{m}(F) = \frac{1}{n}\left[\left(\sum_{i=1}^{n}\hat{F}_i\right) + \Delta F\right] \quad \text{and} \quad \hat{m}(R) = \frac{1}{n}\sum_{j=1}^{n}\hat{R}_j \tag{6.2}$$

In contrast, when calculating the overall availability during a downtime, $\hat{m}(F)$ and $\hat{m}(R)$ have to be determined as stated below:

$$\hat{m}(F) = \frac{1}{n}\sum_{i=1}^{n}\hat{F}_i \quad \text{and} \quad \hat{m}(R) = \frac{1}{n-1}\left[\left(\sum_{j=1}^{n-1}\hat{R}_j\right) + \Delta R\right] \tag{6.3}$$

However, in the following we only consider the first n complete cycles of subsequent uptime and downtime intervals in order to estimate $\hat{m}(F)$ and $\hat{m}(R)$, since the resulting error is negligible in case of a large number of observed uptimes and downtimes.

6.2.3 Influence of Frequency and Sample Size on Accuracy

As already stated before, the accuracy of the observed availability is influenced by the monitoring frequency, which determines the length of the time intervals between the periodic monitoring requests. Since the monitored state of the object under investigation at a certain time interval i_x is not updated until the next monitoring request is evaluated at the beginning of the next time interval i_{x+1}, the real availability is measured with a certain error, denoted as *probing error* in the following. Concerning the length of the probing error, three different approaches of collecting monitoring data can be distinguished in general as depicted in Figure 6.3.

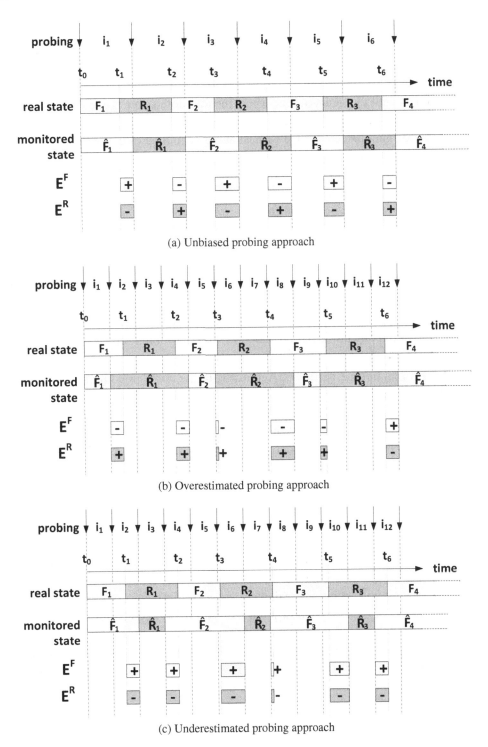

Figure 6.3: Overview of the different probing approaches

Unbiased Probing Approach   In case of an unbiased probing approach, monitoring is conducted in such a manner that the monitored state is always updated immediately after having evaluated a monitoring request and set to the new state that has been detected. In this regard, the time period of the previously observed state is estimated to last until that point in time where the monitored state is updated. However, in most of the cases, changes in state appear in between two subsequent time intervals. Hence, they are either detected at the earliest at the beginning of the next time interval or they are not detected at all. The latter is due to the fact that a monitoring unit will not be able to detect downtimes that are smaller than the period T and occur in between two monitoring intervals. In this regard, we make the following assumption in order to obtain an upper bound for the monitoring frequency and to derive a mathematical model later on. If a downtime exhibits a length of T and exactly lasts from the beginning until the end of a monitoring interval of the size T, a monitoring unit is able to detect that downtime. Therefore, the monitoring frequency depends on the minimum length of a downtime R_{min} that the monitoring system should be able to detect and must be at least equal to or higher than $f = 1/T$ with $T = R_{min}$. In doing so, a downtime period R_j is estimated with a maximum probing error E_j^{Rb} of T at the beginning of the downtime period and a maximum probing error E_j^{Ra} of $-T$ at the end of the downtime period. The opposite applies for the probing errors E_i^{Fb} and E_i^{Fa} before and after an uptime period F_i. According to the corresponding mathematical model introduced in the following, the means of the total probing errors E^R and E^F are both zero. Hence, they are balanced given a large number of samples, so that the bias between the expected values of the downtime and uptime periods and their real values tends to zero. Therefore, this probing approach is denoted as unbiased.

Overestimated Probing Approach   Also an overestimation of the downtime periods can be performed in order to obtain an upper bound for the overall downtime. For this purpose, the monitoring frequency must be at least equal to or higher than $f = 1/T$ with $T = R_{min}/2$, i.e., the distance between the monitoring intervals must be at least equal to or less than half of the minimum length of a downtime R_{min}. In doing so, at least two monitoring results can be obtained for evaluating each downtime period. This permits consideration the downtime periods from a worst-case perspective as follows. In most of the cases, a downtime will start in between two subsequent time intervals. Hence, the real point of failure is unknown. For example, in Figure 6.3b, an uptime is detected at the beginning of the monitoring interval i_2 and the downtime period R_1 starting from the point of failure at t_1 is not recognized before the beginning of the monitoring interval i_3. Therefore, when taking a worst-case perspective without knowing the real point of failure, that failure might have occurred at the earliest directly after having observed an uptime at the beginning of the monitoring interval i_2. The same applies to the real point of recovery of that downtime, which might have occurred at the latest directly before observing the subsequent uptime at the beginning of the monitoring interval i_5. As a consequence, the observed downtime period $\hat{R}_1$ is overestimated lasting from the beginning of the monitoring interval i_2 until the beginning of the monitoring interval i_5. All in all, a downtime period R_j is estimated with a maximum probing error E_j^{Rb} of T at the beginning and a maximum probing error E_j^{Ra} of T at the end of the downtime period. In contrast, an uptime period F_i is observed with a maximum probing error E_i^{Fb} of $-T$ at the beginning and a maximum probing error E_i^{Fa} of $-T$ at the end of the uptime period. As it can be seen from Figure 6.3b, downtime periods are overestimated and uptime periods are underestimated in general in this way.

Underestimated Probing Approach Similar to an overestimation of the downtime periods, an overestimation of the uptime periods can be performed, which constitutes an underestimation of the downtime periods. In doing so, a lower bound for the overall downtime can be obtained. For this purpose, the monitoring frequency must be also at least equal to or higher than $f = 2/R_{min}$. As depicted in Figure 6.3c, for example, the observed uptime period $\hat{F}_2$ is overestimated lasting from the beginning of the monitoring interval i_4 until the beginning of the monitoring interval i_7. In turn, the observed downtime periods $\hat{R}_1$ and $\hat{R}_2$ are both underestimated. In general, when applying an underestimated probing approach, a downtime period R_j is observed with a maximum probing error E_j^{Rb} of $-T$ at the beginning and a maximum probing error E_j^{Ra} of $-T$ at the end of the downtime period. In contrast, an uptime period F_i is observed with a maximum probing error E_i^{Fb} of T at the beginning and a maximum probing error E_i^{Fa} of T at the end of the uptime period.

Mathematical Model Although the total probing error and, thus, the accuracy increases with a higher monitoring frequency in all of the three aforementioned probing approaches, also the impact on system performance grows. Therefore, it is reasonable to determine the monitoring frequency in such a manner that the observed availability reflects the real availability of a cloud service only as closely as required. However, given a certain monitoring frequency, the accuracy of the observed availability not only depends on the monitoring frequency but also on the sample size. Since the real availability is only estimated from a subset of the real uptime and downtime periods, an additional *sampling error* occurs. With an increasing sample size, the sampling error decreases. Now, given a certain monitoring frequency, sample size, and resulting observed availability, a lower confidence bound for the real availability can be computed at a given confidence level $100(1 - \alpha)\%$. Basically, the confidence level expresses that the real availability is at least equal to or higher than the lower bound in $100(1 - \alpha)\%$ of the time when calculating such a one-sided confidence interval from different samples. In this regard, the parameter α expresses the probability of making an error, i.e., in $\alpha \times 100\%$ of the time, the real availability is lower than the lower bound. In this thesis, we express the required accuracy of the point estimate of the real availability in terms of the desired confidence level with which the real availability is at least equal to or greater than the negotiated uptime guarantee (as the lower bound). Now, given a certain number of samples obtained at a certain monitoring frequency, a mathematical model is presented in the following in order to calculate the lower bound for the real availability at the desired confidence level. This model then serves as a foundation for a corresponding method in order to determine an appropriate monitoring frequency and minimum required sample size for achieving the desired level of confidence, provided that the real availability equals the negotiated uptime guarantee. As a preparatory step for our mathematical model, we briefly recall the definition of the real availability A and provide some transformations as follows. In this regard, $m(F)$ and $m(R)$ constitute the real MTTF and MTTR, respectively.

$$\text{real availability } A = \frac{m(F)}{m(F) + m(R)} = \frac{1}{1 + \frac{m(R)}{m(F)}} \tag{6.4}$$

Following Gray and Lewis [82], the problem of finding a confidence interval for A then reduces to determining a confidence interval for the ratio $\frac{m(R)}{m(F)}$, given n independent random samples $\hat{F}_i$ and $\hat{R}_i$ for the observed uptime and downtime periods. The corresponding estimates $\hat{m}(F)$ and $\hat{m}(R)$ are defined as follows when applying our probing approaches mentioned before.

$$\hat{m}(F) = \frac{1}{n} \sum_{i=1}^{n} \hat{F}_i = \frac{1}{n} \sum_{i=1}^{n} (F_i + E_i^F) = \frac{1}{n} \sum_{i=1}^{n} (F_i + E_i^{Fb} + E_i^{Fa}) \tag{6.5}$$

$$\hat{m}(R) = \frac{1}{n} \sum_{j=1}^{n} \hat{R}_j = \frac{1}{n} \sum_{j=1}^{n} (R_j + E_j^R) = \frac{1}{n} \sum_{j=1}^{n} (R_j + E_j^{Rb} + E_j^{Ra}) \tag{6.6}$$

It can be deduced from our probing approaches introduced before that probing errors E_i^{Fb} and E_i^{Fa} are made with respect to the beginning and the end of each real uptime period F_i, respectively, in all of the three approaches. In a similar manner, probing errors E_j^{Rb} and E_j^{Ra} are made with respect to the beginning and the end of each real downtime period R_j, respectively. Now, let E_i^F be the total probing error that is made with respect to a real uptime period F_i and let E_j^R be the total probing error that is made with respect to a real downtime period R_j. Further recall that we consider a similar number n of complete uptime and downtime periods in order to estimate the overall availability in our mathematical model (cf. Section 6.2.2). The estimates $\hat{m}(F)$ and $\hat{m}(R)$ can then be determined as the arithmetic means of the observed uptime periods $\hat{F}_i$ and downtime periods $\hat{R}_j$ according to Equations 6.5 and 6.6. Depending on the probing approach, the distributions of the probing errors differ. Therefore, a confidence interval for A is derived separately for each probing approach in the following.

Unbiased Probing Approach When considering our first probing approach (i.e., unbiased estimation), the errors $E_i^F b$ and $E_j^R b$ measured at the beginning of an uptime i and downtime j, respectively, as well as the errors $E_i^F a$ and $E_j^R a$ measured at the end of an uptime i and downtime j, respectively, all follow a uniform distribution as stated below. Since these probing errors made with respect to each uptime and downtime period constitute independent identically uniform distributed random variables, their sums E_i^F and E_j^R both follow a triangular distribution (abbreviated with *Tri* in the following) as stated below.

$$E_i^F = E_i^{Fb} + E_i^{Fa} \sim Tri(\text{-}T, T) \quad \text{with} \quad E_i^{Fb} \sim U(\text{-}T, 0) \quad \text{and} \quad E_i^{Fa} \sim U(0, T) \quad (6.7)$$

$$E_j^R = E_j^{Rb} + E_j^{Ra} \sim Tri(\text{-}T, T) \quad \text{with} \quad E_j^{Rb} \sim U(0, T) \quad \text{and} \quad E_j^{Ra} \sim U(\text{-}T, 0) \quad (6.8)$$

Furthermore, since the resulting random variables E_i^F and E_j^R are also independent and identically distributed, the central limit theorem states that their arithmetic means approach a normal distribution with an increasing sample size. In this regard, a sample size greater than 30 is usually assumed (e.g., [40]).

$$\hat{m}(F) = \frac{1}{n} \sum_{i=1}^{n} \hat{F}_i = \frac{1}{n} \sum_{i=1}^{n} F_i + E^F \quad \text{with} \quad E^F = \frac{1}{n} \sum_{i=1}^{n} E_i^F \sim N(0, \frac{T^2}{6n}) \quad (6.9)$$

$$\hat{m}(R) = \frac{1}{n} \sum_{j=1}^{n} \hat{R}_j = \frac{1}{n} \sum_{j=1}^{n} R_j + E^R \quad \text{with} \quad E^R = \frac{1}{n} \sum_{j=1}^{n} E_j^R \sim N(0, \frac{T^2}{6n}) \quad (6.10)$$

Further, let $\hat{m}_{orig}(F)$ and $\hat{m}_{orig}(R)$ be the point estimates for the MTTF and MTTR without making any probing error (i.e., only resulting in a sampling error depending on the sample size). Following other works such as, e.g., [40, 191, 211], we assume that the times to failure F_i and the times to repair R_j are exponentially distributed with a failure rate of λ_F and a repair rate of λ_R, respectively. The point estimates $\hat{m}_{orig}(F)$ and $\hat{m}_{orig}(R)$ can then be formally specified as:

$$\hat{m}_{orig}(F) = \frac{1}{n} \sum_{i=1}^{n} F_i \quad \text{and} \quad \hat{m}_{orig}(R) = \frac{1}{n} \sum_{j=1}^{n} R_j$$

$$(6.11)$$

$$\text{with} \quad F_i \sim Exp(\lambda_F), \ R_j \sim Exp(\lambda_R) \quad \text{with} \quad E(F_i) = \frac{1}{\lambda_F}, \ E(R_j) = \frac{1}{\lambda_R}$$

Now, as a preparatory step in order to obtain a lower $100(1-\alpha)\%$ confidence bound for A, we determine the distribution of the ratio $\dfrac{\hat{m}(R)}{\hat{m}(F)}$ as stated below.

$$\frac{\hat{m}(R)}{\hat{m}(F)} = \frac{\hat{m}_{orig}(R)+E^R}{\hat{m}_{orig}(F)+E^F} = \frac{X_R + Y_R}{X_F + Y_F} = \frac{Z_R}{Z_F}$$

with $X_F \sim N\left(\dfrac{1}{\lambda_F}, \dfrac{1}{n\lambda_F^2}\right)$ and $X_R \sim N\left(\dfrac{1}{\lambda_R}, \dfrac{1}{n\lambda_R^2}\right)$

and $Y_F \sim N\left(0, \dfrac{T^2}{6n}\right)$ and $Y_R \sim N\left(0, \dfrac{T^2}{6n}\right)$ $\qquad$ (6.12)

and $Z_F \sim N\left(\dfrac{1}{\lambda_F}, \dfrac{1}{n\lambda_F^2}+\dfrac{T^2}{6n}\right)$ and $Z_R \sim N\left(\dfrac{1}{\lambda_R}, \dfrac{1}{n\lambda_R^2}+\dfrac{T^2}{6n}\right)$

Equation 6.12 is first transformed according to Equations 6.9 to 6.11 and the distributions of the resulting terms in the numerator and denominator are further analyzed in the next step. Following the central limit theorem, a sum of independent and identically distributed random variables is approximately normally distributed. Hence, $\hat{m}_{orig}(R)$ in the numerator and $\hat{m}_{orig}(F)$ in the denominator can be replaced by the two new random variables X_F and X_R, which both follow a normal distribution. Since the error terms E^F and E^R also tend towards a normal distribution (cf. Equations 6.9 and 6.10), the sums of X_F and Y_F in the numerator and of X_R and Y_R in the denominator are also normally distributed with the sums of their individual means and variances. Both resulting sums are represented by the two new normally distributed random variables Z_F and Z_R. In order to determine the distribution of the resulting ratio Z_R/Z_F, Fieller's theorem (cf. [66, 67, 90]) can be applied. According to Motulsky [90], a confidence interval for Z_R/Z_F can be obtained as stated below when following Fieller's theorem.

If the standard error of the mean (SEM) of $\hat{Z}_F$ is small compared to $\hat{Z}_F$, the following approximation can be used with Q being the ratio of the measured $\hat{Z}_R/\hat{Z}_F$, t being the critical value coming from the Student's t distribution, n being the sample size, SE_Q being the standard error (SE) of Q, $SEM_{\hat{Z}_R}$ being the SEM of $\hat{Z}_R$, and $SD_{\hat{Z}_R}$ and $SD_{\hat{Z}_F}$ being the standard deviations of $\hat{Z}_R$ and $\hat{Z}_F$, respectively (cf. [90]):

$$P\left(Q-t_{1-\frac{\alpha}{2};n-2}\times SE_Q \leq \frac{Z_R}{Z_F} \leq Q+t_{1-\frac{\alpha}{2};n-2}\times SE_Q\right) = 1-\alpha$$

with $SE_Q = Q\sqrt{\dfrac{SEM_{\hat{Z}_R}^{\;2}}{\hat{Z}_R^2}+\dfrac{SEM_{\hat{Z}_F}^{\;2}}{\hat{Z}_F^2}}$ $\qquad$ (6.13)

and $SEM_{\hat{Z}_R} = \dfrac{SD_{\hat{Z}_R}}{\sqrt{n}}$ and $SEM_{\hat{Z}_F} = \dfrac{SD_{\hat{Z}_F}}{\sqrt{n}}$

For the case that the SEM of $\hat{Z}_F$ is not small compared to $\hat{Z}_F$, Equation 6.13 has to be modified as provided below (cf. [90]):

$$P\left(\frac{Q}{1-g} - t_{1-\frac{\alpha}{2};n-2} \times SE_Q \le \frac{Z_R}{Z_F} \le \frac{Q}{1-g} + t_{1-\frac{\alpha}{2};n-2} \times SE_Q\right) = 1-\alpha$$

$$\text{with}\quad SE_Q = \frac{Q}{1-g}\sqrt{(1-g)\frac{SEM_{\hat{Z}_R}^2}{\hat{Z}_R^2} + \frac{SEM_{\hat{Z}_F}^2}{\hat{Z}_F^2}} \qquad (6.14)$$

$$\text{and}\quad g = \left(t_{1-\frac{\alpha}{2};n-2} \times \frac{SEM_{\hat{Z}_F}}{\hat{Z}_F}\right)^2$$

If g in Equation 6.14 is greater than or equal to 1.0, the confidence interval cannot be calculated. This happens if the $SEM_{\hat{Z}_F}$ is very large and the confidence interval for Z_F includes zero (cf. [90]), e.g., if the sample size is too small. Now, having determined a lower (B_l) and an upper (B_u) confidence bound for the ratio $Z_R/Z_F = m(R)/m(F)$ (resulting in, e.g., Equation 6.14), a confidence interval for A can then be obtained as follows based on Equation 6.4 (cf. [82]):

$$P\left(\frac{1}{1+B_u} \le A \le \frac{1}{1+B_l}\right) = 1-\alpha$$

$$\text{with}\quad B_u = \frac{Q}{1-g} + t_{1-\frac{\alpha}{2};n-2} \times SE_Q \quad \text{and} \quad B_l = \frac{Q}{1-g} - t_{1-\frac{\alpha}{2};n-2} \times SE_Q \qquad (6.15)$$

In order to derive a lower one-sided confidence bound for A based on B_u, the critical value coming from the Student's t distribution has to be determined for $1-\alpha$ instead of $1-\frac{\alpha}{2}$ resulting in a modified upper confidence bound B'_u:

$$P\left(A \ge \frac{1}{1+B'_u}\right) = 1-\alpha$$

$$\text{with}\quad B'_u = \frac{Q}{1-g} + t_{1-\alpha;n-2} \times SE_Q \qquad (6.16)$$

Overestimated Probing Approach When considering our second probing approach (i.e., an overestimation of downtimes), the errors $E_i^F b$ and $E_j^R b$ measured before an uptime i and downtime j, respectively, as well as the errors $E_i^F a$ and $E_j^R a$ measured after an uptime i and downtime j, respectively, are distributed as follows:

$$E_i^F = E_i^{Fb} + E_i^{Fa} \sim Tri(-2T,0) \text{ with } E_i^{Fb} \sim U(\text{-}T,0) \text{ and } E_i^{Fa} \sim U(\text{-}T,0) \quad (6.17)$$

$$E_j^R = E_j^{Rb} + E_j^{Ra} \sim Tri(0,2T) \text{ with } E_j^{Rb} \sim U(0,T) \text{ and } E_j^{Ra} \sim U(0,T) \quad (6.18)$$

Given that the random variables E_i^F and E_j^R are identically and independently distributed, their arithmetic means approach a normal distribution with an increasing sample size ($n \geq 30$) according to the central limit theorem as follows:

$$E^F = \frac{1}{n} \sum_{i=1}^{n} E_i^F \sim N(\text{-T}, \frac{T^2}{6n}) \quad \text{and} \quad E^R = \frac{1}{n} \sum_{j=1}^{n} E_j^R \sim N(\text{T}, \frac{T^2}{6n}) \qquad (6.19)$$

In order to obtain a two-sided confidence interval for the ratio $Z_R/Z_F = m(R)/m(F)$, we again determine the distribution of that ratio as a preparatory step:

$$\frac{\hat{m}(R)}{\hat{m}(F)} = [\ldots] = \frac{Z_R}{Z_F}$$

$$(6.20)$$

$$\text{with} \quad Z_R \sim N(\frac{1}{\lambda_R} + T, \frac{1}{n\lambda_R^2} + \frac{T^2}{6n}) \quad \text{and} \quad Z_F \sim N(\frac{1}{\lambda_F} - T, \frac{1}{n\lambda_F^2} + \frac{T^2}{6n})$$

The derivation of a lower confidence bound for A can then be performed analogously to the unbiased probing approach using Fieller's theorem.

Underestimated Probing Approach   When considering our third probing approach (i.e., an underestimation of downtimes), the errors $E_i^F b$ and $E_j^R b$ measured before an uptime i and downtime j, respectively, as well as the errors $E_i^F a$ and $E_j^R a$ measured after an uptime i and downtime j, respectively, are distributed as follows:

$$E_i^F = E_i^{Fb} + E_i^{Fa} \sim Tri(0, 2T) \text{ with } E_i^{Fb} \sim U(0, T) \text{ and } E_i^{Fa} \sim U(0, T) \quad (6.21)$$

$$E_j^R = E_j^{Rb} + E_j^{Ra} \sim Tri(-2T, 0) \text{ with } E_j^{Rb} \sim U(-T, 0) \text{ and } E_j^{Ra} \sim U(-T, 0) \quad (6.22)$$

Given that the random variables E_i^F and E_j^R are identically and independently distributed, their arithmetic means approach a normal distribution with an increasing sample size ($n \geq 30$) according to the central limit theorem as follows:

$$E^F = \frac{1}{n} \sum_{i=1}^{n} E_i^F \sim N(T, \frac{T^2}{6n}) \quad \text{and} \quad E^R = \frac{1}{n} \sum_{j=1}^{n} E_j^R \sim N(\text{-T}, \frac{T^2}{6n}) \qquad (6.23)$$

Now, in order to obtain a two-sided confidence interval for the ratio $Z_R/Z_F = m(R)/m(F)$, we again determine the distribution of that ratio as a preparatory step:

$$\frac{\hat{m}(R)}{\hat{m}(F)} = [\ldots] = \frac{Z_R}{Z_F} \qquad (6.24)$$

with $\quad Z_R \sim N(\frac{1}{\lambda_R} - T, \frac{1}{n\lambda_R^2} + \frac{T^2}{6n}) \quad$ and $\quad Z_F \sim N(\frac{1}{\lambda_F} + T, \frac{1}{n\lambda_F^2} + \frac{T^2}{6n})$

Again, a lower confidence bound for A can then be derived analogously to the other two aforementioned probing approaches based on Fieller's theorem.

Application of our Mathematical Model Having presented a mathematical model for calculating a lower bound for the real availability A at a desired level of confidence based on a given point estimate, we now elaborate on how to use that model in conjunction with our monitoring approach CSLAB-Mon.KOM. Basically, the model can be used at design time and at runtime.

At design time, the model enables the determination of the *the minimum number of samples* required in order to obtain a desired level of confidence for different point estimates assuming that the real availability is equal to the prior negotiated uptime guarantee. Such a computation of sample sizes at different levels of confidence has also been performed by Singh and Swaminathan in their work in [191]. However, their model for availability estimation is different from the model in this thesis in this regard that they assume that the real times to failure F_i and times to repair R_j are known. In contrast to their work, we also take a probing error into account. Using our model, the results of an exemplary computation of the minimum required sample sizes at different confidence levels in order to show 99.95% availability are provided in Table 6.2 for different lengths of the probing period T. The considered availability of 99.95% equals the monthly uptime guarantee offered by Amazon for EC2[1] and corresponds to approximately 21.5 minutes downtime per month and 5 minutes downtime per week. Therefore, we have considered the probing periods $T = 5$ minutes and the double value $T = 10$ minutes in our exemplary computation, thereby assuming that, e.g., a downtime may occur every week or every second week. In addition, a probing period of $T = 1$ minute has been considered, since Amazon's own monitoring solution CloudWatch[2] provides system status checks at a one-minute frequency. As it can be deduced from Table 6.2, different combinations of probing periods and sample sizes are applicable in general in order to verify a negotiated uptime guarantee at the desired level of

---

[1]   https://aws.amazon.com/de/ec2/sla/
[2]   https://aws.amazon.com/cloudwatch/details/

confidence given a certain point estimate. Therefore, the following considerations are made in order to provide decision support for customers for choosing and specifying a desired monitoring frequency and confidence level as part of the MLAs (cf. Section 4.3.5).

Basically, the most probable point estimate can be derived by the broker from previous measurements concerning the cloud service to be monitored and disclosed to the customer. Based on that information, a customer can then select the desired monitoring frequency (i.e., probing period), thereby considering the minimum length of a downtime that should be detectable and the waiting time for achieving the desired level of confidence derived from the minimum required sample size. For this purpose, a modified version of Table 6.2 can be presented to customers, in which the waiting times are shown alongside the corresponding required sample sizes. Given a certain sample size n, the corresponding waiting time wt can be determined as $wt = n \times (\hat{m}(F) + \hat{m}(R))$. It can be deduced from Table 6.2 that a larger probing period T leads to an increase in the minimum required sample size and, thus, also the waiting time increases. This effect is most pronounced when the point estimate $\hat{A}$ is close to the negotiated uptime guarantee. With respect to the waiting time, a smaller probing period (i.e., a higher monitoring frequency) is more desirable. However, a higher monitoring frequency will also cause a higher resource consumption and, thus, will be charged at higher costs. Therefore, the waiting time has to be considered in conjunction with the desired minimum detectable length of a downtime. That minimum length is indirectly fixed by the selected monitoring frequency and corresponds to the length of a probing period T when following our unbiased probing approach. Whether a downtime with a certain length should be detectable mainly depends on its severity for associated business activities. A certain length of a downtime may cause different costs for different customers. Accordingly, some customers may not be interested in detecting small downtimes while others require their detection. However, the minimum detectable length of a downtime also depends on the minimum recovery time of a system, since downtimes smaller than the minimum recovery time will not occur and, therefore, are not required to be detectable. Nevertheless, probing periods smaller than the minimum detectable length of a downtime still lead to a higher precision in probing so that a smaller minimum sample size and, thus, a shorter waiting time is required in order to achieve a certain confidence level. Hence, there is a trade-off between the minimum detectable length of a downtime as well as the waiting time and the monitoring costs. Based on the considerations made before, that trade-off must be addressed with respect to the specific business requirements of a customer. Taking the example of Amazon's EC2 mentioned before, it may be beneficial for some customers to increase the minimum detectable length of a downtime to a larger time interval of, e.g., 5 minutes, if smaller downtimes are not business critical. In doing so, the savings in monitoring effort of the broker can then be passed to the customer in terms of a lower monthly monitoring fee.

Table 6.2: Sample sizes at different confidence levels to show 99.95% availability

Point Estimates		Confidence Levels and Sample Sizes			
$\hat{A}$ [%]	$\hat{m}(F)$ [min]	0.8 ($\alpha = 0.2$)	0.9 ($\alpha = 0.1$)	0.95 ($\alpha = 0.05$)	0.99 ($\alpha = 0.01$)
99.951	10199	60	91	117	165
99.952	10412	30	46	59	83
99.953	10633	20	31	39	55
99.954	10865	15	23	29	42
99.955	11106	12	19	24	34
99.956	11359	10	16	20	28
99.957	11623	9	13	17	24
99.958	11900	8	12	15	21
99.959	12190	7	11	13	19

(a) Period $T = 1$ min, $\hat{m}(R) = 5$ min

Point Estimates		Confidence Levels and Sample Sizes			
$\hat{A}$ [%]	$\hat{m}(F)$ [min]	0.8 ($\alpha = 0.2$)	0.9 ($\alpha = 0.1$)	0.95 ($\alpha = 0.05$)	0.99 ($\alpha = 0.01$)
99.951	10199	62	94	121	171
99.952	10412	31	47	61	86
99.953	10633	21	32	41	57
99.954	10865	16	24	30	43
99.955	11106	13	19	24	35
99.956	11359	11	16	20	29
99.957	11623	9	14	18	25
99.958	11900	8	12	15	22
99.959	12190	7	11	14	20

(b) Period $T = 5$ min, $\hat{m}(R) = 5$ min

Point Estimates		Confidence Levels and Sample Sizes			
$\hat{A}$ [%]	$\hat{m}(F)$ [min]	0.8 ($\alpha = 0.2$)	0.9 ($\alpha = 0.1$)	0.95 ($\alpha = 0.05$)	0.99 ($\alpha = 0.01$)
99.951	10199	69	104	134	190
99.952	10412	34	52	67	95
99.953	10633	23	35	45	63
99.954	10865	17	26	33	47
99.955	11106	14	21	27	38
99.956	11359	12	17	22	32
99.957	11623	10	15	19	27
99.958	11900	9	13	17	24
99.959	12190	8	12	15	21

(c) Period $T = 10$ min, $\hat{m}(R) = 5$ min

As already mentioned, our mathematical model can also be used in conjunction with our monitoring approach CSLAB-Mon.KOM at runtime. In this regard, our model enables determining whether prior negotiated uptime guarantees are maintained by computing the confidence level at which the real availability matches the uptime guarantee given the current point estimate. In order to demonstrate the feasibility of our monitoring approach CSLAB-Mon.KOM in conjunction with our mathematical model and to verify that it allows the achievement of accurate monitoring results, we have implemented our monitoring approach as proof-of-concept and performed a corresponding evaluation. A description and the results of that evaluation are provided in Section 8.3.

6.2.4 Influence of Packet Loss on Accuracy

Besides the monitoring frequency and sample size, also network impairments have an influence on the accuracy of the observed availability. Due to the closed nature of cloud environments, measurements can only be performed by sending probing requests from monitoring units placed at remote locations. Since failures in the network between a monitoring unit and the cloud service to be observed may occur, monitoring data may be transmitted with a certain delay or a transmission may fail completely. The first case happens, if an additional latency is introduced in the transmission of the monitoring messages that is caused by, e.g., packet loss and according retransmissions. In the second case, outages in the network or a real downtime of the cloud service may prevent monitoring units to receive any monitoring data. As already mentioned in Section 6.2.1, we consider a cloud service (or the underlying VM) as unavailable during a given time interval i_x from the perspective of a certain monitoring unit if that monitoring unit receives no response to its monitoring request sent at the beginning of that time interval within a predefined timeout period. In order not to lengthen that timeout period unnecessarily and to obtain an efficient monitoring approach, we aim to determine the minimum amount of time required waiting for a response in the context of a certain level of packet loss before considering a cloud service as unavailable. Before we present a corresponding mathematical model that allows the determination of the minimum length of the timeout period given a certain level of packet loss, the following basic considerations are made.

Recall that a monitoring request is sent at the beginning of a certain time interval i_x and that the state derived from such a request characterizes the observed state of the respective cloud service over that time interval. For the case that a monitoring request and/or the corresponding response are affected by an additional latency in the network, the response is received by the respective monitoring unit at a later point in time. If such a response is received after the end of the currently considered time interval i_x, a monitoring unit can hardly decide whether that response still has been sent during the currently considered time interval i_x or not. With increasing latency, the probability that a response to a given monitoring request has been sent after the end of the currently considered time interval i_x increases. Hence, the monitoring unit is more likely to observe a different state of the cloud service at a later point in time instead of the current state, which is actually associated with the currently considered time interval. However, in order to provide a reliable monitoring approach, measurements must be conducted in such a manner that an observed state derived from a response is attributed correctly to the currently considered time interval i_x. Therefore, a monitoring unit must be aware of the observed state at the end of the currently considered time interval at the latest, so that it is reasonable for the timeout period to match the end of a time interval. However, if no response is received within a certain time interval, a monitoring unit will consider the respective cloud service as unavailable, although monitoring data might be available with a certain delay in case of network impairments.

For all the reasons stated above, the earliest point in time to consider a cloud service as available is represented by receiving the first data packet of a response to a monitoring request. That first data packet has to be received within the currently considered time interval in order to ensure that the monitoring request has reached its target, i.e., the cloud service, during that time interval. Otherwise, if the first data packet is received beyond the currently considered time interval, a monitoring unit cannot decide whether there has been a failure of the cloud service before or the transmission has been affected by a large latency. Since a cloud service is considered to be unavailable in this case, the accuracy of the overall availability decreases.

In the following, we present a mathematical model for estimating the time from sending a monitoring request until receiving the first data packet of the corresponding response (referred to as *time to first packet* in the following) in the presence of a certain level of packet loss. In doing so, we lay the foundation for adjusting the monitoring frequency depending on a certain level of packet loss. Specifically, the probing period T must not be smaller than the estimated time to first packet in order to be able to attribute an observed state correctly to the corresponding time interval.

Mathematical Model   Our mathematical model is based on the model for Transmission Control Protocol (TCP) latency proposed by Cardwell et al. in [29], which assumes a TCP implementation that adheres to the TCP standard as defined in RFC793 (cf. [107]). In general, a successful TCP connection starts with a connection establishment phase, denoted as *three-way handshake*, followed by a data transfer phase. The TCP behavior under packet loss during the time to first packet according to our model is depicted in Figure 6.4. Following Cardwell et al., the connection establishment phase proceeds as follows. First of all, the side of the monitoring unit initiates the connection establishment by sending a SYN to the side of the cloud service. Due to packet loss, $i \geq 0$ SYNs are transmitted unsuccessfully, before the $(i+1)^{th}$ SYN is successfully received on the side of the cloud service. Subsequently, SYN+ACKs

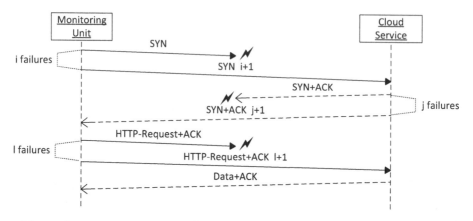

Figure 6.4: TCP behavior under packet loss until receipt of first data packet[3]

being sent from the side of the cloud service are lost $j \geq 0$ times until the $(j+1)^{th}$ SYN+ACK is successfully received on the side of the monitoring unit. Similar to Cardwell et al., we consider that point in time as the end of the connection establishment phase. This is due to the fact that the subsequent ACK $y+1$ discarded in the model is immediately followed by a data segment in conjunction with a redundant ACK $y+1$. According to our model, that data segment initiating the data transfer phase is represented by the http-based monitoring request. The http request+ACK may also fail $l+1$ times until the $l+1$ http request+ACK arrives successfully at the cloud service. The cloud service then answers with the first data+ACK, which constitutes the first data packet of the response received by the monitoring unit.

Now, let $P(i,j,l)$ be the probability of having a TCP behavior as depicted in Figure 6.4, which exhibits exactly i failed SYNs, a subsequent successful SYN, followed by j failed SYN+ACKs, a subsequent successful SYN+ACK, followed by l failures of http request+ACKs, and a subsequent successful http request+ACK, followed by a successful data+ACK. Further let p_f be the packet loss rate in the (forward) direction (of data flow) from the cloud service to the monitoring unit and let p_r be the packet loss rate in the reverse direction (cf. [29]). The overall probability $P(i,j,l)$ can then be formally defined as follows:

$$P(i,j,l) = p_r^i \, (1-p_r) \, p_f^j \, (1-p_f) \, p_r^l \, (1-p_r) \, (1-p_f) \tag{6.25a}$$

$$= p_r^{i+l} \, (1-p_r)^2 \, p_f^j \, (1-p_f)^2 \tag{6.25b}$$

The corresponding latency $L(i,j,l)$ when having such a TCP behavior can be expressed mathematically as stated below. In this regard, RTT represents the average Round

---

3   Lags in time depicted between receiving and sending messages are only for reasons of readability
     of the message descriptions

Trip Time (RTT) between the monitoring unit and the cloud service, T_S constitutes the initial Retransmission Timeout (RTO) of the connection establishment phase, and TD indicates the initial RTO of the data transfer phase. According to Paxson et al. [155], the initial RTO is set to 1 second and increased to 3 seconds before the data transfer phase in case of lost SYNs or SYN+ACKs. We have validated the specified time values in the scope of a small testbed experiment. The corresponding Wireshark[4] trace is provided in Section A.1 in the Appendix. Hence, T_S is 1 second and T_D is 3 seconds in our model. Now, every time an ACK is not received by either side during the respective RTO T_S or T_D, the lost packet is retransmitted and the RTO is doubled (cf. [29, 155]). Whenever an ACK is received, the RTO timer is restarted. The resulting, so-called *exponential backoff* of the RTO can be expressed mathematically as a geometric series, resulting in three sums in Equation 6.26a for each sequence of i, j, and l failures. The two RTTs in that equation refer to the transmission times of the SYN $i+1$ and SYN+ACK $j+1$ as well as the http request+ACK $l+1$ and data+ACK. Finally, the latency $L(i, j, l)$ can be determined as follows:

$$L(i, j, l) = RTT + \left(\sum_{k=0}^{i-1} 2^k \, T_S \right) + \left(\sum_{k=0}^{j-1} 2^k \, T_S \right) + \left(\sum_{k=0}^{l-1} 2^k \, T_D \right) + RTT \quad (6.26a)$$

$$= 2\,RTT + (2^i - 1)\,T_S + (2^j - 1)\,T_S + (2^l - 1)\,T_D \quad (6.26b)$$

$$= 2\,RTT + (2^i + 2^j - 2)\,T_S + (2^l - 1)\,T_D \quad (6.26c)$$

The time to first packet can then be estimated using Equation 6.27c. For the case that the packet loss rate p is similar in both directions, the simplified Equation 6.27d can be used. As a general prerequisite, the packet loss rate(s) must be low enough still to permit a successful handshake, since 4-6 failures lead to the termination of the connection establishment phase in most of the TCP implementations [29].

$$E(L) = \sum_{i=0}^{\infty} \sum_{j=0}^{\infty} \sum_{l=0}^{\infty} L(i, j, l) \, P(i, j, l) \quad (6.27a)$$

$$= \sum_{i,j,l=0}^{\infty} \left(2\,RTT + (2^i + 2^j - 2)\,T_S + \left(2^l - 1\right)\,T_D \right) \left(p_r^{i+l} \, (1 - p_r)^2 \, p_f^j \, (1 - p_f)^2 \right) \quad (6.27b)$$

$$= (1 - p_f) \left(2\,RTT + T_S \left(\frac{1 - p_r}{1 - 2p_r} + \frac{1 - p_f}{1 - 2p_f} - 2 \right) + T_D \left(\frac{1 - p_r}{1 - 2p_r} - 1 \right) \right) \quad (6.27c)$$

$$= (1 - p) \left(2\,RTT + (2\,T_S + T_D) \left(\frac{1 - p}{1 - 2p} - 1 \right) \right) \quad \text{if } p_f = p_r = p \quad (6.27d)$$

---

4   http://www.wireshark.org

Table 6.3: Increase in latency depending on the level of packet loss at different RTTs

RTT (ms)	Packet Loss (%)	Latency with Loss (ms)	Latency w/o Loss (ms)	Difference (ms)	Ratio (%)
20	1	90	40	50	225
20	2	141	40	101	353
20	3	194	40	154	484
20	4	247	40	207	618
20	5	302	40	262	755
50	1	150	100	50	150
50	2	200	100	100	200
50	3	252	100	152	252
50	4	305	100	205	305
50	5	359	100	259	359
100	1	249	200	49	124
100	2	298	200	98	149
100	3	349	200	149	174
100	4	401	200	201	200
100	5	454	200	254	227
500	1	1041	1000	41	104
500	2	1082	1000	82	108
500	3	1125	1000	125	112
500	4	1169	1000	169	117
500	5	1214	1000	214	121
1000	1	2031	2000	31	102
1000	2	2062	2000	62	103
1000	3	2095	2000	95	105
1000	4	2129	2000	129	106
1000	5	2164	2000	164	108

The increase in latency in the presence of different packet loss rates at different RTTs according to our second mathematical model is provided in Table 6.3. We have exemplarily considered typical RTTs and packet loss rates based on the works by Aikat et al. [2] and Cottrell et al. [39]. It can be deduced from the table that the increase in latency is most pronounced in case of small RTTs of 20 ms. In detail, at a higher packet loss rate of 5% the latency is more than seven times higher compared to the latency without packet loss, which translates into an absolute difference of around 262 ms. However, even at lower packet loss rates of 1% the latency nearly doubles given an RTT of 20ms. The impact of packet loss for similar loss rates decreases with an increasing RTT. While there is only a marginal relative increase in latency between 2% and 8% at large RTTs of 1000ms, an absolute difference between 31ms and 164ms is still observed. Although single monitoring requests affected by similar packet loss rates as listed in the table only have a relatively small impact on the additional latency and, thus, the time to first packet, consecutive monitoring requests that fail due to packet loss may affect the overall accuracy to a larger extent. This is not acceptable if guarantees on the accuracy of the monitoring data should be provided. Therefore, we briefly discuss the consideration of the influence of different packet loss rates according to our second mathematical model in the scope of our monitoring approach in the following. Note that mechanisms for adapting the monitoring frequency at runtime are not in the scope of this thesis and may be part of future work.

As already stated, the probing period T utilized in conjunction with our monitoring approach must not be smaller than the estimated time to first packet derived from our mathematical model. A probing period at least equal to or larger than that estimated time is required in order to ensure that the monitored state is correctly associated with the currently considered time interval. For the case that the first packet of the response from the observed cloud service arrives at a later point in time than the end of the currently considered time interval, the monitoring request may have reached the cloud service beyond that time interval. Hence, the time to first packet represents a lower bound for the corresponding probing period T. This lower bound can be considered when initially setting or adjusting the monitoring frequency at runtime. For this purpose, models for predicting the level of packet loss depending on, e.g., different daytimes could be developed in order to adjust the monitoring frequency accordingly. In this regard, the time to first packet with regard to the level of packet loss that is very likely to occur during a certain time period could be considered in parallel to the regular probing period assuming no packet loss. Whenever a response arrives beyond the end of the currently considered probing period but that response is still within the limits defined by the estimated time to first packet the response has very likely been affected by packet loss. In this case, the response could still be considered to be a valid response with regard to the currently considered time interval and the monitoring frequency could be adjusted accordingly. However, in order to avoid an oscillating behavior, the monitoring system could wait to switch back to the regular probing period until no packet loss has been experienced for a predefined amount of time. Moving back to the regular probing period and, thus, a higher monitoring frequency is reasonable in order to achieve a higher level of accuracy as before.

6.3 Summary

In this chapter, we have presented our approach for reliable consumer side availability monitoring CSLAB-Mon.KOM as another major contribution of this thesis. Compared to related approaches, CSLAB-Mon.KOM explicitly addresses the reliability of the monitoring results. For this purpose, CSLAB-Mon.KOM exhibits different properties. First of all, it is *location-aware* and, thus, enables determining whether a downtime occurred due to an incident on the provider side or not. In doing so, real SLA violations can be distinguished from other incidents outside the control sphere of a cloud provider.

This is realized by applying a hybrid monitoring approach that combines monitoring information from monitoring units placed on the broker and the provider side. Secondly, our monitoring approach is *resource-aware*. By combining application-level and VM-level monitoring, the resources affected by an incident can be identified, so that the violated SLA clause can be determined. Thirdly, CSLAB-Mon.KOM provides decision support in two ways in order to obtain monitoring results as *accurate* as required. In this regard, we have created two mathematical models. The first model allows the computation of a lower bound for the real availability at a certain level of confidence based on a given point estimate and can be applied at both, design time and runtime. At design time, the model permits the determination of an appropriate monitoring frequency and required sample size in order to obtain the desired level of confidence assuming that the real availability is equal to the uptime guarantee as specified in the SLA. At runtime, the model allows the calculation of the confidence level at which the real availability matches the negotiated uptime guarantee based on the current point estimate. Our second mathematical model accounts for network impairments in terms of packet loss. It can be used to estimate the time to first packet constituting the earliest point in time at which a cloud service can be considered to be available after having sent a monitoring request given a certain level of packet loss. The estimated time represents a guideline for adjusting the monitoring frequency. Since an observed state cannot be clearly attributed to the currently considered measurement interval, if the time to first packet exceeds the length of that interval, the probing period must be greater or at least equal to the time to first packet. Finally, in order to be able to obtain reliable monitoring results, also the underlying monitoring infrastructure must be *robust*. Therefore, corresponding strategies for robust monitor placement CSLAB-Loc.KOM are presented in the next Chapter 7.

7 Robust Monitor Placement – CSLAB-Loc.KOM

Having described our approach for reliable consumer side availability monitoring in the previous Chapter 6, we will now elaborate on strategies for robust monitor placement in this chapter. As already mentioned in Section 1.2, focusing only on the provisioning of reliable monitoring information itself is not sufficient. In order to enable consumers to monitor the performance of cloud services in a reliable manner, also the reliability of the monitoring infrastructure must be taken into account. Monitoring units themselves or network communication paths in between them may fail, which prevents the monitoring system from collecting and/or delivering certain monitoring information. Following our monitoring approach, we utilize redundant monitor units that are placed at different locations. In doing so, redundant monitor units can substitute for failing monitor units. Nevertheless, since concurrent node and/or link failures may occur, all monitoring units should be placed at reliable locations in order to achieve a robust monitoring infrastructure. Therefore, we propose strategies for robust monitor placement in the following. In contrast to related approaches, we do not limit the number of node and/or link failures. Instead, we consider the probabilities to fail of all candidate nodes for monitor placement as well as all communication paths in between and aim to maximize the reliability of the whole monitoring infrastructure while placing monitoring units. This chapter is structured as follows. In Section 7.1, we describe the Robust Cloud Monitor Placement Problem (RCMPP) [187, 188] in detail. Corresponding formal notations are introduced in Section 7.2. The RCMPP can be formalized as an optimization model, which is presented in Section 7.3. Since the RCMPP constitutes a non-linear, multi-objective optimization problem, multiple solutions exist, which are of the same quality from a mathematical perspective (cf. Section 5.2). Therefore, we propose a set of transformations in Section 7.3 based on a worst-case perspective in order to turn the RCMPP into a linear, single-objective optimization problem. In doing so, we obtain an exact solution approach CSLAB-Loc-Exa.KOM [187, 188] using off-the-shelf algorithms. However, since the RCMPP is NP-hard, an exact solution cannot be obtained for large-scale problem instances in polynomial time. Hence, we also present two heuristic approaches CSLAB-Loc-Start.KOM [188] and CSLAB-Loc-Imp.KOM [188] in Section 7.4. While CSLAB-Loc-Start.KOM represents a Greedy opening procedure, CSLAB-Loc-Imp.KOM constitutes a Tabu Search-based improvement approach. Section 7.5 summarizes the main findings of this chapter.

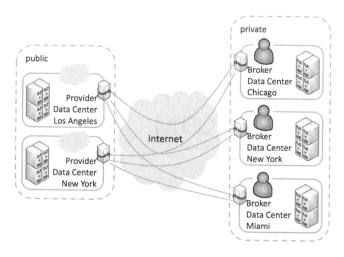

Figure 7.1: Robust cloud monitor placement scenario[1]

7.1 Problem Statement

Recalling Section 4.1, our envisaged SLM broker conducts SLA-related activities on behalf of cloud consumers. Having agreed on SLAs with a certain cloud provider, the SLM broker determines appropriate locations for monitoring units to be placed. The monitoring units then apply our approach for reliable availability monitoring in order to verify the adherence of the cloud services with the prior negotiated SLAs.

In the following, we focus on an enterprise cloud consumer who is about to utilize several cloud applications of a certain cloud provider. We assume that the SLM broker has already agreed on SLAs with that cloud provider on behalf of the enterprise cloud consumer and has to establish appropriate monitoring capabilities in the next step. For this purpose, the SLM broker has to determine appropriate locations for the monitoring units to be placed. In this regard, we assume that the cloud applications to be monitored are running in one or more different data centers of the cloud provider and that the SLM broker is also running several private data centers at different locations worldwide (cf. Figure 7.1). Running cloud applications in different data centers may be reasonable in order to serve different user clusters with specific QoS requirements (cf. [87, 88]). Each VM in a data center of the cloud provider, which is running one or more cloud applications of the enterprise cloud consumer represents a candidate for monitor placement. It should be noted that monitoring units for a certain cloud application are not allowed to be placed on the VM where the application is running. This is due to the fact that such a monitoring unit will not be able to report any outages that affect the cloud application if the underlying VM fails. The same

---

[1]   based on http://docs.aws.amazon.com/AmazonVPC/latest/NetworkAdminGuide/images/Branch/
      _Offices.png

anti-co-location constraint also has to be considered with regard to the VM of the cloud application and the VM of each corresponding monitoring unit being placed on the same physical machine. That issue has already been discussed in the scope of the design of our basic monitoring approach in Section 4.3.4. Summarizing the findings from that discussion, there currently exists no means for influencing the VM placement to a certain extent, but providers could provide according means in the future. Nevertheless, that issue only affects at most one of the monitoring units of each application. This is due to the fact that at most one monitoring unit is placed in the same data center where the application is running, while other monitoring units are placed in different data centers. Besides the VMs in the data centers of the cloud provider, also VMs running in the private data centers of the SLM broker constitute candidates for monitor placement, according to our monitoring approach (cf. Section 4.3.4). As already stated, we utilize redundant monitoring units for each cloud application to be monitored for reasons of fault-tolerance. Therefore, we further assume that a cloud consumer specifies the desired number of redundant monitoring units to be used for each cloud application in advance as part of the MLAs (cf. Section 4.3.5). In practice, the desired level of resilience in terms of a certain number of redundant monitoring units will vary depending on the level of importance of a certain cloud application, since utilizing more resources is more expensive (cf. [16]). However, following our monitoring approach, at least one monitoring unit has to be placed on the provider and on the broker side in order to achieve location-aware monitoring. Furthermore, we demand that each monitoring unit that is responsible for observing the same cloud application be placed in a different data center. This assumption is made since outages in the past have also affected larger parts of a data center. In this case, the remaining monitoring units for a certain cloud application should continue working.

As already mentioned, the main goal in solving the RCMPP is to obtain a robust monitoring infrastructure when placing monitoring units. Therefore, we aim to maximize the probability that at least one of the redundant monitoring units for each cloud application will be working properly. In this thesis, we focus on the initial placement of monitoring units for a given set of cloud applications. Changes concerning their placement that have to be made at run time are out of scope of this thesis and may be part of future work.

A monitoring unit is considered to work properly, if the following conditions hold. First of all, a monitoring unit must be able to perform its monitoring tasks in a reliable manner. This issue has already been addressed with our approach for reliable consumer side availability monitoring presented in the previous chapter. Secondly, the VM where a monitoring unit is placed on must also work properly. Otherwise, neither monitoring information can be collected nor delivered. Finally, a working network connection must exist between a monitoring unit and the cloud application to be observed. Basically, a network connection is considered to be working, if the monitoring unit is able to obtain a response to a corresponding monitoring request sent before within an expected amount of time. In this regard, we assume that the MDA, which is located on the broker side and collects all the monitoring information from the monitoring units (cf. Section 4.3.4), will never fail. Although this assumption is not realistic, monitoring data is also stored locally by each of the monitoring units (cf. Section 4.3.4) and, thus, the MDA can also request the monitoring data from the monitoring units at a later point in time in case of a previous outage of the MDA. In this regard, the MDA will never fail to obtain the monitoring data from the monitoring units. All in all, we consider the reliability of the VMs where monitoring units can be placed and the reliability of the network links between these VMs and the VMs where the cloud applications to be monitored are hosted.

Since the execution of monitoring tasks requires a certain amount of resources, the resource supplies of the VMs that constitute candidates for monitor placement and the resource demands of the monitoring units to be placed must also be taken into account. In general, different types of resources, such as CPU power or memory, can be considered.

Summarizing, the RCMPP can be expressed as follows. Given a set of cloud applications and the desired number of redundant monitoring units for each application, the aim is to determine a placement of the monitoring units that maximizes the reliability of the monitoring system. Thereby, reliability is expressed in terms of the probability that at least one monitoring unit of each application is working properly. Thus, in order to solve the RCMPP, the SLM broker faces the following three challenges. First of all, the reliability of the locations where monitoring units are placed should be maximized for all cloud applications simultaneously. Second, location constraints have to be considered. Monitoring units are not allowed to be placed on the VM where the cloud application to be monitored is running. Furthermore, if monitoring units are in charge of monitoring the same application, they should not be placed in the same data center in order to increase robustness. Third, resource constraints of the VMs must be taken into account. Irrespective of a considered resource type, the given resource supply of a VM must not exceed the specified resource demand of a monitoring unit to be placed on that VM. This is the first work that jointly considers probabilistic reliability values of network links and VMs, monitor redundancy, and location as well as resource constraints (cf. Section 3.3).

7.2 Formal Notations

Before presenting the optimization model corresponding to the RCMPP in conjunction with an exact optimization approach in Section 7.3, some formal notations are introduced in the following as a preparatory step. The basic entities and parameters considered in the RCMPP are related to the available locations for monitor placement, the cloud applications to be monitored, the probabilistic reliabilities of the available locations, and the resource constraints.

Concerning the locations that are available for monitor placement, the basic entities of the RCMPP comprise the different data center sites and the VMs running on each site that are available for hosting monitoring units. In this regard, we distinguish between the data center sites on the broker and the provider side. This can be formally expressed as follows:

- $S = \{1, ..., n\}$: set of n data center sites

- $S'' = \{1, ..., d\}$: subset of broker sites, $S'' \subset S$

- $S' = \{d+1, ..., n\}$: subset of provider sites, $S' \subset S$

- $V_s = \{1, ..., i\}$: set of VM candidates for monitor placement on site $s \in S$

Each VM running in a data center on the provider side is hosting one or more cloud applications that should be monitored. Depending on the level of importance of each cloud application, a certain number of redundant monitoring units to be used is specified by the enterprise cloud consumer. We define the following symbols:

- $C_{s'v'} = \{1, ..., j\}$: set of cloud applications to monitor on VM $v' \in V_{s'}, s' \in S'$

- $rf_{s'v'c} \in \mathbb{N}_{>1}$: redundancy factor for monitoring application $c \in C_{s'v'}$

In order to maximize the reliability of the monitoring system, we consider probabilistic reliability values of the VM candidates for monitor placement and the links interconnecting these VMs with the VMs of the cloud applications. We assume that the SLM broker is able to estimate the reliability values of the VMs based on, e.g., the SLAs offered by the cloud provider, former measurements using our approach for reliable consumer side availability monitoring, and/or predictions derived from internal models. Concerning the reliability values of the links, we further assume that the SLM broker is not aware of the network topologies in the control sphere of the ISP and in the data centers of the cloud provider. Hence, the SLM broker can only make estimates with regard to the end-to-end performance between a VM candidate for monitor placement and a VM running the corresponding cloud application to be monitored. For this purpose, the SLM broker can utilize traditional network measurements tools. In this regard, the following formal expressions are defined:

- $p_{sv} \in [0, 1]$: observed reliability for each VM $v \in V_s$

- $L = \{l(sv \rightleftharpoons s'v')\}$: set of links interconnecting VM candidates for monitor placement V_s and VMs $V_{s'}$ of applications $C_{s'v'}$

- $p_{l(sv \rightleftharpoons s'v')} \in [0, 1]$: observed reliability for each link $l \in L$

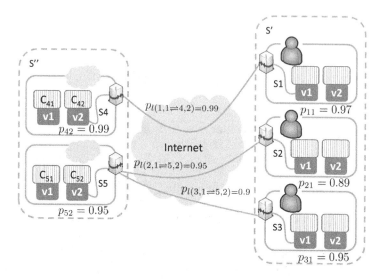

Figure 7.2: Robust cloud monitor placement example

Since each monitoring task requires a certain amount of resources, such as CPU power or memory, for monitoring a certain application, the resource demand of each resource type to be considered must not exceed the available resource supply of a VM where the monitoring unit should be placed on. Thus, we introduce the following definitions:

- $R = \{1, ..., k\}$: set of k considered VM resource types

- $rd_{s'v'cr} \in \mathbb{R}^+$: resource demand for monitoring application $c \in C_{s'v'}$ for resource $r \in R$

- $rs_{svr} \in \mathbb{R}^+$: resource supply of VM $v \in V_s$ for resource $r \in R$

In order to become acquainted with the formal notations, we describe a simplified example of the RCMPP in the following. The example is illustrated in Figure 7.2 and neglects resource constraints for clarity. As it can be seen from the figure, five data center sites $S = \{1, ..., 5\}$ are considered in the example. These sites are further divided into the two sites S_4 and S_5 on the provider side and the three sites $S_1 - S_3$ on the broker side. On each of these sites, two VMs $v1$ and $v2$ are running. Each of the VMs on the provider side is hosting a set of cloud applications to be monitored. For example, the set C_{52} of cloud applications is running on VM $v2$ on data center site $S5$. This VM denoted as $v2$ exhibits a reliability of $p_{52} = 0.95$ and is interconnected with, e.g., VM $v1$ on data center site S_2. The end-to-end connection between these two VMs is represented by the link $l(2, 1 \rightleftharpoons 5, 2)$, for which a reliability of $p_{l(2,1\rightleftharpoons5,2)} = 0.95$ has been estimated. VM $v1$ on data center site S_2 exhibits a reliability value of $p_{21} = 0.89$. In the example, there also exists another link $l(3, 1 \rightleftharpoons 5, 2)$ between VM $v2$ on data center site $S5$ and VM $v1$ on data center site $S3$. Now, if we had to place the first monitoring unit of a cloud application in the set C_{52} on the broker side, given that only the two VMs $v1$ on data center site S_2 and S_3 are available, VM $v1$ on data center site S_3 would be chosen. This is due to the fact, that this VM in conjunction with its corresponding link to the VM $v2$ on data center site $S5$ exhibits a higher total reliability. It has to be noted that although we are focusing only on monitoring applications on the provider side, there may be also applications running on the VMs on the broker side. However, these broker side applications do not constitute cloud applications utilized by consumers, but are used by the broker for further evaluation purposes. We also consider these applications in our optimization model in the form of reduced resource supplies provided by their corresponding VMs. If we assume that each set $C_{s'v'}$ of cloud applications only consists of a single application in the example and that the enterprise cloud user has specified a minimal redundancy factor $rf_{s'v'c} = 2$ for each of these applications, eight monitoring units would have to be placed on VMs in total. In doing so, one monitoring unit would have to be placed on the provider side and one on the broker side for each of the applications.

7.3 Exact Optimization Approach – CSLAB-Loc-Exa.KOM

As already stated, the RCMPP can be formalized as a mathematical optimization model. In the following Section 7.3.1, we will describe the model in detail utilizing the formal notations from the previous section. In this regard, we elaborate on the decision variables, the objective function, as well as the individual constraints. Since the resulting optimization model constitutes a non-linear, multi-objective optimization problem, we propose several transformations in the subsequent Section 7.3.2 in order to obtain an exact solution approach using off-the-shelf algorithms.

7.3.1 Optimization Model

The most important elements of an optimization model are the decision variables. They constitute the foundation for expressing other elements of an optimization model, such as the objective function and the corresponding constraints. Furthermore, the set of decision variables and their range of values represent the options that are available for solving an optimization problem. Therefore, we first introduce the decision variables.

Decision Variables Recalling Section 7.1, the goal of solving the RCMPP is to determine a placement of the monitoring units that maximizes the reliability of the monitoring system. This implies that the options that are available for solving the RCMPP are represented by the set of available placements for the monitoring units.

These options can be formalized by defining binary decision variables. Each decision variable $x_{svs'v'c}$ specifies, whether a monitoring unit that monitors cloud application $c \in C_{s'v'}$ running on VM $v' \in V_{s'}$ on site $s' \in S'$ is placed on VM $v \in V_s$ running on site $s \in S$ (cf. Equation 7.1).

$$x_{svs'v'c} \in \{0,1\} \qquad \forall s \in S, v \in V_s, s' \in S', v' \in V_{s'}, c \in C_{s'v'} \tag{7.1}$$

Objective Function   Based on the decision variables, we can now introduce the objective function. The objective of the RCMPP is to maximize the reliability of the monitoring system while placing monitoring units to VMs on the provider and the broker side. Thereby, reliability is expressed as the probability that at least one monitoring unit of each cloud application is working properly. In this regard, we assume that the downtime events of the different monitoring units are independent of each other.

Hence, the objective of the RCMPP is to maximize that probability for each of the cloud applications. This results in multiple potentially conflicting objective functions that have to be considered simultaneously (cf. Equation 7.2). In each of these objective functions, $p_{s'v'c}^{mon}(x)$ expresses the probability that a certain cloud application $c \in C_{s'v'}$ can be monitored in a reliable manner. The set of all decision variables $x_{svs'v'c}$ is represented as a vector x. The probability $p_{s'v'c}^{mon}(x)$ can be determined based on the probability of the complementary event, i.e., that all monitors for a certain cloud application fail (cf. Equation 7.3). In this regard, $q_{svs'v'}^{path}$ denotes the probability that a monitoring unit, which is placed on VM $v \in V_s$ on site $s \in S$ in order to monitor a certain cloud application $c \in C_{s'v'}$, will fail. The probability $q_{svs'v'}^{path}$, in turn, is calculated by considering the estimated reliability of the link between VM $v \in V_s$ and VM $v' \in V_{s'}$ in conjunction with the estimated reliability of the VM $v \in V_s$ itself (cf. Equation 7.4).

$$Maximize \quad \{p_{s'v'c}^{mon}(x) \mid s' \in S', v' \in V_{s'}, c \in C_{s'v'}\} \tag{7.2}$$

$$p_{s'v'c}^{mon}(x) = 1 - \prod_{s \in S, v \in V_s} (q_{svs'v'}^{path})^{x_{svs'v'c}} \tag{7.3}$$

$$q_{svs'v'}^{path} = [(1 - p_{sv}) + (1 - p_{l(sv \rightleftharpoons s'v')}) - (1 - p_{sv})(1 - p_{l(sv \rightleftharpoons s'v')})] \tag{7.4}$$

Constraints   While placing monitoring units, several constraints have to be considered. As part of the MLAs, consumers specify the number of redundant monitoring units to be used for monitoring a certain application in order to increase the robustness.

Hence, a solution to the RCMPP is only valid, if $rf_{s'v'c}$ monitoring units have been placed for each cloud application $c \in C_{s'v'}$ (cf. Equation 7.5).

$$\sum_{s \in S, v \in V_s} x_{svs'v'c} = rf_{s'v'c} \qquad \forall s' \in S', v' \in V_{s'}, c \in C_{s'v'}, rf_{s'v'c} \geq 2 \qquad (7.5)$$

For the actual monitoring tasks, the monitoring units apply our approach for reliable consumer side monitoring. Since our monitoring approach should be location-aware, at least one monitoring unit has to be placed on the provider side and one on the broker side (cf. Equations 7.6 and 7.7) .

$$\sum_{s \in S, v \in V_s} x_{svs'v'c} \geq 1 \qquad \forall s' \in S', v' \in V_{s'}, c \in C_{s'v'}, s \in S' \qquad (7.6)$$

$$\sum_{s \in S, v \in V_s} x_{svs'v'c} \geq 1 \qquad \forall s' \in S', v' \in V_{s'}, c \in C_{s'v'}, s \in S'' \qquad (7.7)$$

Each monitoring unit requires a certain amount of resources $rd_{s'v'cr}$ from a certain resource type r for observing a certain application $c \in C_{s'v'}$. In doing so, the sum of the resource demands of all monitoring units that have been assigned to the same VM $v \in V_s$ must not exceed the resource supplies rs_{svr} of that VM $v \in V_s$ (cf. Equation 7.8).

$$\sum_{s' \in S', v' \in V_{s'}, c \in C_{s'v'}} rd_{s'v'cr} \, x_{svs'v'c} \leq rs_{svr} \qquad \forall s \in S, v \in V_s, r \in R \qquad (7.8)$$

Often, outages may affect large parts of a data center. Therefore, we demand that all monitoring units for a certain application $c \in C_{s'v'}$ have to be placed on VMs running on different data center sites (cf. Equation 7.9).

$$\sum_{v \in V_s} x_{svs'v'c} \leq 1 \qquad \forall s \in S, s' \in S', v' \in V_{s'}, c \in C_{s'v'} \qquad (7.9)$$

Finally, a monitoring unit will not be able to detect and report any downtime concerning a certain cloud application $c \in C_{s'v'}$ if they are both assigned to the same VM $v' \in V_{s'}$ on site $s' \in S'$ and that VM fails. Thus, we demand that a monitoring unit is not allowed to be placed on the same VM where the cloud application to be monitored is running (cf. Equation 7.10).

$$x_{svs'v'c} = 0 \qquad \forall c \in C_{s'v'}, \ s = s' \text{ and } v = v' \qquad (7.10)$$

Table 7.1: Symbols used in the optimization model

Symbol	Description
$S = \{1,...,n\}$	set of n data center sites
$S'' = \{1,...,d\}$	broker sites, $S'' \subset S$
$S' = \{d+1,...,n\}$	provider sites, $S' \subset S$
$V_s = \{1,...,i\}$	VM candidates for monitor placement on site $s \in S$
$C_{s'v'} = \{1,...,j\}$	cloud applications to monitor on VM $v' \in V_{s'}, s' \in S'$
$L = \{l(sv \rightleftharpoons s'v')\}$	links interconnecting VM monitor candidates V_s and VMs of applications $C_{s'v'}$
$R = \{1,...,k\}$	set of k considered VM resource types
$rd_{s'v'cr} \in \mathbb{R}^+$	resource demand for monitoring application $c \in C_{s'v'}$ for resource $r \in R$
$rs_{svr} \in \mathbb{R}^+$	resource supply of VM $v \in V_s$ for resource $r \in R$
$rf_{s'v'c} \in \mathbb{N}_{>1}$	redundancy factor for monitoring application $c \in C_{s'v'}$
$p_{l(sv \rightleftharpoons s'v')} \in \mathbb{R}^+$	observed reliability for each link $l \in L$
$p_{sv} \in \mathbb{R}^+$	observed reliability for each VM $v \in V_s$

Table 7.1 summarizes the symbols used in the optimization model. The complete optimization model is depicted in Model 6. As it can be deduced from the model, it comprises multiple objective functions (cf. Equation 7.11) that have to be solved simultaneously. Therefore, it represents a multi-objective optimization problem. As already mentioned, a main characteristic of multi-objective optimization problems is that no unique solution exists (cf. Section 5.2). Instead, multiple solutions exist, which exhibit no differences in quality from a mathematical point of view. An option for obtaining a unique solution when solving a multi-objective optimization problem is to assign a certain weight to each of the objective functions and to optimize the weighted sum of the objective functions. However, in doing so, an increased reliability of the set of monitoring units of some cloud applications is traded against a decreased reliability of the set of monitoring units of other cloud applications. Since this decrease in reliability is not predefined in advance, this cannot be considered to be an acceptable option in a business scenario. An enterprise cloud consumer rather aims to quantify the risk for the monitoring units of each cloud application to fail. Therefore, we take a worst-case perspective in the following, based on which we aim to minimize that risk, i.e., the worst possible outcome, over all cloud applications. In doing so, we can transform the multi-objective optimization problem into a single-objective optimization problem. However, the multi-objective optimization problem is also nonlinear due to the products of the values in Equation 7.12. Hence, we have to linearize that problem first before applying other transformations in order to be able to utilize off-the-shelf algorithms for solving that problem later on.

Model 6 Robust Cloud Monitor Placement Problem

$$Maximize \quad \{p_{s'v'c}^{mon}(x)|s' \in S', v' \in V_{s'}, c \in C_{s'v'}\} \tag{7.11}$$

$$p_{s'v'c}^{mon}(x) = 1 - \prod_{s \in S, v \in V_s} (q_{svs'v'}^{path})^{x_{svs'v'c}} \tag{7.12}$$

$$q_{svs'v'}^{path} = [(1 - p_{sv}) + (1 - p_{l(sv \rightleftharpoons s'v')}) - (1 - p_{sv})(1 - p_{l(sv \rightleftharpoons s'v')})] \tag{7.13}$$

subject to

$$\sum_{s \in S, v \in V_s} x_{svs'v'c} = rf_{s'v'c} \quad \forall s' \in S', v' \in V_{s'}, c \in C_{s'v'}, rf_{s'v'c} \geq 2 \tag{7.14}$$

$$\sum_{s \in S, v \in V_s} x_{svs'v'c} \geq 1 \quad \forall s' \in S', v' \in V_{s'}, c \in C_{s'v'}, s = \{d+1, ..., n\} \tag{7.15}$$

$$\sum_{s \in S, v \in V_s} x_{svs'v'c} \geq 1 \quad \forall s' \in S', v' \in V_{s'}, c \in C_{s'v'}, s = \{1, ..., d\} \tag{7.16}$$

$$\sum_{s' \in S', v' \in V_{s'}, c \in C_{s'v'}} rd_{s'v'cr} x_{svs'v'c} \leq rs_{svr} \quad \forall s \in S, v \in V_s, r \in R \tag{7.17}$$

$$\sum_{v \in V_s} x_{svs'v'c} \leq 1 \quad \forall s \in S, s' \in S', v' \in V_{s'}, c \in C_{s'v'} \tag{7.18}$$

$$x_{svs'v'c} = 0 \quad \forall c \in C_{s'v'}, s = s' \ and \ v = v' \tag{7.19}$$

$$x_{svs'v'c} \in \{0, 1\} \quad \forall s \in S, v \in V_s, s' \in S', v' \in V_{s'}, c \in C_{s'v'} \tag{7.20}$$

7.3.2 Linearization and Single Objective Transformation

This section presents the linearization and transformations to be applied in order to obtain a single-objective optimization model. In doing so, we obtain an exact solution approach by utilizing off-the-shelf optimization algorithms, such as branch-and-bound (e.g., [95]).

In order to linearize the RCMPP, we propose two transformations that are described in detail in the following. The first transformation constitutes a preparatory step based on considering the complementary objectives of the initial Model 6 while changing the direction of optimization. Instead of maximizing the probability $p_{s'v'c}^{mon}(x)$ that at least

---

Model 7 Linearized Optimization Model of the RCMPP

$$Minimize \quad \{q^{log}_{s'v'c}(x)|s' \in S', v' \in V_{s'}, c \in C_{s'v'}\} \tag{7.23}$$

$$q^{log}_{s'v'c}(x) = \sum_{s\in S, v\in V_s} x_{svs'v'c} \, log(q^{path}_{svs'v'}) \tag{7.24}$$

$$q^{path}_{svs'v'} = [(1 - p_{sv}) + (1 - p_{l(sv \rightleftharpoons s'v')}) - (1 - p_{sv})(1 - p_{l(sv \rightleftharpoons s'v')})] \tag{7.25}$$

$$q^{path}_{svs'v'} > 0 \quad \forall s \in S, v \in V_s, s' \in S', v' \in V_{s'} \tag{7.26}$$

... followed by the constraints (55) to (61) from the initial model

---

one monitoring unit is working properly for each cloud application $c \in C_{s'v'}$, we can minimize the probability $q^{mon}_{s'v'c}(x)$ that all monitoring units for each cloud application $c \in C_{s'v'}$ will fail. In doing so, we obtain a new set of objective functions and the problem turns into a minimization problem (cf. Equations 7.21 and 7.22).

$$Minimize \quad \{q^{mon}_{s'v'c}(x)|s' \in S', v' \in V_{s'}, c \in C_{s'v'}\} \tag{7.21}$$

$$q^{mon}_{s'v'c}(x) = \prod_{s\in S, v\in V_s} (q^{path}_{svs'v'})^{x_{svs'v'c}} \tag{7.22}$$

For the second transformation, we follow an approach, which has also been applied by, e.g., Andreas and Smith in [7]. We take the logarithm of both sides of Equation 7.22, so that the product of the probability values can be rewritten as the sum of their logarithms (cf. Equations 7.27 and 7.28). This second transformation represents the actual linearization of the problem. The resulting linearized optimization problem is depicted in Model 7. Since the logarithm of zero is not defined, we have to assume that $q^{path}_{svs'v'} > 0$. This assumption can be considered to be reasonable, since no system is without failure. It should be noted that the constraints of the initial Model 6 are not affected by the two aforementioned transformations. Therefore, they have been neglected in Model 7.

$$log(q^{mon}_{s'v'c}(x)) = log(\prod_{s\in S, v\in V_s} (q^{path}_{svs'v'})^{x_{svs'v'c}}) \tag{7.27}$$

leads to

$$q^{log}_{s'v'c}(x) = \sum_{s\in S, v\in V_s} x_{svs'v'c} \, log(q^{path}_{svs'v'}) \tag{7.28}$$

Model 8 Robust Cloud Monitor Placement Problem after Transformation

$Minimize \quad z$ (7.31)

subject to

$$q^{log}_{s'v'c}(x) \leq z \qquad \forall s' \in S', v' \in V_{s'}, c \in C_{s'v'}, z \in \mathbb{R}$$ (7.32)

$$q^{log}_{s'v'c}(x) = \sum_{s \in S, v \in V_s} x_{svs'v'c} \, log(q^{path}_{svs'v'})$$ (7.33)

$$q^{path}_{svs'v'} = [(1 - p_{sv}) + (1 - p_{l(sv \rightleftharpoons s'v')}) - (1 - p_{sv})(1 - p_{l(sv \rightleftharpoons s'v')})]$$ (7.34)

$$q^{path}_{svs'v'} > 0 \qquad \forall s \in S, v \in V_s, s' \in S', v' \in V_{s'}$$ (7.35)

... followed by the constraints from the initial model

Finally, we propose a last transformation in order to turn the Model 7 into an optimization problem with a single-objective function. For this purpose, a so-called *minimax strategy* is applied (cf. [105]). That is we take a worst-case perspective and minimize the worst (i.e., maximum) possible outcome. In doing so, the set of multiple objective functions each minimizing the logarithm $q^{log}_{s'v'c}(x)$ of the probability that all monitoring units for a certain cloud application $c \in C_{s'v'}$ will fail, is turned into a single-objective function that aims at minimizing the maximum value of all $q^{log}_{s'v'c}(x)$. In this regard, a new decision variable $z \in \mathbb{R}$ has to be introduced, which represents that maximum value and is to be minimized in the new single-objective function (cf. Equation 7.29).

$Minimize \quad z$ (7.29)

subject to

$$q^{log}_{s'v'c}(x) \leq z \qquad \forall s' \in S', v' \in V_{s'}, c \in C_{s'v'}, z \in \mathbb{R}$$ (7.30)

In addition, $|C_{s'v'}|$ new constraints $\forall s' \in S', v' \in V_{s'}$ have to be added to the new single-objective optimization model in order to define z as the upper bound for the value of $q^{log}_{s'v'c}(x)$ of each cloud application (cf. Equation 7.30). Again, all other constraints of the initial Model 6 are not affected by this last transformation, so that they have been neglected in the final single-objective optimization model. The complete model is provided in Model 8. It can be seen from the model, that the resulting optimization problem represents a MILP problem (cf. Section 3.3) for which off-the-shelf solution algorithms, such as branch-and-bound [95], are applicable. Although having presented an exact solution approach in this section, a MILP is known to be NP-hard (cf., e.g., [73, 75]). Hence, an exact solution cannot be determined for large-scale problems, i.e., real-world scenarios with large-scale data centers, in polynomial time. This is due to the fact that the solution space grows exponentially with an increasing problem size in the number of integer decision variables. In case of the RCMPP, we consider specific integer variables, namely binary decision variables, which can only take the two values zero or 1. Each decision variable represents two different options with regard to a certain VM for placing a monitoring unit of a certain cloud application (cf. Section 7.3.1). Consequently, the number of options for placing monitoring units doubles with each additional decision variable that has to be considered. Since the total number of VM candidates for placing monitoring units of each cloud application corresponds to the total number of VMs on the broker and the provider side, the total number of decision variables for monitor placement for all cloud applications corresponds to $|S| \times |V_s| \times |S'| \times |V_{s'}| \times |C_{s'v'}|$. Recalling that each of these decision variables can take two different values, the worst-case time complexity of solving the RCMPP is $\mathcal{O}(2^{|S| \times |V_s| \times |S'| \times |V_{s'}| \times |C_{s'v'}|})$. Therefore, we propose two different heuristics in the next section. The basic idea of developing heuristics is to trade solution quality for reduced computation time. That is to develop an algorithm, which is able to solve a given problem in a considerably smaller amount of time at the cost of a less optimal solution. However, in the best case, such a heuristic is able to obtain near optimal results while exhibiting polynomial time complexity, thus being applicable to large-scale problems. In this regard, our exact solution approach constitutes a baseline for evaluating the performance of our heuristic approaches (cf. Chapter 8).

7.4 Heuristic Placement Strategies

In this section, we propose two heuristic approaches for solving the RCMPP. The first heuristic (*CSLAB-Loc-Start.KOM*) represents a Greedy approach and constitutes an opening procedure searching for a first feasible solution. The goal of the second heuristic is further to improve that initial solution. Therefore, we combine our Greedy heuristic with a Tabu-Search-based improvement procedure (*TSearch*) in order to obtain our second heuristic, denoted as *CSLAB-Loc-Imp.KOM*. The heuristics are partly inspired from approaches for solving the related generalized assignment problem and its bottleneck variant (e.g., [95], [146]). However, these existing solution approaches are not applicable to the RCMPP, since the RCMPP cannot be fully mapped to these related optimization problems.

7.4.1 Heuristic Optimization Approach - CSLAB-Loc-Start.KOM

This section describes our first heuristic, denoted as *CSLAB-Loc-Start.KOM*, which follows an intuitive, a so-called Greedy approach. The conceptual design of our first heuristic is presented in the following.

Conceptual Design   The basic idea behind this heuristic is to select a specific location for a monitoring unit to be placed iteratively among the remaining available locations that exhibits the maximum reliability. This results in a maximum improvement in each step with regard to the total reliability of all the monitoring units that have been placed so far. In doing so, our heuristic is inspired from the *steepest ascent approach* (cf. [95]), which constitutes a form of local search procedure. However, a local search procedure starts from an initial solution and iteratively aims to improve the solution obtained so far to a maximum extent in each step. Hence, it belongs to the group of improvement procedures. In contrast, our heuristic aims to determine an initial solution, and thus, belongs to the group of opening procedures.

A tangible example is provided in Figure 7.3 in conjunction with the three subtables in Table 7.2. Based on that example, we will elaborate on the conceptual design of our heuristic CSLAB-Loc-Start.KOM. As a preparatory step for applying our heuristic, we build the list of connections (cf. Table 7.2a). This list comprises the result of the cross product $l(sv \rightleftharpoons s'v') \times C_{s'v'}$ of the links, which interconnect VM candidates for monitor placement V_s and VMs on the provider side $V_{s'}$, and the cloud applications $C_{s'v'}$ to be monitored. Basically, each entry in that list represents an option for placing monitoring units of a certain cloud application $c_{s'v'}$. The list is then sorted in decreasing order of reliability values $p_{svs'v'}^{path} = 1 - q_{svs'v'}^{path}$. In this regard, $p_{svs'v'}^{path}$ expresses the probability for a monitoring unit being placed on VM $v \in V_s$ in order to monitor a cloud application running on VM $v' \in V_{s'}$ not to fail. Besides the list of connections, our heuristic also requires a list of the remaining monitor requirements (cf. Table 7.2b) and a list of the remaining VM resource capacities (cf. Table 7.2c). The list of the remaining monitor requirements comprises an entry for each cloud application $c_{s'v'}$, for which not all of the $rf_{s'v'c}$ redundant monitoring units have been placed, yet. Each of these entries specifies the number rm_b and rm_p of remaining monitoring units to be placed on the broker side and the provider side, respectively. In addition, the resource demand rd in percent of each monitoring unit is specified. For clarity, we only make use of a single abstract resource type in the example. The list of remaining VM resource capacities indicates the amount of remaining resource supply of each VM candidate for monitor placement v_s. The two last-mentioned lists are dynamically updated after each iteration of our heuristic.

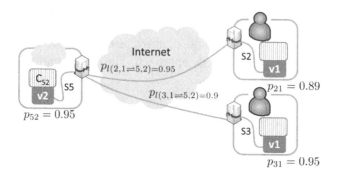

Figure 7.3: Example for applying our heuristic CSLAB-Loc-Start.KOM

Greedy Algorithm   All in all, our heuristic proceeds as follows. The list of connections is explored in descending order of reliability values, until - in the best case - all monitoring units have been placed for all cloud applications. In each iteration, the next entry in the list is checked for its feasibility. We consider an entry to be feasible, if a monitoring unit can be placed on the candidate location v_s, represented by the corresponding link $l(sv \rightleftharpoons s'v')$ in the list, in order to monitor the cloud application $c_{s'v'}$, as specified in the entry. A placement is not feasible if any constraints are violated, e.g., if the resource supply of the candidate location is not sufficient. In this case, the list of connections is further explored, until a feasible entry is found. If an entry is feasible, the monitoring unit is placed on the specified location, the auxiliary lists are updated, and the heuristic starts with a new iteration. If not all of the monitoring units have been placed when reaching the end of the list, no feasible solution could be found.

Concerning the tangible example in Figure 7.3, which constitutes an excerpt of our RCMPP example provided in Figure 7.2, we assume that two cloud applications 1_{52} and 2_{52} to be monitored are part of the set C_{52} on site $S5$. If we consider the next entry in the list of connections in Table 7.2a, the maximum improvement with regard to the total reliability would be achieved, if a monitoring unit of application 1_{52} is placed on VM 1 on site $S3$. However, it can be seen from the monitoring requirements in Table 7.2b, that a monitoring unit of application 1_{52} has a resource demand of $rd = 40\%$, which exceeds the remaining resource supply of $rs = 30\%$ of VM 1_3. Note that the indices of the parameters have been neglected in the table for clarity. Therefore, the currently considered entry in the list of connections is not feasible. Proceeding to the next entry reveals that the corresponding placement is feasible. Hence, a monitoring unit for application 2_{52} is placed on VM 1 on site $S3$ and the auxiliary lists are updated. The next (third) entry in the list is also feasible, but the placement concerning the last (fourth) entry in the list cannot be realized. This is due to the fact that a monitoring unit for application 2_{52} has already been placed on the broker side, so that the corresponding number rm^b of remaining monitoring units equals zero. However, application 2_{52} has not been removed from the list of remaining monitoring units, since there is still one monitoring unit to be placed on the provider side, i.e., $rm^p = 1$.

The complete pseudocode of our heuristic CSLAB-Loc-Start.KOM is provided in Algorithm 9 and is described in detail in the following. As input parameters, the algorithm receives the three auxiliary lists mentioned before. The final placements of the monitoring units are stored in a list P, which represents the output of the algorithm. This list is initialized at the beginning and the list of connections is sorted in descending order of reliability values using the auxiliary function SORTDESCREL (line 3). Subsequently, the algorithm explores the list of connections in descending order (line 4). In each iteration, the parameters of the currently considered entry in the list are retrieved using the auxiliary functions GETAPP, GETSOURCE, and GETTARGET (lines 5-7). These parameters comprise the cloud application $c_{s'v'}$ to be monitored, the VM candidate for monitor placement v_s^{src}, and the VM $v_{s'}^{trgt}$ where the cloud application is running. If not all desired monitoring units for the currently considered cloud application have been placed so far (line 8), the algorithm checks, whether a monitoring unit can be placed on VM v_s^{src} of the currently considered entry. For this purpose, the auxiliary function CHECKCONSTRAINTS verifies whether any constraints are violated or not when placing that monitoring unit (line 9). If the placement does not violate any constraints, the placement is stored in the final result set P and an update of the auxiliary list is performed (lines 10-13). If no more monitoring

$c_{s'v'}$	**Candidate location**	**Total reliability**
...		
1_{52}	$l(3, 1 \rightleftharpoons 5, 2)$	85.5%
2_{52}	$l(3, 1 \rightleftharpoons 5, 2)$	85.5%
1_{52}	$l(2, 1 \rightleftharpoons 5, 2)$	84.55%
2_{52}	$l(2, 1 \rightleftharpoons 5, 2)$	84.55%
...		

(a) List of connections

$c_{s'v'}$	**Monitor requirements**
...	
1_{52}	$rm^b = 1, rm^p = 0, rd = 40\%$
2_{52}	$rm^b = 1, rm^p = 1, rd = 5\%$
...	

(b) Remaining monitoring units

v_s	**Remaining resource supply**
...	
1_2	$rs = 30\%$
1_3	$rs = 75\%$
...	

(c) Remaining VM resource capacities

Table 7.2: Auxiliary lists to the example in Figure 7.3

Algorithm 9 Greedy Heuristic CSLAB-Loc-Start.KOM

---

input: *list of connections C, remaining VM resource capacities V, remaining monitoring units R*

output: *monitor placements P*

1: **procedure** GREEDY(C, V, R)
2:     $P \leftarrow \emptyset$
3:     SORTDESCREL(C)
4:     **for all** $con \in C$ **do**
5:         $c_{s'v'} \leftarrow$ GETAPP(con)
6:         $v_s^{src} \leftarrow$ GETSOURCE(con)
7:         $v_{s'}^{trgt} \leftarrow$ GETTARGET(con)
8:         **if** $(c_{s'v'} \in R)$ **then**
9:             $violation \leftarrow$ CHECKCONSTRAINTS($c_{s'v'}, v_s^{src}, v_{s'}^{trgt}, V, R, P$)
10:            **if** $(violation \neq true)$ **then**
11:                $P \leftarrow P \cup \{con\}$
12:                UPDATE($c_{s'v'}, v_s^{src}, v_{s'}^{trgt}, V, R$)
13:            **end if**
14:            $n \leftarrow$ GETREMUNITS($c_{s'v'}, R$)
15:            **if** $n = 0$ **then**
16:                $R \leftarrow R/\{c_{s'v'}\}$
17:            **end if**
18:        **end if**
19:    **end for**
20:    $l \leftarrow$ GETLENGTH(R)
21:    **if** $l > 0$ **then**
22:        $P \leftarrow NULL$ ▷ no feasible solution could be found
23:    **end if**
24:    **return** P
25: **end procedure**

---

units to be placed are left for the currently considered application, it is removed from the set R of remaining monitoring units (line 14-17). Having explored all entries in the list of connections, the algorithm checks, whether all monitoring units have been placed for each application or not (line 21). If there are still some monitoring units left to be placed, the algorithm could not find a feasible solution and, thus, returns an empty result set P (line 22). In any other case, the final placements are returned in the set P (line 24).

Although choosing the most reliable location among the remaining feasible locations in each step, the resulting monitor placements will most likely not be optimal. This is due to the fact that the RCMPP is NP-hard. Furthermore, a maximum improvement is made in each step with regard to the total reliability of all the monitoring units of all the applications. In doing so, the reliabilities of the locations that are chosen for placing monitoring units are not "balanced" across the different cloud applications. However, due to the low complexity of the performed computations, the Greedy heuristic is suitable in order to obtain a valid solution in a small amount of time (cf. Chapter 8).

7.4.2 Heuristic Improvement Approach - CSLAB-Loc-Imp.KOM

In this section, we describe our second heuristic CSLAB-Loc-Imp.KOM. This heuristic aims to provide an improved solution quality in comparison to solutions that are obtained using our Greedy heuristic. For this purpose, CSLAB-Loc-Imp.KOM utilizes our Greedy heuristic as an opening procedure in order to obtain an initial solution, which is further improved using a *Tabu Search*-based improvement procedure.

Tabu Search   Basically, *Tabu Search* constitutes a meta-heuristic that was coined by Glover in his seminal work in 1986 [77] and is based on the following principles (cf., e.g., [77, 78, 79]). As a meta-heuristic, Tabu Search guides another method in the form of a local search procedure. Starting from a first solution, Tabu Search strategically explores the solution space over a number of iterations. In each iteration, the so-called *neighborhood* of the currently considered solution is determined. The neighborhood comprises the set of solutions that can be obtained from the currently considered solution by performing so-called *moves*. Such a move specifies transformations to be applied to some elements of the currently considered solution in order to obtain a related solution. Typically, moves consist of modifying an element, deleting an element and adding another element, or interchanging the position of two elements of the current solution. The attractiveness of each move is expressed in terms of, e.g., the change with regard to the objective function. Among all the moves in the current neighborhood, the best admissible move is chosen in each iteration. In order to avoid running in circles, i.e., to repeat the same sequence of moves thereby returning to the same set of solutions, Tabu Search utilizes an adaptive memory. A so-called *tabu list* keeps track of the attributes that have changed recently when moving from a given solution to a neighboring solution. In this regard, the moves recently performed are put on the tabu list in conjunction with a certain *tabu tenure* indicating that they are not allowed to be reversed for a certain amount of time. In doing so, the tabu list prevents solutions recently observed from being revisited. This allows local optimality to be overcome by directing the search into other regions of the solution space and, thus, to approach a global optimum. Although the reversal of moves on the tabu list is forbidden, so-called *aspiration criteria* can be defined, which allow to overwrite the tabu status of a certain move. For example, a simple aspiration criterion can allow a move to be performed despite being on the tabu list if it results in a better solution

Figure 7.4: Steps in each iteration of the TSearch procedure

than the overall best solution obtained so far. In doing so, that aspiration criterion still prevents cycling the same region of the solution space, since the new solution has not been visited before and, thus, permits the access to new regions. In general, a Tabu Search procedure is executed until a predefined stopping criterion (e.g., a certain number of iterations) is met and the last best solution is returned as result.

Tabu Search has been chosen for the following reasons. First of all, it is often utilized for solving hard combinatorial optimization problems and it is applicable to any kind of optimization problem in general, regardless of the type (e.g., linear, nonlinear) of the objective function [79]. Secondly, additional constraints can be easily added and it has outperformed other methods in terms of solution quality in a variety of problem settings [78]. Hence, Tabu Search constitutes a very flexible and powerful meta-heuristic. By designing a Tabu Search-based improvement procedure, our resulting heuristic will not be trapped in a local optimum and individual stopping criteria, such as a maximum number of iterations or a certain quality level of the current solution, can be defined in advance according to the specific needs of the party executing the heuristic. Furthermore, our heuristic can be easily adapted if further constraints should be taken into account.

Conceptual Design   In the following, we describe the conceptual design of our second heuristic CSLAB-Loc-Imp.KOM. Basically, our heuristic is inspired by the work of Karsu and Azizoglu [146]. The authors address the multi-resource agent bottleneck generalized assignment problem and propose a tabu search-based solution procedure. However, the authors focus on balancing the workload distribution among a given set of agents while considering multiple periods. In line with their work, we also build the initial neighborhood around the bottleneck element in each iteration and overwrite the tabu status if a resulting solution outperforms the current best solution. The steps performed in each iteration of our Tabu Search-based improvement procedure (denoted as TSearch) are depicted in Figure 7.4. As already mentioned, our TSearch procedure starts with building the neighborhood of the bottleneck element, which corresponds to the cloud application of which the monitoring units exhibit the overall worst reliability. That application is denoted as *bottleneck application* in the following. Its neighborhood is determined by the union of the *admissible moves* in

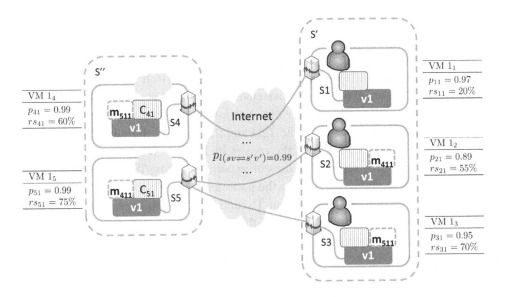

Figure 7.5: Example for applying our heuristic CSLAB-Loc-Imp.KOM

its swap and shift neighborhood. In this regard, the *swap neighborhood* comprises all the moves, in which a monitoring unit of the bottleneck application and another monitoring unit of a non-bottleneck application interchange their positions. In contrast, the *shift neighborhood* incorporates the set of moves, in which a monitoring unit of the bottleneck application is moved to another position. Having determined the combined neighborhood, the best move is chosen from that neighborhood. That move either constitutes the move with the highest improvement or lowest decrease with regard to the currently considered solution. Recalling that the aim of Tabu Search is to overcome local optimality, accepting moves that result in a decrease of the current solution may also be reasonable, since they permit to access other regions of the solution space. For the case that no move is admissible, the combined neighborhood of the cloud application of which the monitoring units exhibit the overall second (up to i^{th}) worst reliability is considered in the next iteration. We consider a move as admissible if it does not violate any of the constraints of the RCMPP (cf. Section 7.3).

A tangible example is provided in Figure 7.5 in conjunction with the two subtables in Table 7.3. The reliabilities of all connections are set to $p_{l(sv \rightleftharpoons s'v')} = 99\%$ for simplicity. Hence, the total reliabilities of the monitoring units of both applications, denoted as m_{411} and m_{511}, only depend on the difference of the reliabilities of the VMs, where the monitoring units are placed on. It can be easily deduced from Figure 7.5 that the cloud application 1_{41} represents the bottleneck application. In the example, there are no admissible moves on the provider side. This is due to the fact that a monitoring unit is not allowed to be placed on the same VM where the application to monitor is running. Furthermore, according to our monitoring approach (cf. Section 4.3.4, at least one monitoring unit has to be placed on the provider side. Therefore, Table 7.3b only lists the moves with regard to the monitoring unit m_{411} of the bottleneck application that has been placed on the broker side. All in all, three moves are conceivable. The first move demands that the monitoring units m_{411} and m_{511} on the broker side swap their positions. The second and third move envisage a shift of the monitoring unit m_{411} to the VM 1_1 and the VM 1_3, respectively. According to the resource demands rd of the monitoring units provided in Table 7.3a and the resource supplies rs_{sv} specified for each VM in Figure 7.5, each of the moves in Table 7.3b would not result in a violation of the resource supplies of the corresponding VMs. Thus, all these moves are admissible. Note that the indices of the parameters have been neglected again in the table for clarity. In each iteration, our TSearch procedure chooses the best move among all admissible moves with regard to the change of the current solution. In this regard, moving the monitoring unit m_{411} to VM 1_1 yields the highest improvement, so that the second move is chosen by the TSearch procedure.

Tabu Search-based Improvement Algorithm   The main procedure of our heuristic CSLAB-Loc-Imp.KOM is provided in Algorithm 10 and is described in detail in the following. Besides the initial solution *Sol* obtained using our Greedy heuristic and a maximum number of iterations *max*, three auxiliary lists are passed as input parameters to our TSearch procedure. The three lists C, V, and *Req* are nearly identical to the lists that have already served as input for our Greedy heuristic. Only the list *Req* differs from the list R as it comprises the requirements of all monitoring units and does not change throughout the TSearch procedure. As output parameter, the TSearch procedure returns the final monitor placements P.

At the beginning of the TSearch procedure, several auxiliary variables are defined (line 2). Afterwards, starting from the initial solution stored in P, the objective value of the current solution constituting the best result obtained so far is retrieved using the auxiliary function GETOBJVAL (line 3). From that point on, the TSearch procedure is executed over a number of *max* iterations while trying further to improve the current solution (line 4). Each iteration starts with updating the tabu list, i.e., removing all the moves of which the tabu tenure is lower than the current *round*, and with resetting

$c_{s'v'}$	**Monitor requirements**
1_{41}	$rf = 2, rd = 10\%$
1_{51}	$rf = 2, rd = 20\%$

(a) Monitor requirements

Type of move	$v_s^b, m_{s'v'c}^b$	$v_s, m_{s'v'c}$
SWAP	$1_2, m_{411}$	$1_3, m_{511}$
SHIFT	$1_2, m_{411}$	$1_1, m_{411}$
SHIFT	$1_2, m_{411}$	$1_3, m_{411}$

(b) List of admissible moves

Table 7.3: Auxiliary lists to the example in Figure 7.5

Algorithm 10 Tabu-Search-based Improvement Procedure of CSLAB-Loc-Imp.KOM

---

input: *initial solution Sol, iteration limit max, connections C, remaining VM resource capacities V, application monitor requirements Req*

output: *monitor placements P*

 1: **procedure** TSEARCH(*Sol, max, C, V, Req*)
 2:     $P \leftarrow Sol, T \leftarrow \emptyset, moveperf \leftarrow false, round \leftarrow 1$
 3:     $bestobjval \leftarrow$ GETOBJVAL(P,C)
 4:     **while** *round <= max* **do**
 5:         $T \leftarrow$ UPDATE(T)$, AM \leftarrow \emptyset$
 6:         **if** (*moveperf = true*) **then**
 7:             $i \leftarrow 0$
 8:         **else**
 9:             $i \leftarrow i+1$
10:         **end if**
11:         **if** ($i < size(Req)$) **then**
12:             $c_{s'v'}^{b} \leftarrow$ GETBOTTLENECKAPP(i,P,C)
13:         **else**
14:             **return** P ▷ no improvement can be found anymore
15:         **end if**
16:         $M_{s'v'c}^{b} \leftarrow$ GETMONITORS($c_{s'v'}^{b}, P$)
17:         **for all** $m_{s'v'c}^{b} \in M_{s'v'c}^{b}$ **do**
18:             $NB_{SWAP} \leftarrow$ GETSWAPNEIGHBORHOOD($P, m_{s'v'c}^{b}, C, V, Req$)
19:             $NB_{SHIFT} \leftarrow$ GETSHIFTNEIGHBORHOOD($P, m_{s'v'c}^{b}, C, V, Req$)
20:             $AM \leftarrow AM \cup NB_{SWAP} \cup NB_{SHIFT}$
21:         **end for**
22:         $AM \leftarrow$ SORTDESCOBJVAL(AM)
23:         **for all** $am \in AM$ **do**
24:             **if** ($am \notin T$) $|$ ($objval(am) > bestobjval$) **then**
25:                 $P \leftarrow$ DOMOVE(am, P, V)
26:                 $T \leftarrow T \cup \{am_{rev}\}$
27:                 **if** ($objval(am) > bestobjval$) **then**
28:                     $bestobjval \leftarrow objval(am)$
29:                 **end if**
30:                 $moveperf \leftarrow true$
31:                 **break**
32:             **end if**
33:         **end for**
34:         $round \leftarrow round + 1$
35:     **end while**
36:     **return** P
37: **end procedure**

---

the list AM of admissible moves (line 5). Subsequently, the index i of the bottleneck application is determined (lines 6 to 10). As already mentioned before, if there are no moves admissible in a certain iteration, the cloud application of which the monitoring units exhibit the ith worst reliability is considered to be the bottleneck application in the next iteration. While not all applications have already been considered to be the bottleneck application, the current bottleneck application to be considered is retrieved using the auxiliary function GetBottleneckApp (lines 11 and 12). Otherwise, the final monitor placements P are returned since no improvement can be found anymore and the TSearch procedure ends (lines 13 to 15). By utilizing the auxiliary function GETMONITORS, the set of monitoring units of the current bottleneck application is retrieved (line 16). For each monitoring unit in that set, the shift and swap neighborhood are determined by invoking the two subroutines GETSWAPNEIGHBORHOOD and GETSHIFTNEIGHBORHOOD and the resulting moves are added to the set AM of admissible moves (lines 17 to 21). The set AM of admissible moves is then sorted in descending order of changes in the objective value of the current solution using the auxiliary function SortDescObjVal (line 22). In the subsequent steps, the best move, which is not on the tabu list or despite being on that list satisfies the aspiration criterion is selected among the moves in the set AM (lines 23 to 25). The reverse move is put on the tabu list, the best objective value found so far is updated if the new solution exhibits a higher value, and the auxiliary variable $moveperf$ is updated since an admissible move has been found (lines 26 to 30). The TSearch procedure then proceeds to the next round (line 34). If the maximum number of iterations has been reached, the final monitor placements P are returned (line 36). The steps performed in order to determine the swap and shift neighborhood are provided in detail in the Algorithms 11 and 12, respectively.

Swap Neighborhood Algorithm It can be deduced from Algorithm 11 that the subroutine GETSWAPNEIGHBORHOOD receives the following input parameters: the current solution, the monitoring unit of the bottleneck application for which to determine the neighborhood, as well as the three auxiliary lists specifying the connections, the resource capacities of all VMs, and the monitor requirements. As output parameter, a set comprising all moves in the swap neighborhood of the currently considered monitoring unit is returned. The subroutine GETSWAPNEIGHBORHOOD then proceeds as follows.

Having initialized the variable NB_{SWAP} specifying the swap neighborhood later on, the VM v_s^b where the monitoring unit $m_{s'v'c}^b$ of the bottleneck application is currently placed on and the resource demand rd^b of that monitoring unit are retrieved by calling the auxiliary functions GETVM and GETRESDEMAND, respectively (line 2 to 4). Afterwards, we determine a random subset of cloud applications with the cardinality $\log_2(|C_{s'v'}^{nb}|)$ from the set $C_{s'v'}^{nb}$ of all cloud applications, which exhibit a higher reliability with regard to their monitoring units than the currently considered bottle-

---

Algorithm 11 Procedure GETSWAPNEIGHBORHOOD

---

input: *current solution P, monitor unit of bottleneck application* $m^b_{s'v'c}$, *connections C, remaining VM resource capacities V, application monitor requirements Req*

output: *swap neighborhood* NB_{SWAP}

1: **procedure** GETSWAPNEIGHBORHOOD(P, $m^b_{s'v'c}$, C, V, Req)
2:     $NB_{SWAP} \leftarrow \emptyset$
3:     $v^b_s \leftarrow$ GETVM($m^b_{s'v'c}$)
4:     $rd^b \leftarrow$ GETRESDEMAND($m^b_{s'v'c}$)
5:     $C^{nb}_{s'v'} \leftarrow$ GETRANDOMNONEBOTTLENECKAPPS(i, P, C)
6:     **for all** $c^{nb}_{s'v'} \in C^{nb}_{s'v'}$ **do**
7:        $M^{nb}_{s'v'c} \leftarrow$ GETMONITORS($c^{nb}_{s'v'}$)
8:        **for all** $m^{nb}_{s'v'c} \in M^{nb}_{s'v'c}$ **do**
9:           $v^{nb}_s \leftarrow$ GETVM($m^{nb}_{s'v'c}$)
10:           **if** $\left(v^b_s \neq v^{nb}_s\right)$ **then**
11:              $rd^{nb} \leftarrow$ GETRESDEMAND($m^{nb}_{s'v'c}$)
12:              $rs^b \leftarrow$ GETRESCAPACITY(v^b_s, V) $+ rd^b - rd^{nb}$
13:              $rs^{nb} \leftarrow$ GETRESCAPACITY(v^{nb}_s, V) $+ rd^{nb} - rd^b$
14:              **if** $\left(rs^b \geq 0\right)$ & $\left(rs^{nb} \geq 0\right)$ **then**
15:                 $violation \leftarrow$ CHECKCONSONSWAP(v^b_s, $m^b_{s'v'c}$, v^{nb}_s, $m^{nb}_{s'v'c}$, V, R, P)
16:                 **if** $(violation \neq true)$ **then**
17:                    $move \leftarrow$ CREATEMOVE("SWAP", v^b_s, $m^b_{s'v'c}$, v^{nb}_s, $m^{nb}_{s'v'c}$)
18:                    $NB_{SWAP} \leftarrow NB_{SWAP} \cup \{move\}$
19:                 **end if**
20:              **end if**
21:           **end if**
22:        **end for**
23:     **end for**
24:     **return** NB_{SWAP}
25: **end procedure**

---

neck application using the auxiliary function GETRANDOMNONEBOTTLENECKAPPS (line 5). A random subset of the cloud applications is explored in order to reduce the computational complexity of the neighborhood search. In this regard, we take the rounded binary logarithm of the total number of cloud applications in order to achieve a logarithmic growth of the neighborhood with an increasing problem size. Subsequently, the algorithm explores the monitoring units of each of these non-bottleneck applications (lines 6 to 8). For each of these monitoring units $m^{nb}_{s'v'c}$, the algorithm checks whether that monitoring unit and the currently considered monitoring unit $m^b_{s'v'c}$ of the bottleneck application can interchange their positions. For this purpose, the algorithm first checks that both monitoring units have not already been placed on the same VM in the current solution (lines 9 and 10). If this is not the case, the resource demand rd^{nd} of the monitoring unit observing the non-bottleneck application is determined and the remaining resource capacities rs^b and rs^{nb} of the respective VMs if both monitoring units swap their places are calculated (line 11 to 13). In this regard, the auxiliary functions GETRESDEMAND and GETRESCAPACITY are used in order to retrieve the resource demand of the monitoring unit $m_{s'v'c}^{nb}$ and the current resource supplies of the VMs. If the envisaged swap does not exceed the resource capacities of both VMs (line 14), the algorithm still has to check that the move does not violate any further constraints, such as placement restrictions (cf. Section 7.3.1). In this regard, the result of the auxiliary function CHECKCONSONSWAP indicates whether a violation would occur (line 15). If the move turns out to be admissible the move is added to the swap neighborhood (lines 16 to 19). Having explored all the candidate monitoring units for swapping places with the monitoring unit of the bottleneck application, the final swap neighborhood is returned as result (line 24).

Shift Neighborhood Algorithm   The subroutine GETSHIFTNEIGHBORHOOD for computing the shift neighborhood provided in Algorithm 12 proceeds in a very similar manner. It receives the same input parameters as the subroutine GETSWAP-NEIGHBORHOOD and returns the final shift neighborhood of the currently considered monitoring unit as output parameter. Also similar to the previous subroutine, the variable NB_{SHIFT} specifying the shift neighborhood later on, the VM v_s^b where the monitoring unit $m_{s'v'c}^b$ of the bottleneck application is currently placed on and the resource demand rd^b of that monitoring unit are retrieved by calling the auxiliary functions GETVM and GETRESDEMAND, respectively (line 2 to 4). From that point on, both subroutines differ.

First of all, we determine a random subset of VMs with the cardinality $\log_2(|V_s^{nb}|)$ from the set V_s^{nb} of all VMs, which are different from the VM v_s^b of the currently considered monitoring unit $m_{s'v'c}^b$ of the bottleneck application using the auxiliary function GETRANDOMNONEBOTTLENECKVMS (line 5). Similar to the subroutine GETSWAPNEIGHBORHOOD, we explore a random subset of the total number of VMs in order to reduce the computational complexity of the neighborhood search. Again, the rounded binary logarithm is used for determining the subset size so that a logarithmic growth of the neighborhood with an increasing problem size is achieved. The algorithm then explores each VM v_s^{nb} (line 6) in order to examine whether the currently considered monitoring unit $m_{s'v'c}^b$ of the bottleneck application can be moved to that VM. For this purpose, the algorithm checks that the envisaged move does not exceed the resource capacities rs^{nb} of the candidate VM v_s^{nb} (lines 7 and 8), i.e., if a shift is feasible. However, since that shift could still violate any further constraints, the auxiliary function CHECKCONSONSHIFT is invoked subsequently in order to determine whether that move is also admissible (line 9). For the case that a shift does

---

Algorithm 12 Procedure GETSHIFTNEIGHBORHOOD

---

input: *current solution P, monitor unit of bottleneck application $m^b_{s'v'c}$, connections C, remaining VM resource capacities V, application monitor requirements Req*
output: *shift neighborhood NB_{SHIFT}*

1: **procedure** GETSHIFTNEIGHBORHOOD(P, $m^b_{s'v'c}$, C, V, Req)
2: $\quad$ $NB_{SHIFT} \leftarrow \emptyset$
3: $\quad$ $v^b_s \leftarrow$ GETVM($m^b_{s'v'c}$)
4: $\quad$ $rd^b \leftarrow$ GETRESDEMAND($m^b_{s'v'c}$)
5: $\quad$ $V^{nb}_s \leftarrow$ GETRANDOMNONEBOTTLENECKVMS(i, P, C)
6: $\quad$ **for all** $v^{nb}_s \in V^{nb}_s$ **do**
7: $\qquad$ $rs^{nb} \leftarrow$ GETRESCAPACITY(v^{nb}_s, V)
8: $\qquad$ **if** $\left(rs^{nb} - rd^b \geq 0 \right)$ **then**
9: $\qquad\quad$ $violation \leftarrow$ CHECKCONSONSHIFT($v^b_s, m^b_{s'v'c}, v^{nb}_s, V, R, P$)
10: $\qquad\quad$ **if** ($violation \neq true$) **then**
11: $\qquad\qquad$ $move \leftarrow$ CREATEMOVE(*"SHIFT"*, $v^b_s, m^b_{s'v'c}, v^{nb}_s, m^b_{s'v'c}$)
12: $\qquad\qquad$ $NB_{SHIFT} \leftarrow NB_{SHIFT} \cup \{move\}$
13: $\qquad\quad$ **end if**
14: $\qquad$ **end if**
15: $\quad$ **end for**
16: $\quad$ **return** NB_{SHIFT}
17: **end procedure**

---

not cause any violation, the corresponding move is added to the shift neighborhood (lines 10 to 13). Having explored all the candidate VMs for moving the currently considered monitoring unit of the bottleneck application, the final shift neighborhood is returned as result (line 16).

When comparing our second heuristic CSLAB-Loc-Imp.KOM with our exact optimization approach CSLAB-Loc-Exa.KOM, it becomes apparent that the bottleneck application in the TSearch procedure has a pivotal role for calculating the objective value z of our optimization model. Since z is equal to the overall highest probability that all monitoring units fail for a certain cloud application, that application directly corresponds to the bottleneck application, which exhibits the worst total reliability with regard to its monitoring units. Therefore, building the neighborhood around that application in each iteration of the TSearch procedure is very effective. However, the effectiveness of the TSearch procedure does not only depend on choosing a reasonable neighborhood, but is also affected by the tabu tenure. Recalling that elements are put on the tabu list in order to avoid cycling the same regions of the solution space, it is also important to choose a reasonable tabu tenure. While in the early days of tabu search best tabu list sizes were often linked to the "magic number seven", more recent experiments have revealed that preferred tabu list sizes are often related to the problem size [78]. Finally, we restrict the swap and shift neighborhoods to a size that matches the rounded binary logarithm of the number of objects to be considered, i.e., the cloud applications and VMs. In this regard, we take the binary logarithm in order to achieve a logarithmic growth of the neighborhood with the problem size while maintaining a maximum neighborhood size that still allows the computation of a high quality solution.

7.5 Summary

In this chapter, the Robust Cloud Monitor Placement Problem (RCMPP) was described in detail and a corresponding mathematical formalization was presented in the form of an optimization model. Based on that model, we proposed an exact optimization approach for the RCMPP, denoted as CSLAB-Loc-Exa.KOM. Since the resulting optimization model constitutes a non-linear, multi-objective optimization problem, we also proposed several transformations in order to turn that problem into a linear, single-objective optimization problem. In doing so, off-the-shelf algorithms can be applied for solving the problem. In this regard, we chose a worst case perspective in order to minimize the maximum risk for the monitoring units of a cloud application to fail. Since the corresponding optimization problem is NP-hard and, thus, cannot be solved for real-world scenarios in polynomial time, we also proposed two heuristic solution approaches CSLAB-Loc-Start.KOM and CSLAB-Loc-Imp.KOM. In general, heuristic approaches trade solution quality for reduced computation time, so that the placement concerning RCMPP instances becomes computationally tractable, while still trying to maintain a high solution quality. Our first heuristic follows an intuitive Greedy approach with the aim to obtain an initial solution in a very small amount of time. Thus, it can serve as an opening procedure for our second heuristic, which represents an improvement procedure aiming further to improve that initial solution. In contrast to related work, our placement approaches jointly consider the reliability of all the nodes and links in the system and also take resource constraints into account. An extensive evaluation of our placement approaches is provided in Chapter 8.

8 Evaluation

Having presented our three major contributions of this thesis, we evaluate their performance in this Chapter 8 in order to validate that the prior identified research goals have been met. This chapter is structured as follows. As a preparatory step, we first state the major objectives with regard to the evaluation of our three contributions in Section 8.1. In this regard, our evaluation aims to show that (i) our negotiation mechanism CSLAB-Neg.KOM is able to approach Pareto-efficient outcomes, that (ii) our monitoring approach CSLAB-Mon.KOM allows the achievement of accurate monitoring results, and that (iii) our strategies for monitor placement CSLAB-Loc.KOM permit to obtain a robust monitoring infrastructure. Subsequently, we describe the evaluation of our three contributions in the next Sections 8.2, 8.3, and 8.4. Each of these sections concerns one of our contributions and first explains the simulation environment and experimental setup, followed by the presentation and discussion of the results of the evaluation. Finally, Section 8.5 summarizes the main findings of this chapter.

8.1 Major Objectives

8.1.1 Pareto-Efficient Negotiations

Following our generic model of negotiation performance (cf. Section 4.2.2), the performance metrics concerning a negotiation mechanism can address either the *contractual performance* or the *computational performance*. Pareto-efficiency corresponds to the contractual performance of a negotiation mechanism. Although the major objective of the evaluation regarding our negotiation mechanism CSLAB-Neg.KOM is to assess the Pareto-efficiency of the outcome of a negotiation, the computational performance of CSLAB-Neg.KOM must also be taken into account. This is due to the fact that metrics expressing the computational performance reflect the effort for achieving a certain level of contractual performance. Besides a *parameter evaluation* of CSLAB-Neg.KOM, we also perform a *comparative evaluation* to an approach that applies a pure Alternate-Offers protocol in conjunction with time-dependent strategies (cf. Sections 2.3.1 and 5.3).

Concerning the computational performance, the two metrics *Pareto-efficiency* and *success rate* are considered in the evaluation. In order to assess the Pareto-efficiency, we follow our ex post Pareto-efficiency reference model (cf. Section 5.2) and determine the distance of a certain outcome from the Pareto frontier. However, the Pareto frontier comprises multiple agreements, which differ in the amounts of utility provided to a consumer and a provider but which are all equally good from a mathematical perspective. Therefore, we determine the maximum utilities U_c^{max} and U_p^{max} that both parties could have obtained given their preferences without making the opposing party worse off. Let C and D be the agreements that would provide these maximum amounts in utility to the consumer and provider, respectively, and let $A = (U_p, U_c)$ be the agreement achieved from a certain negotiation. The distance to the Pareto frontier can then be expressed in terms of the differences ΔU_c and ΔU_p between the maximum amounts in utility U_c^{max} and U_p^{max} and the consumer's and provider's total utilities U_c and U_p obtained from A, respectively. Mathematically, these differences correspond to the *euclidean distances* of the achieved agreement A to the agreements C and D (cf. Figure 5.1). This can be formalized as follows:

$$\Delta U_c = \|C - A\| \quad \text{with} \quad C = (U_p, U_c^{max}) \tag{8.1}$$

$$\Delta U_p = \|D - A\| \quad \text{with} \quad D = (U_p^{max}, U_c) \tag{8.2}$$

In the evaluation, the distance to the Pareto frontier is specified in percent. This is due to the fact that the absolute differences ΔU_c and ΔU_p each correspond to a certain percentage of the maximum amount in utility of 1 (= 100%) that is theoretically achievable. We consider Pareto-efficiency expressed as the distance to the Pareto frontier as *dependent variable* and examine the influence of the parameters *greed factor*, *risk factor*, and *patience* as *independent variables* in the parameter evaluation. Regarding a comparative evaluation, we also compare the Pareto-efficiency of CSLAB-Neg.KOM to a pure Alternate Offers-based approach using time-dependent strategies. Besides the Pareto-efficiency, we also examine the success rate, which expresses the ratio of the number of successful negotiations n_{succ} resulting in an agreement to the overall number of negotiations n_{all}:

$$success\ rate = \frac{|n_{succ}|}{|n_{all}|} \tag{8.3}$$

CSLAB-Neg.KOM utilizes the Alternate-Offers protocol in the first instance in order to obtain an initial agreement, which is then iteratively improved towards a Pareto-efficient solution in the second phase (cf. Section 5.3.1). Hence, the success rate of CSLAB-Neg.KOM is equal to the success rate of a pure Alternate-Offers-based approach. However, we also examine the success rate, since an initial solution is a prerequisite for CSLAB-Neg.KOM to succeed. Since the success rate depends highly on the selected strategies, we consider the *success rate* as dependent variable and explore the impact of the *strategy setting* as independent variable.

Regarding the computational performance, we evaluate the scalability of CSLAB-Neg.KOM in terms of the *execution time* and the *number of exchanged messages* in accordance with our generic model of negotiation performance. For each of the dependent variables, we examine the impact of the *number of providers* as independent variable in the parameter evaluation and the impact of the *patience* as independent variable in the comparative evaluation. For the parameter evaluation, the number of providers is selected as independent variable, since the number of exchanged messages and, thus, the execution time both increase with a growing number of participants. For the comparative evaluation, the patience is selected as independent variable in order to explore the additional effort of the search for improvements in the Trade-Off Phase in comparison to the search for an initial agreement in the Agreement Phase. The details of the setup and selected results of our evaluation of CSLAB-Neg.KOM are provided in Section 8.2.

8.1.2 Reliable Monitoring

In order to demonstrate the practical applicability of our monitoring approach, the major objective of the evaluation of CSLAB-Mon.KOM is to validate the *accuracy* of the monitoring results as dependent variable. As already mentioned in Section 6.2.3, given a certain point estimate of the real availability, we express the accuracy of the monitoring results in terms of the achieved confidence level at which the real availability at least matches or exceeds the negotiated uptime guarantee, i.e., if it is considered to be the lower bound. In this regard, we explore the impact of the utilized *monitoring frequency*, specified in terms of the corresponding probing period, and the required *sample size* as independent variables. Recall that the monitoring frequency has an influence on the probing error, while the sample size directly affects the sampling error.

For the purpose of assessing the impact of our consumer side monitoring approach compared to a provider side approach, we measure the *ratio of sample size* as well as the absolute *difference in sample size*. The ratio and the difference are calculated between the sample size required when using our monitoring approach and the sample size required if the exact values of the real TTF and TTR are known, i.e., without making any probing error. The latter number of samples is referred to as "exact sample size" in the following.

Finally, we also evaluate the *ratio of availability* and the *difference in availability*. While the former reflects the ratio of the estimated availability and the real availability, i.e., $\hat{A}/A$, the latter expresses the absolute difference between these two values, i.e., $\hat{A} - A$. Specifically, we analyze the amount of deviation of the current point estimate from the real availability in conjunction with the required sample size. This not only permits assessing the precision of the point estimate but also allows the convergence of the point estimate to the negotiated uptime guarantee to be explored, assuming that the real availability matches that uptime guarantee. Further details regarding the experimental setup of the evaluation as well as the subsequent presentation and discussion of the results are provided in Section 8.3.

8.1.3 Robust Monitor Placement

One major objective of the evaluation of our strategies for monitor placement CSLAB-Loc.KOM is to analyze their ability to establish a robust monitoring infrastructure. For this purpose, we consider the dependent variables *solution quality* and *computation time* in our evaluation. While the solution quality expresses the achieved reliability of the monitoring infrastructure, the computation time expresses the corresponding effort for achieving a certain level of reliability. In this regard, the solution quality refers to the decision variable z of our mathematical model, which represents the worst case total reliability among the sets of redundant monitoring units over all cloud applications (cf. Section 7.3.2). In order to better assess the effects of applying a certain strategy, we transform the resulting reliability in terms of the objective value z into the maximum expected overall downtime of the monitoring units on a yearly basis. For example, "four nines", i.e., 99.99% translate into around 50 minutes downtime per year (cf., e.g., [83]). Concerning the independent variables considered in our evaluation, we explore the impact of the *total number of data center sites* on the provider side and the broker side, the *number of VMs* running on each site, the *number of cloud applications* co-located on each VM, and the *redundancy factor* for placing monitoring units.

Besides the parameter evaluation mentioned before, we also aim to assess the practical applicability of our heuristic strategies CSLAB-Loc-Start.KOM and CSLAB-Loc-Imp.KOM as second major objective. Recall that our exact solution approach CSLAB-Loc-Exa.KOM is NP-hard and, thus, cannot be applied for solving large-scale problems in practice. Therefore, our heuristic solution approaches trade solution quality against computation time and should be able to achieve near optimal results in polynomial time in the best case. Hence, we also perform a comparative evaluation, in which we compare our heuristic solution approaches against our exact solution approach CSLAB-Loc-Exa.KOM and a random placement approach CSLAB-Loc-Rand.KOM. While our exact solution approach constitutes a baseline in terms of solution quality, the random placement approach can be considered to be a baseline in terms of computation time. In addition, a comparison with a random placement approach in terms of solution quality also allows the demonstration of the improvement achieved by applying a more sophisticated approach. The setup of the evaluation of our placement strategies CSLAB-Loc.KOM is described in detail in Section 8.4, followed by the presentation and discussion of the corresponding results.

8.2 Pareto-Efficient Negotiations - CSLAB-Neg.KOM

This section presents the details of our evaluation of CSLAB-Neg.KOM and is structured as follows. Section 8.2.1 introduces the simulation environment, Section 8.2.2 describes the experimental setup of our evaluation, and Section 8.2.3 presents and discusses selected results. Further results are provided in the Appendix in Section A.2.

8.2.1 Simulation Framework

In order to evaluate our negotiation mechanism, CSLAB-Neg.KOM as well as a pure Alternate-Offers-based approach using time-dependent strategies have been both prototypically implemented using the agent-based simulation platform Repast Simphony[1]. Repast Simphony is based on the Java programming language. An overview of our simulation environment comprising the implemented Java packages and classes as well as the utilized files for configuration and logging purposes is provided in Figure 8.1. In the following, we briefly describe the implemented Java packages and the overall interaction in our simulation environment.

Basically, the packages in the simulation environment are split into two groups. While one group comprises the packages for simulating the actual negotiations using the simulation platform Repast Simphony, the other group incorporates all the packages for analyzing the negotiation results. In accordance with Figure 8.1, we first describe the latter group in the following.

- *evaluation:* This package contains the classes required to analyze the results of the evaluation. By utilizing Repast Simphony, two different output files *param.txt* and *log.txt* are obtained from each execution of a certain test case. Each test case itself comprises a predefined number of negotiations, denoted as negotiation runs in the following. While the former output file contains all the configuration parameters that have been used in each negotiation run, the latter output file contains the results of each run. Concerning the implemented Java packages, *Evaluation* constitutes the main class for initiating the evaluation over certain test cases, *LogFileParser* is used to import the results by utilizing the class *NegotiationRecord* as data structure, and *Analytics* provides all the methods to analyze the imported results. Finally, the class *Visualizer* provides methods for generating plots and for saving them as pdf files. For plot generation purposes the JFreeChart library[2] has been used.

---

[1]   http://repast.sourceforge.net/
[2]   http://www.jfree.org/jfreechart/

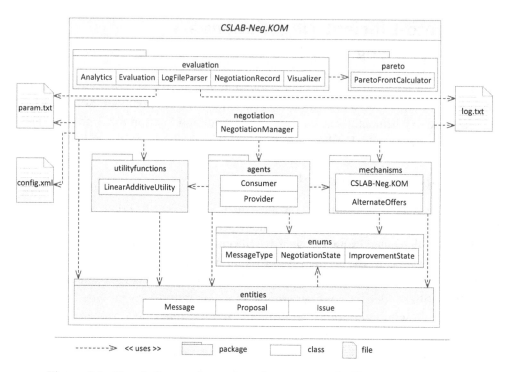

Figure 8.1: Simulation environment of our approach CSLAB-Neg.KOM

- *pareto:* In order to determine the distance to the Pareto frontier of a certain negotiation outcome, the class *ParetoFrontCalculator* computes a representation of the Pareto frontier based on the *adaptive weighted sum method* as proposed by Kim and de Weck [99] (cf. Section 5.2).

The second group consists of the packages, which have been implemented in conjunction with Repast Simphony for simulating the actual negotiations. These packages are described in the following.

- *negotiation:* The class *NegotiationManager* constitutes the main class for selecting a certain test case to be executed and for controlling the interactions with Repast Simphony. In order to specify the configuration of a certain test case in Repast Simphony, an input file *config.xml* can be defined. This file indicates the number of negotiation runs to be conducted amongst all other parameters, which are required by the considered negotiation mechanism.

- *agents:* This package represents the negotiating parties in the form of the two classes *Consumer* and *Provider*. For each object of these classes, a corresponding agent is created in Repast Simphony.

- *utilityfunctions:* Generic types of utility functions are defined in this package. As already mentioned, we exemplarily consider linear additive utility functions in this thesis for reasons of computational simplicity. However, our simulation environment can be easily extended by other types of utility functions.

- *mechanisms:* The actual negotiation mechanisms are contained in this package. While our negotiation mechanism has been implemented in the class *CSLAB-Neg.KOM*, the class *AlternateOffers* realizes a pure Alternate-Offers-based approach using time-dependent strategies.

- *entities:* This package comprises the basic entities required to model a negotiation, namely the classes *Message*, *Proposal*, and *Issue*.

- *enums:* In Java, an *enum* is used to define a special data type. Variables from this type can only hold values from a predefined set of constants. This package defines the enums *MessageType* specifying the available message types, *NegotiationState* defining the possible states during the Agreement Phase, and *ImprovementState* indicating the possible states during the Trade-Off Phase.

8.2.2 Experimental Setup

For the evaluation of CSLAB-Neg.KOM, we apply a one-factor-at-a-time design [20]. This means that we explore the impact of each independent variable on a certain dependent variable separately. Hence, we only modify the value of the currently considered independent variable and make use of default values for all of the remaining independent variables at a single point in time. As already mentioned, we conduct a parameter evaluation and a comparative evaluation. The former evaluates the performance of our negotiation mechanism CSLAB-Neg.KOM and the latter compares the performance of CSLAB-Neg.KOM to a pure Alternate-Offers-based approach. Recall that we analyze the contractual performance as well as the computational performance in both cases. An overview of the corresponding experimental setup is provided in the Tables 8.1 to 8.3 and elaborated on in detail in the following. All experiments have been conducted on a laptop with an Intel Core i5 CPU with 2.40 GHz and 6 GB RAM running Microsoft Windows 7 (64 Bit) as operating system.

Experimental Setup concerning the Contractual Performance Concerning the dependent variable Pareto-efficiency in the parameter evaluation of CSLAB-Neg.KOM, we explore the influence of the three parameters greed factor, risk factor, and patience as independent variables. The corresponding values can be obtained from Table 8.1. In the table, the underlined values represent the default values of the independent variables. Such a default value is used for an independent variable if the impact of that variable is not the focus of a certain test case. Furthermore, we

Table 8.1: Parameters of the GRiP-based strategies

Independent Variable	Symbol and Values
Risk factor (%):	$\rho_i^a \in \{0.001, 0.005, \underline{0.01}, 0.05, 0.1, 0.25, 0.5\}$
Greed factor (%):	$\gamma_i^a \in \{0.05, \underline{0.1}, 0.15, 0.2, 0.25\}$
Patience (no. of trials):	$\pi_i^a \in \{1, 3, \underline{5}, 10, 20, 30\}$
Cooling factors:	$\tau_j^{a1}, \tau_j^{a2} = 0.0025$

Table 8.2: Parameters of the time-dependent strategies

Variable	Values
Consumer concession:	boulware: 0.5 | linear: 1 | conceder: 2.5
Provider concession:	boulware: $U(0.0, 1.0)$ | linear: 1.0 | conceder: $(1.0, 5.0]$
Number of providers:	$n_{prov} = \{10, 20, 30, 40, 50, 60, 70, 80, 90, 100\}$
Deadline interval (rounds):	$d_1 = U[1,5], d_2 = U[6,10], d_3 = U[11,15],$ $d_4 = U[16,20], d_5 = U[21,25]$

Table 8.3: Ranges for consumer and provider proposals

Issue	Consumer		Provider	
	best:	worst:	best:	worst:
Price ($/month):	$U[5,10]$	$U[15,20]$	$U[17,22]$	$U[7,12]$
Exec. time (ms):	$U[100,400]$	$U[600,900]$	$U[700,1000]$	$U[200,500]$
Availability (%):	$U[98.95,99.95]$	$U[97.55,98.55]$	$U[97.5,98.5]$	$U[98.9,99.9]$

have used a constant value for the cooling factors that was suggested by Di Nitto et al. in [143]. By using a one-factor-at-a-time design, we obtain 18 different test cases with respect to the GRiP-based strategies.

Regarding the comparative evaluation, we also examine the Pareto-efficiency of our negotiation mechanism CSLAB-Neg.KOM in comparison to a pure Alternate-Offers-based approach that utilizes time-dependent strategies. Recall that CSLAB-Neg.KOM also applies time-dependent strategies in conjunction with the Alternate Offers protocol during the *Agreement Phase*. The overall setup used in both cases regarding the time-dependent strategies is provided in Table 8.2. In order to evaluate the influence of different strategy settings on the success rate as another dependent variable, we vary the time-dependent strategies as follows. In each negotiation run, the broker acting on behalf of a consumer and all of the providers apply one of the three common types of strategies (i.e., boulware, linear, or conceder). Although the type of strategy is similar for all of the providers, each provider makes different amounts of concession due to different concession factors and/or different constraint intervals for the issues under negotiation. While we draw the concession factors randomly from a continuous uniform distribution in case of a boulware or conceder strategy applied on the provider side, we keep the concession factor fixed in case of a linear strategy. On the consumer side, we keep all concession factors constant for all types of strategies. By comparing three types of strategies on the consumer side against three types of strategies on the provider side, nine different strategy settings are obtained in total. Since we compare each of the 18 test cases mentioned before in each strategy setting, we obtain 162 test cases in total. For each test case, we conduct 2500 different negotiation runs, in which we vary the number of providers, the individual deadlines, as well as the individual ranges of the constraint intervals for each issue under negotiation. In detail, we vary the number of providers from 10 up to 100 in steps of 10 providers over five different deadline intervals resulting in 50 different settings. For each of these settings, we generate 50 negotiation instances randomly, in which the bounds of the constraint intervals for proposal generation are drawn from a uniform distribution. The corresponding ranges for the constraint intervals are provided in Table 8.3. Concerning the price ranges, we have exemplarily analyzed the monthly prices of the SaaS offers from the field of project management as a reference on the AWS Marketplace[3] of Amazon. The ranges for the execution time have been created around the response time intervals used by Wang et al. in their experiments in [210]. Regarding availability, the upper and lower bounds have been created around the penalty classes of the SLAs from Amazon EC2[4] and Rackspace[5]. Besides the constraint intervals, the values for the weights utilized by the negotiating parties indicating their individual levels of importance of the issues under negotiation are also drawn from a uniform distribution in the open interval $(0, 1)$. In addition, the resulting values are normalized, so that all the weights used by a single party have a total sum of 1.

Experimental Setup concerning the Computational Performance

We further evaluate the scalability of our approach CSLAB-Neg.KOM in terms of the two dependent variables execution time and the number of exchanged messages. For this purpose, we also determine the values of these two dependent variables while executing our 162 test cases mentioned before in conjunction with 2500 negotiation runs for each test case. Based on the results, we explore the influence of an increasing number of providers from 10 up to 100 in steps of 10 providers on the number of exchanged messages and the execution time at different deadline intervals in the parameter evaluation. In doing so, we are able to explore the impact of the number of providers as independent variable independently from an additional impact that would be caused by varying deadline intervals. Furthermore, we evaluate the impact of an increasing patience level from 1 over 3, 5, 10, and 20 trials up to a patience

---

3   https://aws.amazon.com/marketplace/
4   https://aws.amazon.com/de/ec2/sla/
5   https://www.rackspace.com/information/legal/cloud/sla

level of 30 trials on the number of exchanged messages and the execution time in the comparative evaluation. As already stated in Section 8.1.1, the impact of the patience level is explored since it reflects the additional effort for searching improvements in the Trade-Off Phase in comparison to the effort for searching an initial agreement in a pure Alternate-Offers-based approach as well as in the Agreement Phase. The results of our evaluation of CSLAB-Neg.KOM are presented in the next section.

8.2.3 Results and Discussion

While Figures 8.2 to 8.5 show selected results concerning the contractual performance of CSLAB-Neg.KOM, selected results concerning the computational performance can be obtained from Figures 8.6 and 8.7. All figures are elaborated on in detail in the following.

Results concerning the Contractual Performance Figures 8.2 to 8.4 depict the impact of each of the three independent variables risk factor, greed factor, and patience on the Pareto-efficiency. Each of these figures is further divided into four different subfigures. While the first two subfigures show the results of the parameter evaluation of our negotiation mechanism CSLAB-Neg.KOM with respect to one of the independent variables, the last two subfigures provide the results of the comparative evaluation with a pure Alternate-Offers-based approach. In each of the two aforementioned cases, the first and the second subfigure show the overall best and worst outcomes, respectively, which are obtained in different strategy settings. For the results from the parameter evaluation, the Pareto-efficiency is specified on the y-axis in terms of the distance to the Pareto frontier of the achieved agreement from a consumer's and provider's perspective, i.e., ΔU_c and ΔU_p (cf. Section 8.1.1). For the results from the comparative evaluation, the y-axis displays the difference in the distances to the Pareto frontier of the agreement achieved with CSLAB-Neg.KOM and the agreement achieved with a pure Alternate-Offers-based approach. Hence, the results of the comparative evaluation reveal the improvement in comparison to the initial agreement. In all subfigures of Figures 8.2 to 8.4, the x-axis displays the values of the respective independent variable. All results are displayed with the respective confidence intervals at a confidence level of 95%. A thorough discussion of the results follows.

Impact of the Risk Factor on the Pareto-efficiency Concerning the impact of the risk factor in the parameter evaluation of CSLAB-Neg.KOM, the distance to the Pareto frontier could be reduced in the best case to 0.65% on average on the consumer side and to 0.88% on average on the provider side (cf. Figure 8.2a). In the worst case, the distance could be reduced to around 1.5% and 1.6% on average on the consumer side and the provider side, respectively (cf. Figure 8.2b). In general, the distance to

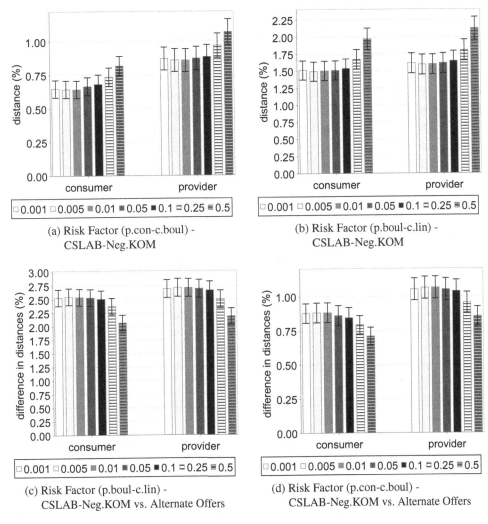

(a) Risk Factor (p.con-c.boul) -
CSLAB-Neg.KOM

(b) Risk Factor (p.boul-c.lin) -
CSLAB-Neg.KOM

(c) Risk Factor (p.boul-c.lin) -
CSLAB-Neg.KOM vs. Alternate Offers

(d) Risk Factor (p.con-c.boul) -
CSLAB-Neg.KOM vs. Alternate Offers

Figure 8.2: Impact of the Risk factor on the Pareto-efficiency

the Pareto frontier increases with a risk factor of 0.5 up to more than 2.1% on average in the worst case on the provider side. The best results could be achieved with a risk factor less or equal to 0.01. All in all, a smaller risk factor allows the achievement of higher improvements.

Regarding the comparison with a pure Alternate-Offers-based approach, CSLAB-Neg.KOM is able further to improve an initial solution in the best case by around 2.5% on the consumer side and by around 2.75% on the provider side (cf. Figure 8.2c) and in the worst case using the most promising risk factor of 0.01 by around 0.88% on the consumer side and by around 1.05% on the provider side (cf. Figure 8.2d). As it can be seen from Figures 8.2a and 8.2b, the best results of CSLAB-Neg.KOM could be achieved when using the strategy setting *provider: conceder - consumer: boulware* and the worst results have been obtained in the strategy setting *provider: boulware - consumer: linear*. The opposite applies to the results of the comparative evaluation in Figures 8.2c and 8.2d. This is due to the fact that the distance to the Pareto frontier of the initial agreement in the strategy setting *provider: boulware - consumer: linear* is much higher than the distance when using the strategy setting *provider: conceder - consumer: boulware*. In the latter, there is less room for improvement, since the area of joint gains has already become very small. In this case, it is also more difficult to identify trade-offs that lead to joint gains. Nevertheless, the results confirm that our negotiation approach is still able to achieve considerable improvements in this case.

Impact of the Greed Factor on the Pareto-efficiency   The results concerning the impact of the greed factor are depicted in Figure 8.3. The order of the subfigures is similar to the results presented before with respect to the risk factor. To start with, the best results in the parameter evaluation exhibit a reduction of the distance to the Pareto frontier to 0.62% on average on the consumer side and to 0.83% on average on the provider side (cf. Figure 8.3a). In the worst case, a reduction of the distance to the Pareto frontier to 1.55% on average on the consumer side and to 1.65% on average on the provider side could be obtained (cf. Figure 8.3b). Similar to the influence of the risk factor, the distance to the Pareto frontier increases with an increasing greed factor and also grows to more than 2.1% on average in the worst case on the provider side when using a very high greed factor of 0.25. To summarize, a greed factor of 0.1 or less has yielded the best results.

Concerning the results from the comparative evaluation, Figure 8.3c shows the largest improvement of the initial agreement of around 2.5% on average on the consumer side and of 2.7% on average on the provider side. In the worst case, the highest reduction of 0.89% on average on the consumer side and of 1.08% on average on the provider side could be obtained using a greed factor of 0.05 (cf. Figure 8.3d). Regarding the influence of the applied strategies, the greatest reduction of the distance to the Pareto frontier with respect to the initial agreement could be achieved in the strategy setting *provider: boulware - consumer: linear* and the smallest reduction resulted from the strategy setting *provider: conceder - consumer: boulware*. Hence, the best and the worst improvements could be observed in strategy settings similar to the strategy settings already observed in the comparative evaluation concerning the risk factor.

All in all, the greed factor shows a similar behavior in comparison with the risk factor. By applying a smaller greed factor higher improvements can be obtained in general.

Impact of the Patience on the Pareto-efficiency   The impact of the patience level can be deduced from Figure 8.4. Again, the order of the subfigures follows

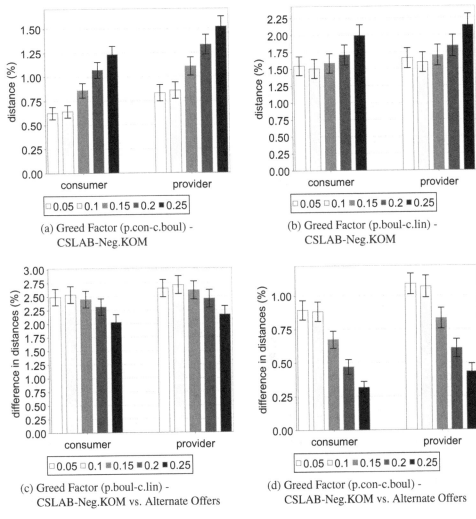

Figure 8.3: Impact of the Greed factor on the Pareto-efficiency

the order of the previous subfigures first showing the best and worst results of the parameter evaluation followed by the best and worst results from the comparative evaluation. The results from the parameter evaluation reveal that the greatest reduction in the distance to the Pareto frontier already occurs when using a patience level of 3 instead of 1. When the patience level is further increased to 10, the distance to the Pareto frontier drops below 1% on average on both sides. A further increase of the patience level only results in marginal improvements from that point on. Thus, CSLAB-Neg.KOM is able to already improve an initial agreement to a large extent at a low patience level. Hence, a small patience level will be sufficient in most of the

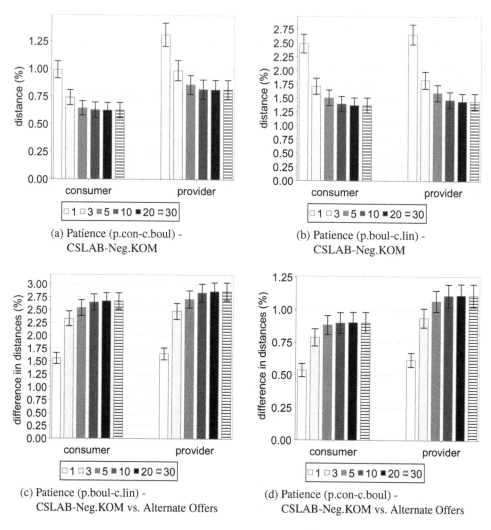

(a) Patience (p.con-c.boul) -
    CSLAB-Neg.KOM

(b) Patience (p.boul-c.lin) -
    CSLAB-Neg.KOM

(c) Patience (p.boul-c.lin) -
    CSLAB-Neg.KOM vs. Alternate Offers

(d) Patience (p.con-c.boul) -
    CSLAB-Neg.KOM vs. Alternate Offers

Figure 8.4: Impact of the Patience on the Pareto-efficiency

cases in practice, since higher patience levels are also tied to higher communication costs. Overall, a reduction to 0.63% on average on the consumer side and to 0.81% on average on the provider side could be achieved in the best case (cf. Figure 8.4a). When using a large patience level greater than 10, a distance to the Pareto frontier of 1.36% on average on the consumer side and of 1.43%on average on the provider side has been obtained in the worst case (cf. Figure 8.4b).

When comparing our negotiation mechanism to a pure Alternate-Offers-based approach, Figure 8.4c reveals that an initial agreement is improved in the best case by 2.68% on average on the consumer side and by 2.88% on average on the provider side when using a patience level of 10 or higher. In contrast, a patience level of 10 or higher only leads to a reduction of 0.9% on average on the consumer side and of 1.11% on average on the provider side in the worst case (cf. Figure 8.4d). Similar to the results from the two aforementioned independent variables, the best results with respect to the influence of the patience level could be obtained in the strategy setting *provider: boulware - consumer: linear*, whereas the worst results occurred in the strategy setting *provider: conceder - consumer: boulware*. It follows from these observations that a risk-adverse strategy yields better results in favor for the consumer and that a risk-seeking behavior is more beneficial from a provider's perspective.

Impact of the Strategy Setting on the Success Rate   The types of time-dependent strategies applied by the negotiating parties during the Agreement Phase or in case of a pure Alternate-Offers-based approach have not only a major influence on the utilities obtained by the negotiating parties from an (initial) agreement, but do also affect the probability of a successful negotiation resulting in any kind of agreement overall. This is due to the fact that the strategies determine the speed of convergence of the conflicting interests of the negotiating parties towards mutually acceptable proposals by making larger or smaller amounts of concession in each round. However, the impact of the utilized strategies on the success rate is most pronounced in case of very low deadlines and is negligible in case of higher deadlines since the success rate then becomes very close to 100%.

The influence of the deadline interval on the success rate is exemplarily depicted for the strategy setting *provider: boulware - consumer: boulware* in Figure 8.5b, since that strategy setting shows the overall lowest success rate among all strategy settings in case of a deadline interval d_1 (cf. Table 8.2). In case of higher deadline intervals all strategy settings show very similar success rates. The sensitivity of the success rate depending on the strategies applied is mostly pronounced at a deadline interval d_1, since there is only a small amount of time available to reach an agreement. Therefore, larger differences in the amounts of concession may occur, so that no mutual acceptable agreement can be found. In contrast, when negotiating with higher deadlines, the amounts of concession are smaller, since they are distributed over a larger interval of time and, thus, the issued proposals become more similar near the end of a negotiation. Nevertheless, we also explore the impact of the strategies on the success rate at a very low deadline interval d_1. This is due to the fact that a short deadline for SLA negotiation is reasonable in a cloud computing scenario in order to allow for on-demand service provisioning. The impact of different strategy settings at a short deadline interval d_1 is depicted in Figure 8.5a. It can be deduced from the figure that a risk-averse behavior on both sides in the strategy setting *provider: boulware - consumer: boulware* results in the lowest success rate overall of around 70% on average. In contrast, by applying more risk-seeking strategies higher success rates of around 85% on average can be obtained.

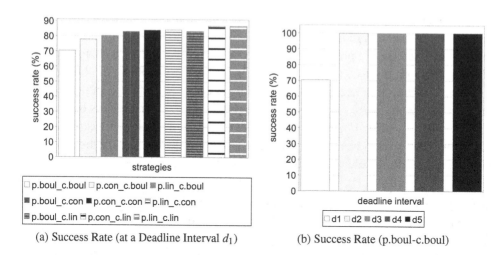

(a) Success Rate (at a Deadline Interval d_1)   (b) Success Rate (p.boul-c.boul)

Figure 8.5: Impact of the strategies on the success rate - CSLAB-Neg.KOM

Results concerning the Computational Performance   The impact of each of the two independent variables number of providers and patience on the two dependent variables number of exchanged messages and execution time is shown in Figures 8.6 and 8.7. Again, the figures also include the respective confidence intervals at a confidence level of 95%. While Figure 8.6 shows the results of the parameter evaluation of CSLAB-Neg.KOM with respect to its scalability with an increasing number of providers, Figure 8.7 provides the results of the comparative evaluation indicating the additional effort for improving an initial agreement depending on the applied level of patience. In each of the figures, the y-axis displays one of the dependent variables, while the currently considered independent variable is specified on the x-axis. Regarding the independent variables, we have varied the number of providers from 10 up to 100 in steps of 10 providers. Concerning the level of patience, the results obtained by using a pure Alternate-Offers-based approach and the results obtained with our negotiation mechanism CSLAB-Neg.KOM at different patience levels ranging from 1 over 3, 5, 10, and 20 up to a patience level of 30 are displayed next to each other.

Impact of the No. of Providers on the No. of Exchanged Messages
Regarding the impact of the number of providers on the number of exchanged messages at a deadline interval d_2 (cf. Table 8.2) shown in Figure 8.6a, we observe a linear growth in the number of exchanged messages while the number of providers increases. These results confirm the scalability of our negotiation mechanism CSLAB-Neg.KOM. Dividing the total number of exchanged messages by the number of providers, 10 messages are exchanged on average with each provider, which can be considered to

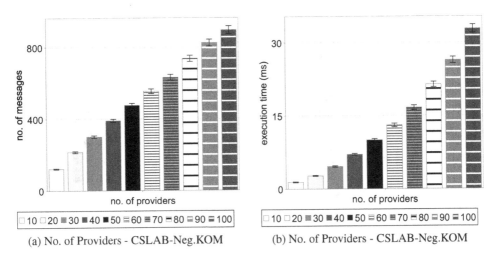

(a) No. of Providers - CSLAB-Neg.KOM   (b) No. of Providers - CSLAB-Neg.KOM

Figure 8.6: Impact of the no. of providers on the no. of exchanged messages and the execution time at a deadline interval d_2

be tractable in an automated negotiation. Basically, the results at a deadline interval d_2 comprising negotiations between 6 and 10 rounds have been selected for presentation, since it constitutes the deadline interval with the lowest deadlines, which at the same time result in an overall success rate near 100% (cf. Figure 8.5b). Hence, in order to realize automated SLA negotiations in the context of on-demand cloud service provisioning, i.e., in a small amount of time, with a success rate near 100%, a deadline interval d_2 can be considered to be the most adequate interval. Results concerning other deadline intervals are provided in Figure A.11 in Section A.2 of the Appendix and also confirm the scalability of our approach.

Impact of the No. of Providers on the Execution Time The results concerning the impact of the number of providers on the execution time at a deadline interval d_2 (cf. Table 8.2) are depicted in Figure 8.6b. Similar to the number of exchanged messages, the execution time grows linearly with an increasing number of providers. Hence, also with respect to the execution time, our negotiation mechanism CSLAB-Neg.KOM shows a scalable behavior. Furthermore, with a total execution time lower than 1 second, the results also confirm the applicability of our negotiation mechanism in the context of instant on-demand cloud service provisioning. Again, additional results concerning the execution time can be obtained from Figure A.12 in the Appendix. Furthermore, a comparison of the execution time of our negotiation mechanism with a pure Alternate-Offers-based approach is provided in the following.

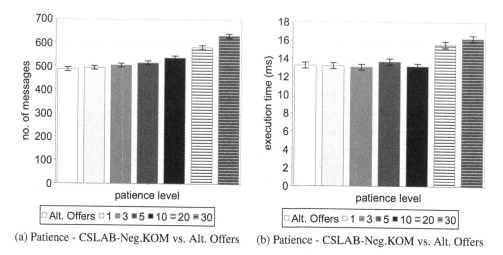

(a) Patience - CSLAB-Neg.KOM vs. Alt. Offers   (b) Patience - CSLAB-Neg.KOM vs. Alt. Offers

Figure 8.7: Impact of the Patience on the no. of exchanged messages and the execution time at a deadline interval d_2

Impact of the Patience on the No. of Exchanged Messages As part of our comparative evaluation, we have analyzed the impact of the patience level on the number of exchanged messages in comparison with a pure Alternate-Offers-based approach. In doing so, we are able to determine the additional effort for improving an initial agreement. The corresponding results at a deadline interval d_2 (cf. Table 8.2) in case of a pure Alternate Offers-based approach or during the Agreement Phase of CSLAB-Neg.KOM are provided in Figure 8.7a. In case of a pure Alternate Offers-based approach, 485 messages are exchanged on average. It can be further deduced from the figure that only a small amount of up to 55 additional messages on average is exchanged up to a patience level of 10. In case of a higher patience level of 30, around 140 messages are additionally exchanged on average. This results in around 11% of additional messages in case of a patience level of 10 and around 29% of additional messages in case of a patience level of 30. However, as already mentioned before, only marginal improvements regarding the Pareto-efficiency are made when the patience level is further increased beyond 10 (cf. Figure 8.4). Therefore, an additional number of around 11% of exchanged messages on average will already be sufficient in most of the cases for improving an initial agreement to a large extent. Additional results regarding other deadline intervals are provided in Figure A.13 of the Appendix.

Impact of the Patience on the Execution Time Besides the number of exchanged messages, we have also considered the execution time as dependent variable in conjunction with a varying patience level. The results in Figure 8.7b at a deadline interval d_2 (cf. Table 8.2) show that there is no significant difference in the execution time up to a patience level of 10 in comparison with a pure Alternate Offers-based approach. Also in case of a patience level of 30, the execution time is only further increased by around 3 ms on average. Hence, the additional effort in terms of execution time required to improve an initial agreement is very low. Again, further results with respect to other deadline intervals can be obtained from Figure A.14 in the Appendix.

8.3 Reliable Monitoring - CSLAB-Mon.KOM

In this section, we describe the evaluation of our monitoring approach CSLAB-Mon.KOM in detail. Specifically, Section 8.3.1 briefly explains the prototypical implementation of our approach, Section 8.3.2 introduces our experimental setup, and finally, we present and discuss selected results in Section 8.3.3.

8.3.1 Prototypical Implementation

For evaluation purposes, we have prototypically implemented our monitoring approach CSLAB-Mon.KOM in the Java programming language. Our prototypical implementation is illustrated in Figure 8.8. The figure depicts the implemented Java packages and classes as well as the different log files. It should be noted that the Java packages with the prefix "java." in their package name constitute existing packages of the Java framework and have been added to the overview for clarification. All other packages and classes have been implemented by the author of this thesis. In order to demonstrate the practical applicability of our approach, we have utilized a real cloud service to be monitored in the evaluation, namely the community version of the Kaltura[6] video platform. Besides the open-source community edition, this video platform is also available as a commercial SaaS variant[7] to be deployed on the infrastructure of a commercial cloud provider such as Amazon. In the scope of our evaluation, we have deployed that video platform on a VM running Ubuntu 14.04.4 in the blade center of our department. On that VM, we have also deployed the component corresponding to the simulator package of CSLAB-Mon.KOM (cf. Figure 8.8), in the following referred to as *Downtime Simulator*. That component enables the simulation of downtimes of the cloud service without actually affecting it in practice. For this purpose, the Downtime Simulator utilizes the iptables[8] utility in the linux kernel for modifying the packet filter ruleset. Specifically, in order to initiate a downtime, we add a rule to the packet filter ruleset stating that all incoming TCP packets on port 80 should be dropped. That rule is deleted later on in order to initiate a subsequent uptime. The monitoring unit itself has been placed on a local laptop with an Intel Core i5 CPU with 2.40 GHz and 6 GB RAM running Microsoft Windows 7 (64 Bit) as operating system. It periodically

---

6   http://corp.kaltura.com
7   http://corp.kaltura.com/Products/Deployment-Options
8   http://www.netfilter.org/projects/iptables/

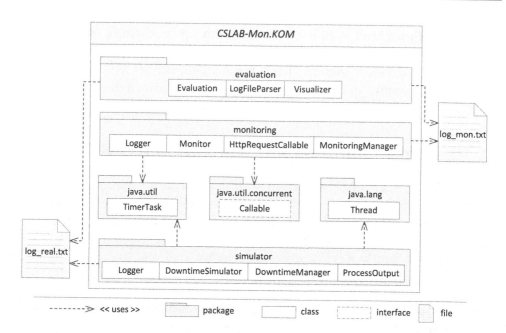

Figure 8.8: Prototypical implementation of our approach CSLAB-Mon.KOM

checks the availability of the cloud service by sending HTTP Get requests to the cloud service, thereby requesting some metadata of a specific video file. In the following, we give a brief overview of the Java packages utilized in our prototypical implementation and describe their role in the overall interaction of CSLAB-Mon.KOM. The packages and classes, which are part of the Java framework, are only elaborated implicitly.

- *simulator:* This package comprises the classes of the Downtime Simulator. In detail, the *DowntimeManager* class constitutes the main class in order to control the Downtime Simulator, i.e., to start the simulator at a specific point in time. From that point on, downtimes are generated as defined in the *DowntimeSimulator* class. The latter class constitutes the actual class for simulating downtimes by utilizing the iptables utility as described above. For this purpose, it extends the *TimerTask* class provided by the Java framework, so that it can be scheduled at a specific time and is executed by a separate thread. The uptimes and downtimes to be simulated are generated by random according to our mathematical model in Section 6.2.3 and cause the thread to sleep for the respective amount of time. In between each two time intervals, iptables commands are executed. The output from these commands is processed in the *ProcessOutput* class, which is also realized as a thread. The timestamps when executing these commands are written to a log file using the Logger class and reflect the real changes in availability of the cloud service.

- *monitoring:* Our actual monitoring approach is realized by the classes in this package. The *MonitoringManager* represents the main class in order to control the monitoring unit and proceeds in a similar manner to the DowntimeManager in the simulator package. Hence, it invokes the respective monitoring unit at a specific point in time, which subsequently checks the availability of the cloud service to be monitored at regular time intervals. The monitoring unit itself is realized in the *Monitor* class and also extends the *TimerTask* class in order to run as a timed separate thread. Monitoring requests are sent by instances of the *HttpRequestCallable* class. As the name already indicates this class implements the interface *Callable* provided by the Java framework. In doing so, a monitoring request is executed by a special separate thread, which is able to return an object in the future to the respective instance of the Monitor class containing the result of the monitoring request. The results of the monitoring requests are written into a log file using the *Logger* class.

- *evaluation:* All classes for assessing the results of the evaluation are part of this package. While the class *LogFileParser* is used in order to process the log files obtained from the Downtime Simulator and the monitoring, the class *Evaluation* provides different methods for analyzing the results. The findings obtained from that analysis can then be visualized by utilizing the *Visualizer* class. Again, the JFreeChart library[9] has been used for generating plots.

8.3.2 Experimental Setup

In order to validate the *accuracy* of our monitoring approach CSLAB-Mon.KOM as dependent variable, thereby demonstrating its practical applicability, we explore the impact of different *monitoring frequencies* and *sample sizes* as independent variables. Furthermore, we evaluate the *ratio of sample size* as well as the *difference in sample size* in order to assess the impact of the probing error on the sample size as well as the *ratio of availability* and the *difference in availability* in order to explore the convergence of $\hat{A}$ to the agreed uptime guarantee (cf. Section 8.1.2). Table 8.4 depicts the parameters and their values used in the evaluation. As it can be seen from the table, we exemplarily assume two different uptime guarantees in the evaluation. The verification of the adherence to each uptime guarantee by applying our monitoring approach is explored at three different monitoring frequencies. For each uptime guarantee, we generate two different traces and collect monitoring data up to a sample size of $n = 100$ in each trace, which corresponds to $n = 100$ different uptime and downtime cycles. A minimum downtime R_{min} of 10s is considered due to the time required to modify and apply the packet filter rules as described in Section 8.3.1. In order to avoid time intervals below the minimum downtime of 10s, the generation of

---

9   http://www.jfree.org/jfreechart/

Table 8.4: Parameters and their values used in the evaluation

Parameter	Symbol and Values
Uptime Guarantee:	$A_{SLA} \in \{80\%, 90\%\}$
Probing Period:	$T \in \{4s, 6s, 8s\}$
Minimum Downtime:	$R_{min} = 10s$
Time to Repair:	$R_j \in Exp(1/10) + 10s$
Time to Failure:	$F_i^{80\%} \in Exp(1/70) + 10s, \; F_i^{90\%} \in Exp(1/170) + 10s$

the time to repair R_j and time to failure F_i intervals must be adapted accordingly as stated in Table 8.4. The lengths of these time intervals are drawn from an exponential distribution in line with our mathematical model resulting in MTTR and MTTF values that match the respective uptime guarantee.

8.3.3 Results and Discussion

The results in case of an uptime guarantee of 90% are depicted in Figures 8.9 to 8.12 and in case of an uptime guarantee of 80% in Figures 8.13 to 8.14 and will be discussed in the following.

Regarding an uptime guarantee of 90%, we have exemplarily selected one real trace, which is depicted in Figure 8.9 along with the three corresponding monitoring traces for the different monitoring frequencies. As it can be deduced from the figure, an overestimation of the real availability is performed in case of a probing period of 8s and an underestimation occurs if the probing period is decreased to 4s. In contrast, when using a probing period of 6s the results are very close to the real availability. That observation derived from a single trace already reflects the general behavior of the monitoring tasks at the different monitoring frequencies in the considered test cases, i.e., given a minimum downtime $R_{min} = 10s$ and an $MTTR = 20s$. That result will be confirmed in the further course of this discussion.

The average ratio of sample size and difference in sample size for all real traces are illustrated in the subfigures of Figure 8.10. The subfigures show that a higher number of samples is required when monitoring with a probing period of 4s (cf. Figure 8.10a) compared to the exact sample size, i.e., the number of samples required without making an additional probing error besides the sampling error (cf. Section 8.1.2). In case of a probing period of 6s, the required sample size is very close to the exact sample size. If the probing period is increased to 8s, the average required sample size is nearly half of the exact sample size (cf. Figure 8.10b). These results are in line with the observation from the single trace presented before. Since the 8s monitoring trace overestimates the real availability, higher point estimates in terms of availability are achieved so that the number of required samples decreases. In contrast, the monitoring trace at 4s requires a higher number of samples in order to achieve the same confidence

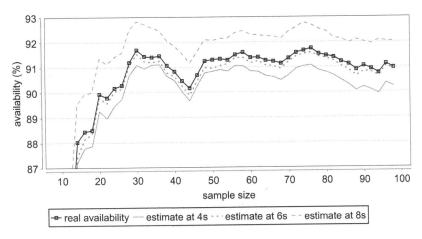

Figure 8.9: Selected trace at an uptime guarantee of 90%

level in comparison with the other two monitoring traces. This is due to the fact that the 4s trace underestimates the real availability, i.e., achieves smaller point estimates on average and, thus, requires a larger sample size. Figures 8.10c and 8.10d showing the absolute differences in sample size also confirm this observation. However, while the results obtained from the 4s monitoring trace only differ from the exact sample size by at most 4 additional samples, the 8s monitoring trace nearly requires 20 samples less than the exact sample size. Although a probing period of 8s can be considered to be the most preferable in terms of the monitoring effort with respect to the required sample size, it constitutes the probing period with the largest probing error, which is obvious from the large deviation from the exact sample size. Therefore, the 8s probing period also results in the highest deviation from the real availability among the considered probing periods as outlined in the following.

Concerning the ratio and absolute difference of the estimated availability and the real availability, the subfigures of Figure 8.11 depict the corresponding results of the evaluation. These results also reflect the observations made before. A probing period of 4s underestimates the real availability in general (cf. Figure 8.11a) while an 8s probing period leads to an overestimation of the real availability (cf. Figure 8.11c). Again, when using a 6s probing period, the estimated availability is very close to the real availability (cf. Figure 8.11b). In detail, a probing period of 4s underestimates the real availability by at most 1% on average given a sample size greater than 30 while an 8s probing period overestimates the real availability by at most 1.5% on average at similar sample sizes. The 6s probing period shows an overall deviation from the real availability of less than 0.5% on average. These ratios translate into nearly similar absolute values of additional or less percent in availability in case of an uptime guarantee of 90% (cf. Figures 8.11d to 8.11f).

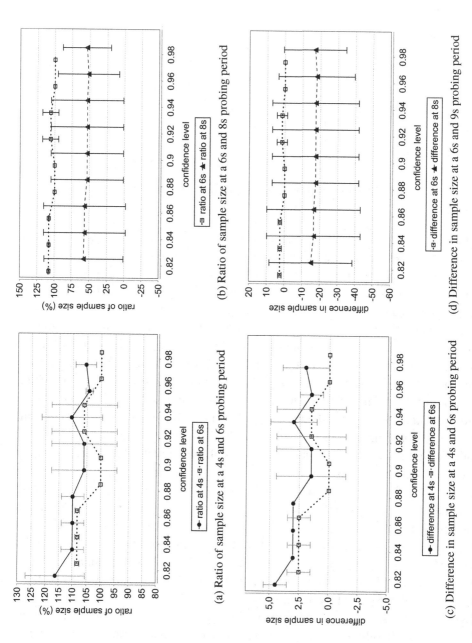

Figure 8.10: Ratio and absolute difference of the required sample size and the exact sample size at 90% uptime guarantee

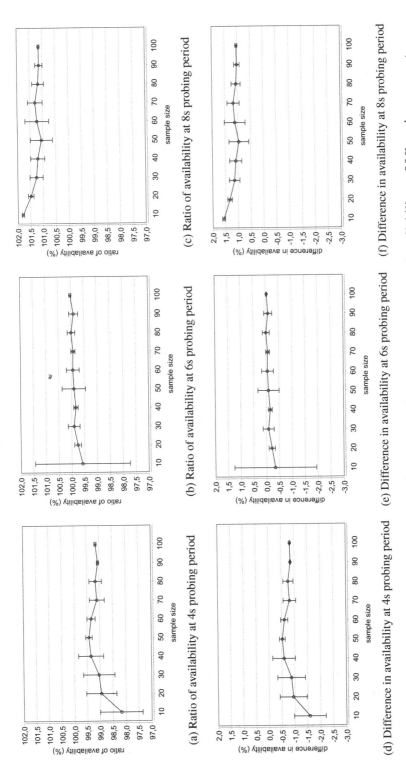

Figure 8.11: Ratio and absolute difference of the estimated availability and the real availability at 90% uptime guarantee

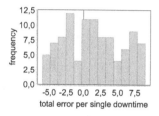 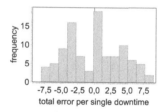 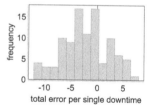

(a) Error at 4s probing period   (b) Error at 6s probing period   (c) Error at 8s probing period

Figure 8.12: Error per single downtime for different probing periods ($A_{SLA} = 90\%$)

All in all, the achieved results confirm the accuracy of our monitoring approach. At higher monitoring frequencies, such as 6s or 4s probing periods, the overall deviation from the real availability is at most 1% for all the monitoring traces. Hence, the estimated availability only deviates from the real availability to a small extent.

Basically, all monitoring traces tend to approach the real availability and, thus, the negotiated uptime guarantee on the long run given that the observed cloud service adheres to the negotiated uptime guarantee. However, depending on the utilized monitoring frequency different probing errors occur, which affect the difference of the estimated availability from the real availability. The aforementioned results reveal that although the resulting point estimates in availability differ depending on the utilized monitoring frequency, the point estimates still allow to verify the adherence to the negotiated uptime guarantee at a certain confidence level.

According to our mathematical model in Section 6.2.3, the probing error decreases with an increasing monitoring frequency, i.e., smaller probing periods permit to lower the difference between the estimated availability and the real availability. While the results of the evaluation basically confirm this relation regarding a decrease of the probing period from 8s to 6s or from 8s to 4s, the probing error slightly increases when the probing period is decreased from 6s to 4s. In order to explore this behavior, we have compiled histograms showing the empirical frequencies of the different values that occur with respect to the total error per single downtime at different probing periods. The histograms are depicted in Figure 8.12 and correspond to the monitoring traces obtained for one selected real trace. As it can be deduced from the histograms the negative and positive deviations from the real downtime intervals are not balanced, i.e., so that they (nearly) add up to zero, over the whole trace for all the considered probing periods. Specifically, a total balance is nearly achieved in case of a 6s probing period, which explains the close approximation of the real availability throughout the measurements. In addition, the histograms reveal the imbalance of the total error when switching from a probing period of 6s to 4s or from 6s to 8s, which explains the underestimation and overestimation of the real availability in these cases. Regarding our mathematical model, we have claimed that the total errors per single downtime E_j^R (or uptime E_i^F) follow a triangular distribution. However, the histograms only approximately show a triangular distribution. The best approximation is achieved in case of an 8s probing period (cf. Figure 8.12c) but the negative and positive deviations are still imbalanced. That imbalance is caused by the fact that we encounter a minimum downtime $R_{min} = 10s$ in our evaluation, which can arise in practice since systems exhibit minimum recovery times of the order of seconds. However, in case of the existence of a minimum downtime R_{min}, the errors made before a downtime E_j^{Rb} and after a downtime E_j^{Ra} are not uniformly distributed anymore. Nevertheless, we approximate their distribution by a uniform distribution in our mathematical model, which results in a certain error, referred to as E^X in the following. Due to this error E^X the sum E_j^R of the error made before a downtime E_j^{Rb} and after a downtime E_j^{Ra} only approximately follows a triangular distribution. Although the results of the evaluation reveal that our mathematical model still constitutes a good approximation, the incorporation of the error E^X into our mathematical model may be part of future work in order further to increase the accuracy of our approach.

The results of our evaluation concerning an uptime guarantee of 80% basically confirm the results achieved with regard to an uptime guarantee of 90%. In detail, regarding the ratio and difference in sample size (cf. Figure 8.13) a probing period of 4s also requires a higher number of up to 5 additional samples in order to achieve the same confidence level in contrast to an approach without making any probing error. Again, the sample size required in case of the 6s monitoring traces is very close to the exact sample size but still deviates from that exact sample size by around 2 samples less in case of a confidence level of 0.96 (cf. Figure 8.13c). In case of a probing period of 8s a reduction of the required sample size by around 10 samples is sufficient on average for achieving similar confidence levels (cf. Figure 8.13d). Concerning the ratio and difference of the estimated availability and the real availability, a 4s probing period results in an underestimation of the real availability by up to 2% on average given a sample size greater than 30 and an 8s probing period overestimates the real availability by up to 3% on average given similar sample sizes (cf. Figures 8.14a and 8.14c). Also in case of an uptime guarantee of 80% the best results are achieved when utilizing a probing period of 6s (cf. Figure 8.14b). In comparison with the results obtained given an uptime guarantee of 90% the relative and absolute differences between the estimated availability and the real availability are larger in case of a 4s and an 8s probing period. This is due to the fact that the MTTR is the same in both test cases but the MTTF is smaller in case of an uptime guarantee of 80%. Hence, a similar probing error has a larger impact on a smaller MTTF than on a larger MTTF, which results in larger deviations from the real availability. In detail, a 4s probing period underestimates the real availability to a larger extent while an 8s probing period results in a larger overestimation. That observation also gives an explanation for the differences in sample size in case of an uptime guarantee of 80% in comparison with the results obtained given an uptime guarantee of 90% as presented above.

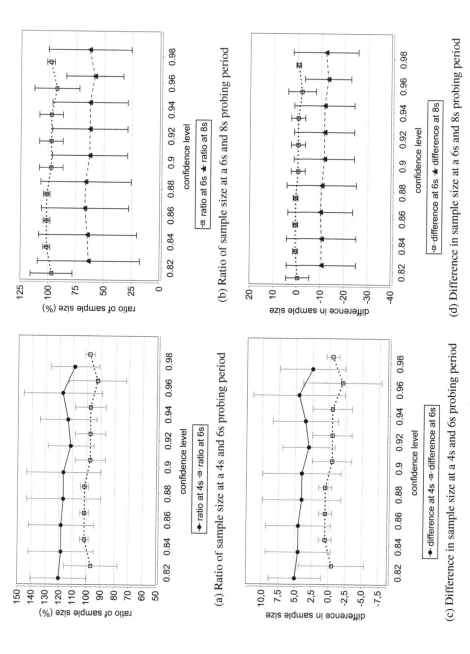

(a) Ratio of sample size at a 4s and 6s probing period

(b) Ratio of sample size at a 6s and 8s probing period

(c) Difference in sample size at a 4s and 6s probing period

(d) Difference in sample size at a 6s and 8s probing period

Figure 8.13: Ratio and absolute difference of the required sample size and the exact sample size at 80% uptime guarantee

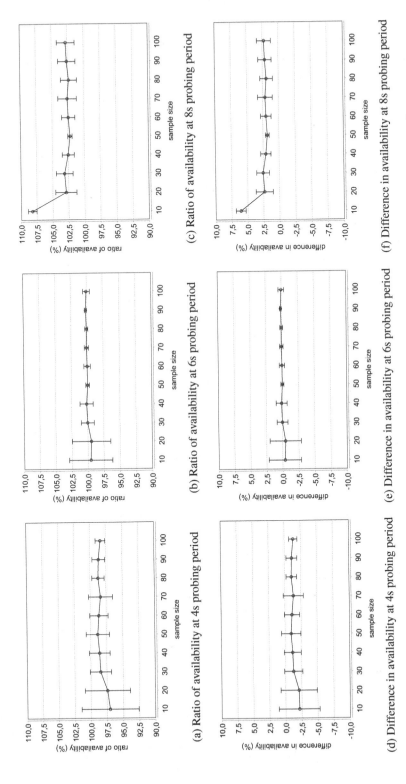

(a) Ratio of availability at 4s probing period   (b) Ratio of availability at 6s probing period   (c) Ratio of availability at 8s probing period

(d) Difference in availability at 4s probing period   (e) Difference in availability at 6s probing period   (f) Difference in availability at 8s probing period

Figure 8.14: Ratio and absolute difference of the estimated availability and the real availability at 80% uptime guarantee

In detail, the differences in sample size achieved in case of an uptime guarantee of 80% show that a smaller number of samples is required in order to achieve a similar confidence level when monitoring tasks are conducted at an 8s probing period and that a larger number of samples is required in case of 4s monitoring tasks compared to the results in case of an uptime guarantee of 90%. This is due to the fact that the overestimation at an 8s probing period as well as the underestimation at a 4s probing period both increase as stated above. Hence, a "better" availability is estimated in the first case while a "worse" availability is deduced in the second case so that a lower or higher number of samples is required accordingly. For these reasons, the selection of an adequate monitoring frequency must not only be conducted with regard to the negotiated uptime guarantee, i.e., the resulting error made compared to the maximum overall downtime to be observed, but also the MTTR and MTTF, specifically their ratio, must be taken into account. According to the results discussed above, a similar monitoring frequency will result in a decreased accuracy if the MTTF decreases given that the MTTR remains the same. In these cases it may be reasonable further to increase the monitoring frequency in order to achieve the same level of accuracy.

Regarding limitations of our evaluation, we have assumed that all components in the system are working correctly, except for the cloud service to be observed. In doing so, we have focused on the main objective of our monitoring approach to achieve accurate monitoring results at a certain confidence level and to determine an appropriate monitoring frequency and required sample size for this purpose. However, in practice, further aspects exist, which have an influence on the accuracy of the monitoring results, such as the properties of the underlying network. In this regard, our mathematical model can serve as approximation in the first instance and the probability distributions assumed in the current model can be replaced by other distributions that account for these additional aspects in future work.

8.4 Robust Monitor Placement - CSLAB-Loc.KOM

In this section, we present the setup and results of the evaluation of our strategies for monitor placement CSLAB-Loc.KOM. In detail, Section 8.4.1 describes the utilized optimization framework, Section 8.4.2 elaborates on the experimental setup, and Section 8.4.3 presents the results of our evaluation in conjunction with a thorough discussion.

8.4.1 Optimization Framework

For the evaluation, we have prototypically implemented our four strategies for monitor placement CSLAB-Loc-Exa.KOM, CSLAB-Loc-Start.KOM, CSLAB-Loc-Imp.KOM, and CSLAB-Loc-Rand.KOM in the Java programming language. In order to obtain an exact solution for our ILP-based approach CSLAB-Loc-Exa.KOM, we have utilized

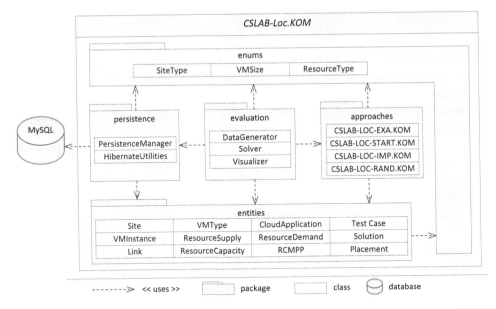

Figure 8.15: Optimization framework of our placement strategies CSLAB-Loc.KOM

the commercial solver framework IBM ILOG CPLEX[10] and the JavaILP framework[11] in order to be able to specify the corresponding optimization model in Java. An overview of our optimization framework is provided in Figure 8.15. It comprises the Java packages and classes that have been implemented and a MySQL[12] database for storing the generated problem instances as well as the results. In order to map Java classes and objects to tables and records in the database, the Java persistence framework Hibernate[13] has been used. The implemented Java packages of our optimization framework and the overall interaction are briefly described in the following.

- *evaluation:* This package contains all the classes required to manage the evaluation. In detail, the class *DataGenerator* is used to randomly generate RCMPP instances (cf. Chapter 7) for our considered test cases, which are then stored in the database using the *persistence* package. The *Solver* class constitutes the main class for conducting the evaluation. It is responsible for loading RCMPP instances associated with a certain test case from the database, for invoking a certain placement strategy in order to solve these problem instances, and to store the final results in the database. For plot generation, the class *Visualizer* has been implemented. Similar to the evaluations of our other major contributions, we have utilized the JFreeChart library[14] for plot generation.

---

10   http://www.ibm.com/software/integration/optimization/cplex-optimizer
11   http://javailp.sourceforge.net/
12   http://www.mysql.com/
13   http://hibernate.org/
14   http://www.jfree.org/jfreechart/

- *approaches:* Our strategies for monitor placement are contained in this package. While our exact solution approach implemented in the class *CSLAB-Loc-EXA.KOM* utilizes the solver framework IBM ILOG CPLEX in order to compute an exact solution, the other three placement strategies constitute heuristic solution approaches. In contrast to CSLAB-Loc-Exa.KOM, the heuristics do not depend on an external solver framework, so that their logic is encapsulated within the respective Java class.

- *entities:* This package comprises the basic entities required to model a *TestCase*, an *RCMPP* instance, a corresponding *Solution*, which is obtained by applying a certain placement strategy, as well as an associated *Placement*. In order to model an RCMPP instance in turn, further classes are required. Each monitoring unit is to be placed on a certain *VMInstance* located at a certain data center *Site* and utilizes a certain *Link* in order to monitor a specific *CloudApplication*. Such a monitoring unit has a certain *ResourceDemand* and each VM candidate for monitor placement is of a certain *VMType* exhibiting a certain *ResourceCapacity* in general and a certain remaining *ResourceSupply* after monitoring units have been placed on that VM.

- *enums:* As already stated in Section 8.2.1, an *enum* defines a special data type in Java that is used to hold values from a predefined set of constants. This package defines the enums *SiteType* indicating a broker or provider site, *VMSize* specifying the available VM types, and *ResourceType* defining the different resource types to be considered in the optimization.

- *persistence:* The classes for mapping Java classes and objects to tables and records in the MySQL database are defined in this package. While the class *HibernateUtilities* is used for configuration purposes of the Hibernate framework, the class *PersistenceManager* provides methods for storing and loading test cases, RCMPP instances, and corresponding solutions.

8.4.2 Experimental Setup

Similar to the evaluation of our negotiation mechanism CSLAB-Neg.KOM, we explore the impact of each independent variable on the dependent variables separately, i.e., we follow a one-factor-at-a-time design [20]. As already mentioned in Section 8.1.3, we consider the two dependent variables *computation time* and *solution quality* expressed in terms of the maximum expected overall downtime of the monitoring units. Furthermore, regarding the independent variables, we analyze the impact of the *total number of data center sites* on the provider side and the broker side, the *number of VMs* running on each site, the *number of cloud applications* co-located on each VM, and the *redundancy factor* for placing monitoring units. The values for the independent

Table 8.5: Independent variables and values used in the evaluation

Independent Variable	Symbol and Values
Number of sites:	$|S'|, |S''| \in \{\underline{2}, 3, 4, 5\}$
Number of VMs:	$|V_s| \in \{3, 4, \underline{5}, 6, 7\}$
Number of applications:	$|C_{s'v'}| \in \{\underline{1}, 2, 3\}$
Redundancy factor:	$rf_{s'v'c} \in \{2, \underline{3}, 4\}$

Table 8.6: Parameters for the generation of the RCMPP instances

Parameter	Symbol and Values
VM Resource Capacity:	$rc_{svr} \in \{100\%, 150\%, 225\%\}$
VM Load:	$rl_{svr} \sim N(0.6, 0.2)$
Monitoring Unit Resource Demand:	$rd_{s'v'cr} \in \{3\%, 12\%, 25\%\}$
Broker VM Reliability:	$p_{s''v''} \sim N(0.99, 0.02)$
Provider VM Reliability:	$p_{s'v'} \sim N(0.999, 0.02)$
Broker to Provider Link Reliability:	$p_{l(s''v'' \rightleftharpoons s'v')} \sim U(\text{packet loss EU} \leftrightarrow \text{US})$
Provider to Provider Link Reliability:	$p_{l(s'v' \rightleftharpoons s'v')} \sim U(\text{packet loss US} \leftrightarrow \text{US})$

variables used in the evaluation are listed in Table 8.5. As it can be seen from the table, the evaluation comprises 15 different test cases in total. For each of these test cases, we have randomly generated 100 different problems, i.e., RCMPP instances. All problems have been created by incorporating realistic data as described in the following.

The utilized VM types have been created based on the specification of Amazon's EC2 general purpose M3 instance types[15], namely m3.medium, m3.large, and, m3.xlarge exhibiting 1, 2, and, 4 virtual CPUs (vCPUs), respectively. In order to derive the maximum CPU capacity rc_{svr} of each VM type, the application speedup depending on the number of cores (with 1 vCPU $\cong 100\%$) has been considered. The speedup has been subject of a performance evaluation of different processor types conducted by Barker et al. in [10]. In our evaluation, we have exemplarily considered CPU as resource type, since CPU demand turned out to be a major determinant when executing different monitoring tasks in our early experiments. The initial remaining resource supply rs_{svr} of each VM before placing any monitoring units has been determined after generating a synthetic workload rl_{svr} for each VM based on the work by [182]. Among the monitoring tasks explored in our early experiments ranging from a simple http get request up to a complex task comprising a file download, we have selected three types of monitoring tasks with different CPU requirements $rd_{s'v'cr}$, each corresponding to a specific application type to be observed in our evaluation. The reliabilities of the VMs on the broker and the provider side have been drawn from normal distributions with

---

15   https://aws.amazon.com/ec2/instance-types

means and variances derived from the SLAs and corresponding penalty classes from Amazon EC2[16] and Rackspace[17]. Normal distributions are assumed since the uptime guarantees constitute the most probable values while the probability of deviating from these uptime guarantees decreases with an increasing amount of deviation in both directions. In order to model link reliability, packet loss statistics from the PingER project[18] have been used.

In detail, monthly packet loss statistics of Internet links between the United States and Europe have been used for specifying the reliabilities of the links connecting the broker and the provider side VMs and monthly packet loss statistics of Internet links within the United States have been used for defining the reliabilities of the links connecting two VMs on the provider side. In this regard, we exemplarily consider a provider operating several data centers across the United States and a broker running several data centers at different locations in Europe. From the two resulting lists of packet loss values, different values have been drawn based on a uniform distribution in order to model a varying link reliability throughout the different test cases. Recall that we assume that our envisaged broker is not aware of the underlying network topologies of the ISP and the cloud provider's data centers and therefore, can only estimate the end-to-end performance between two given VMs by applying traditional network measurement tools (cf. Section 7.2). For these reasons, links representing end-to-end connections have been created between each given pair of VMs in all of our test cases.

Each of the 100 randomly generated problems has been solved by applying our four placement strategies CSLAB-Loc-Exa.KOM, CSLAB-Loc-Start.KOM, CSLAB-Loc-Imp.KOM, and CSLAB-Loc-Rand.KOM in all of our 15 test cases. As already mentioned, we conduct a parameter evaluation and a comparative evaluation. For the latter, we have added the random placement approach CSLAB-Loc-Rand.KOM, since it can be considered to be a baseline in terms of computation time. Furthermore, it allows pointing out the loss in solution quality over a more sophisticated approach. Basically, the random placement approach randomly selects a monitoring unit to be placed and a corresponding location while only considering adherence with all the constraints. In addition, we compare our heuristic solution approaches with the performance of our exact solution approach CSLAB-Loc-Exa.KOM, which constitutes a baseline in terms of solution quality. In case of the exact solution approach, we have set a timeout of 2400 seconds (i.e, 40 minutes) for solving a single problem. This is due to the fact that CSLAB-Loc-Exa.KOM is NP-hard and, thus, large RCMPP instances cannot be deterministically solved in polynomial time and small problems already require a large amount of time to be solved. Concerning our heuristic approach CSLAB-Loc-Imp.KOM, we have set the maximum number of iterations of the Tabu-

---

[16]   https://aws.amazon.com/de/ec2/sla/
[17]   https://www.rackspace.com/information/legal/cloud/sla
[18]   http://www-iepm.slac.stanford.edu/pinger/

Search-based improvement procedure to 100 and we have used a tabu tenure of 10. Both values have turned out to be the most promising within the scope of our former experiments. Similar to CSLAB-Neg.KOM, a laptop with an Intel Core i5 CPU with 2.40 GHz and 6 GB RAM running Microsoft Windows 7 (64 Bit) as operating system has been used for conducting all the experiments.

8.4.3 Results and Discussion

The results of the parameter evaluation and the comparative evaluation are jointly depicted in each of Figures 8.16 to 8.18 with respect to our four placement strategies CSLAB-Loc-Exa.KOM, CSLAB-Loc-Start.KOM, CSLAB-Loc-Imp.KOM, and CSLAB-Loc-Rand.KOM. While Figure 8.16 shows the absolute computation times, Figures 8.17 and 8.18 depict the solution quality expressed in terms of the corresponding maximum expected overall downtime of the monitoring units on a yearly basis (cf. Section 8.1.3). In all of the figures, the confidence intervals at a confidence level of 95% are provided.

Computation Time   Concerning the absolute computation times, Figure 8.16 is further divided into four different subfigures, each showing the impact of one of the four independent variables. Please note the logarithmic scale in each of these subfigures. As it can be deduced from Figure 8.16a, the exact solution approach CSLAB-Loc-Exa.KOM shows an exponential growth of the computation times from 100 ms up to more than 100000 ms with an increasing *number of data center sites* on the provider side and the broker side. This effect is most pronounced when the *number of cloud applications* co-located on each VM increases from 1 to 2 (cf. Figure 8.16c). However, an increase in the *redundancy factor* for placing monitoring units has considerably less influence on the computation times when utilizing the exact solution approach. This also applies to the other three solution approaches and is due to the fact that although the number of monitoring units to be placed increases, the overall number of options for placing a monitoring unit stays the same. All in all, the results of the evaluation underline the limited applicability of the exact solution approach in practice. Although small problem sizes are considered in this evaluation, the exponential growth already results in large computation times in comparison with the other solution approaches. This emphasizes the need for developing heuristic solution approaches, which trade solution quality against computation time.

The random placement approach CSLAB-Loc-Rand.KOM exhibits the overall smallest computation times. Nonetheless, serving as a baseline it can be deduced from Figure 8.16 that our Greedy approach CSLAB-Loc-Start.KOM is close to the computation times of the random placement approach. Also in case of a total number of 10 data center sites (i.e., 5 on the provider and 5 on the broker side), CSLAB-Loc-Start.KOM still exhibits computation times less than 10 ms (cf. Figure 8.16a).

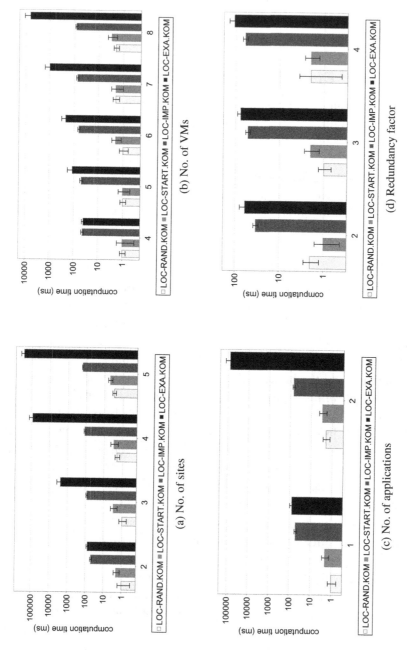

Figure 8.16: Absolute computation times

Summarizing, both approaches show a linear growth in computation time with an increasing problem size and are therefore highly applicable - with respect to computation time - to large-scale problems in practice. In comparison with the other solution approaches, our second Tabu Search-based heuristic CSLAB-Loc-Imp.KOM yields smaller computation times than the exact placement approach, but exceeds the computation times of CSLAB-Loc-Start.KOMand CSLAB-Loc-Rand.KOM. However, CSLAB-Loc-Imp.KOM also exhibits a linear growth in computation time in contrast to the exact approach. All in all, CSLAB-Loc-Imp.KOM is able to already reduce the computation times of the exact approach by around 99% in case of 7 VMs running on each of 4 data center sites in total (cf. Figure 8.16b) and by more than 99.9% in case of 10 data center sites and 5 VMs deployed on each site (cf. Figure 8.16a).

Although the exact solution approach performs worst with respect to computation time, it constitutes a baseline for assessing the solution quality of our heuristic approaches as discussed in the following.

Solution Quality The results concerning the solution quality are illustrated in Figures 8.17 and 8.18. When using CSLAB-Loc-Rand.KOM, the worst overall downtime (on a yearly basis) of the monitoring units ranges from up to more than 9.7 hours (35.000 s) in the worst case with a redundancy factor of 2 (cf. Figure 8.17d) over around 13 minutes (800 s) if the redundancy factor is increased to 3 (cf. Figure 8.17a) down to around 20 s in case of a redundancy factor of 4 (cf. Figure 8.17d). Although the overall downtime of the monitoring units can be further decreased by increasing the redundancy factor, as expected, a higher level of redundancy will be charged with higher costs in practice. Hence, a redundancy factor of 2 or 3 will be more likely in practice than a redundancy factor of 4 in terms of costs. Despite the lower costs incurred at a redundancy factor of 2, the high downtimes obtained when conducting a random placement cannot be considered to be acceptable when business critical applications are involved. In case of having an uptime guarantee of, e.g., 99.95%, similar to Amazon EC2, an overall downtime of the corresponding cloud service of not more than around 4.5 hours is allowed on a yearly basis. Hence, the monitoring units themselves would exhibit nearly twice as much downtime in the worst case than the maximum amount of downtime to be monitored, assuming that the overall uptime of the respective cloud service matches the uptime guarantee. These results achieved by the random placement approach CSLAB-Loc-Rand.KOM, i.e., without performing any optimization, emphasize the need for developing more sophisticated placement approaches. As it can be deduced from Figure 8.17, our exact solution approach CSLAB-Loc-Exa.KOM as well as our two heuristic approaches CSLAB-Loc-Start.KOM and CSLAB-Loc-Imp.KOM are all able further to improve the solution quality to a large extent compared to the random placement approach CSLAB-Loc-Rand.KOM.

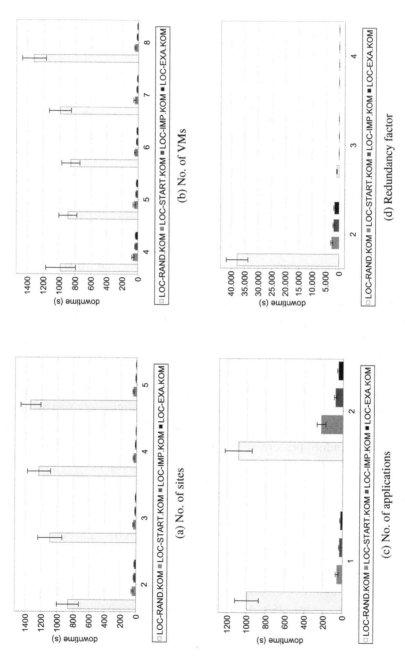

Figure 8.17: Solution quality in terms of downtime (on a yearly basis). For a magnified view please look at Figure 8.18.

Since the differences between the first three approaches can hardly be recognized from Figure 8.17, a magnified view of the results with respect to the solution quality is provided in Figure 8.18. In terms of solution quality, our Greedy heuristic CSLAB-Loc-Start.KOM
shows the second highest overall downtime of the monitoring units of around 45 minutes (2700 s) in case of a redundancy factor of 2 (cf. Figure 8.18d, note the logarithmic scale). However, in comparison with the random placement approach, this already constitutes a decrease in downtime of around 92%. Nevertheless, CSLAB-Loc-Start.KOM thereby still exceeds the downtimes of around 1600 s achieved by the exact approach CSLAB-Loc-Exa.KOM by around 68%. When applying our Tabu Search-based heuristic CSLAB-Loc-Imp.KOM, the overall downtime of the monitoring units further decreases to around 1900 s in case of a redundancy factor of 2, i.e., only adds up around 19% of downtime compared to the exact solution approach CSLAB-Loc-Exa.KOM. However, in case of an uptime guarantee of 99.95%, the results achieved by our heuristic approaches as well as the exact solution approach still make up 9.88% to 16.67% of downtime in comparison to the maximum expected downtime of the cloud service. By increasing the redundancy factor up to 3, the downtime of the monitoring units can be further decreased to 50 s when using CSLAB-Loc-Start.KOM, 25 s when using CSLAB-Loc-Imp.KOM, and 18 s when using CSLAB-Loc-Exa.KOM. These results constitute reductions in downtime of around 94%, 97%, and 98% in comparison with the random placement approach CSLAB-Loc-Rand.KOM. The results also reveal, that a redundancy factor of 3 is more suitable for monitoring an uptime guarantee of 99.95%, resulting in at most 0.3% downtime of the monitoring units compared to the maximum expected downtime of 4.5 hours of the cloud service.

Figures 8.17a to 8.17c and 8.18a to 8.18c all depict results at a redundancy factor of 3. As it can be deduced from Figures 8.17a and 8.17b, the solution quality slightly decreases when increasing the number of sites from 2 to 4 or the number of VMs from 4 to 8 in case of conducting a random placement. In contrast, the solution quality slightly increases with an increasing number of sites or VMs when applying our heuristic CSLAB-Loc-Imp.KOM or the exact solution approach CSLAB-Loc-Exa.KOM. These effects are due to the fact that the number of options for placement grows slightly faster than the number of monitoring units to be placed when increasing the number of sites or VMs while keeping the other parameters fixed. Consequently, the probability that the random placement approach selects a more inadequate location increases while the other optimization-based approaches obtain more options to search for an improvement. However, the solution quality decreases for all approaches with an increasing number of applications co-located on each VM (on the provider side). This is due to the fact that the number of monitoring units to be placed doubles while the number of options for placing monitoring units of each application remains the same. In addition, an increase in the number of applications results in an increased complexity for solving the corresponding problems, since more monitoring units

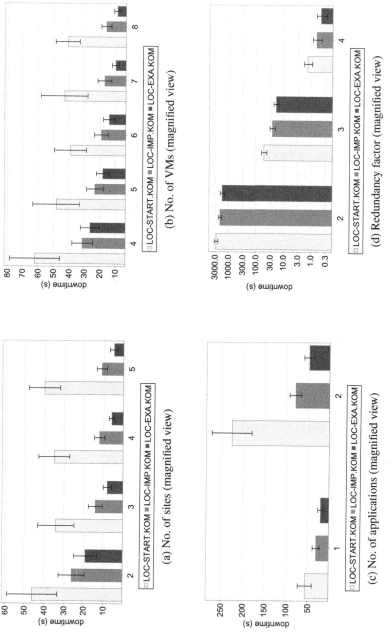

Figure 8.18: Solution quality in terms of downtime (on a yearly basis) - magnified views

have to be placed and the available resources become more sparse when co-locating monitoring units on the same VM. This effect also explains the large increase in computation time of the exact solution approach in Figure 8.16c when increasing the number of applications from 1 to 2.

Finally, when using a redundancy factor of 4, the overall downtime of the monitoring units drops below 1 s (cf. Figure 8.18d). Such a high redundancy factor would be appropriate if we assume a more stringent uptime guarantee than 99.95% in the order of, e.g., "five nines" (i.e., 99.999%), which corresponds to not more than around 5 minutes downtime per year.

Concerning potential shortcomings of our evaluation, we have only considered very small problems in the experiments. While this permits preventing vast time intervals for completing the evaluation due to the exponential time complexity of our exact approach, the results cannot be necessarily generalized to large-scale problems in practice. Nevertheless, the results are appropriate to demonstrate the exponential time complexity of our exact approach and the relative improvements achieved by our heuristic approaches. Due to the consistent behavior of the results with regard to solution quality and computation time, we assume that similar results will also be achieved in case of larger problem sizes.

8.5 Summary

In this chapter, we have presented the evaluation and discussed the corresponding results of our three major contributions in this thesis. The main findings from the discussion of the results are summarized in the following.

Concerning our negotiation mechanism CSLAB-Neg.KOM, the results of the evaluation show that our negotiation mechanism is able to approach Pareto-efficient outcomes. In detail, a reduction of the distance to the Pareto frontier up to a remaining distance of 0.62% on average could be achieved in the best case on the consumer side and of 0.83% on average on the provider side. In doing so, our negotiation mechanism permits an improvement of up to 2.68% to be achieved on average on the consumer side and of 2.88% to be achieved on the provider side compared to a pure Alternate-Offers-based approach. This translates into considerable improvements with regard to the QoS parameters by around, e.g., 1 hour less of monthly downtime in conjunction with 200 ms less execution time. Note that these improvements can be achieved by applying our negotiation mechanism without making any of the negotiating parties worse-off and that existing approaches fail to take that opportunity.

The evaluation also confirms the scalability of CSLAB-Neg.KOM. With an increasing number of providers, the number of exchanged messages and the execution time both grow linearly. We have further evaluated the additional effort required during the second phase for improving an initial agreement obtained in the first phase. The results reveal that the number of exchanged messages increases by at most 11% and that no significant difference in the execution time occurs up to a patience level of 10 trials. Beyond that patience level the execution time only increases by around 3 ms on average in case of a patience level of 30 trials.

Regarding the evaluation of our monitoring approach CSLAB-Mon.KOM, the results confirm that our monitoring approach allows the achievement of accurate monitoring results. In case of an uptime guarantee of 90%, the estimated availability only deviates from the real availability by 1% or less at lower probing periods of 4s or 6s. Furthermore, the results reveal that our corresponding mathematical model constitutes a good approximation in case of the existence of a minimum downtime. However, since such a minimum downtime is very likely to exist in practice, e.g., due to a minimum recovery time of a system to be observed, it may be of interest to incorporate that minimum downtime into the mathematical model as part of future work. This would further increase the accuracy of our monitoring approach in the presence of a minimum downtime.

Considering our strategies for monitor placement CSLAB-Loc.KOM, the evaluation confirms the limited applicability of the exact solution approach CSLAB-Loc-Exa.KOM to large-scale problems in practice due to the exponential growth in computation time with an increasing problem size. By comparison, the Tabu Search-based heuristic CSLAB-Loc-Imp.KOM can be considered to be the best trade-off when focusing on solution quality, followed by the Greedy heuristic constituting the best trade-off when computation time is more important. All in all, the worst solution quality is obtained from the random placement approach CSLAB-Loc-Rand.KOM, as expected, although exhibiting the best results with respect to computation time. The results of the evaluation also revealed that the solution quality achieved by applying one of the four approaches can be further improved to a certain extent by introducing redundant monitoring units, which is tied, however, to higher costs. In this regard, the solution quality must always be considered in conjunction with the negotiated uptime guarantee to be observed as discussed before. An appropriate redundancy factor can then be chosen accordingly. In doing so, higher costs incurred by a higher redundancy factor will also reflect the severity of a downtime of the cloud service to be monitored.

9 Summary and Outlook

In this thesis, we present and discuss approaches enabling an efficient and reliable control over cloud service performance from an enterprise consumer's perspective. In the following, Section 9.1 summarizes the major contributions of this thesis and Section 9.2 points out some directions for future work.

9.1 Summary

Since the era of cloud computing, arbitrary, highly-configurable computing resources are provided on-demand as a service and delivered over the Internet, similar to utilities such as electricity or water (cf. [25]). However, the shift of responsibility to cloud providers for managing these cloud resources is accompanied by a loss of control for cloud consumers over certain aspects, specifically cloud service performance. Cloud providers address that issue by offering quality guarantees in terms of SLAs. However, these SLAs are mainly static and cannot be considered as being appropriate from a business perspective. Since IT constitutes a major enabler for realizing efficient business processes, cloud service performance is critical. Therefore, appropriate means are required in order to obtain individual SLAs according to individual business constraints. In the context of on-demand cloud service provisioning, a time-consuming process of manual negotiations is not viable, so that an automation of SLA negotiations is required (cf. [215]). Furthermore, solely obtaining quality guarantees is not sufficient since the respective cloud service must also comply with these quality guarantees at runtime. For this purpose, cloud providers usually offer their own monitoring solutions and oblige cloud consumers to report any SLA violations [152]. However, these monitoring solutions do not provide an independent evidence base for SLA violations from a consumer's perspective so that appropriate means for non-provider-based quality assessment are required.

In order to address these issues, we focus on a cloud service broker residing in the market, acting as an intermediary between cloud providers and consumers and also offering services to cloud consumers for automated SLA negotiation and independent SLA monitoring. In doing so, the broker enhances market efficiency by successfully mediating trades, given the large number of providers and consumers and constitutes a trusted third party when performing monitoring tasks (cf. [33]). However, to realize such broker-based SLA negotiation and SLA monitoring provided to enterprise cloud consumers effectively, we have addressed the following three research goals in this thesis (cf. Section 1.3): First of all, when negotiating SLAs, enterprise cloud consumers aim to achieve the best available outcome given their time and cost constraints and will therefore strive for Pareto-efficient agreements. Secondly, the monitoring results provided by the broker must be reliable in order for consumers to be able to verify whether a cloud provider adheres to the agreed quality guarantees or not. Thirdly, reliable monitoring results can only be obtained if the underlying monitoring infrastructure itself is robust and, thus, continues working correctly even in the presence of failures. The aforementioned research goals have been addressed in this thesis by developing the following three major contributions, thereby overcoming the limitations of existing approaches.

Our first major contribution consists of a mechanism for Pareto-efficient concurrent multiple-issue negotiations, referred to as CSLAB-Neg.KOM. In order to create that mechanism, we have proposed a two-phase meta-strategy. During the first phase, denoted as the *Agreement Phase*, the negotiating parties explore their mutual interests with the aim of reaching an initial agreement. The second phase, denoted as the *Trade-Off Phase*, then serves further to improve the initial agreement towards a Pareto-efficient outcome. We have realized that meta-strategy by developing a corresponding negotiation protocol, which constitutes an enhancement of the well-known Alternate-Offers protocol. Our negotiation protocol is applied in conjunction with different negotiation strategies. In detail, we apply existent time-dependent negotiation strategies in the Agreement Phase in order to account for the individual time constraints of the negotiating parties and to concede towards an initial agreement. For the Trade-Off Phase, we have developed a negotiation strategy based on greed, risk, and patience levels of the negotiating parties, referred to as GRiP-based strategy. Following this strategy, a negotiating party determines his/her own MRS from the current agreement in order to identify promising trade-offs that may result in joint gains. Improvement proposals specifying trade-offs between a specific QoS parameter and the price are then made by deviating from the own MRS based on the individual greed and risk level. The maximum number of improvement proposals to be made with respect to each QoS parameter is thereby indicated by the individual patience level. In doing so, negotiating parties become able to approach Pareto-efficient agreements while their privacy and strategic behavior is maintained. These properties overcome the drawbacks of related approaches, in which the negotiating parties have to disclose private information and their proposals depend on the former values proposed by the opponent. In addition, none of the existing approaches has considered a consumer who concurrently negotiates with multiple providers over multiple issues in conjunction with Pareto-efficient outcomes. We have evaluated our negotiation mechanism with respect to its contractual and computational performance by conducting simulations, in which we incorporate realistic data from cloud providers. For the purpose of evaluating the Pareto-efficiency, we have developed an ex post Pareto-efficiency reference model. The model permits a representation of the set of Pareto-optimal solutions, serving as a baseline, to be computed. Concerning the contractual performance, the distance to the Pareto frontier could be reduced in the best case to a remaining distance of 0.62% on average on the consumer side and to 0.83% on average on the provider side. Furthermore, the results revealed that the impact of the selected time-dependent strategies on the success rate of achieving an initial agreement in the first phase, as a prerequisite for the second phase, is negligible in case of deadlines greater than 5 rounds. The success rate then becomes very close to 100%. In comparison to a pure Alternate Offers approach, we are able further to improve an initial agreement in the best case by 2.68% on average on the consumer side and by 2.88% on average on the provider side. Concerning the computational performance, our negotiation mechanism shows a linear growth in the number of exchanged messages as well as in the execution time with an increasing number of providers. These results confirm the scalability of our approach. In order to demonstrate the additional effort required to improve an initial agreement, we have explored the impact of the patience level on the number of exchanged messages and the execution time. From the results, it can be determined that at most 11% of additional messages are exchanged and that there is no significant difference in execution time up to a patience level of 10. When the patience level further increases up to 30, the additional effort is still very low in terms of an additional execution time of around 3 ms on average.

Our second major contribution is an approach for reliable consumer side availability monitoring, denoted as CSLAB-Mon.KOM. We have focused on availability monitoring in this thesis, since the SLAs offered by most of today's cloud providers only comprise some uptime guarantees. However, our approach can be easily enhanced in order to consider other QoS parameters as well. In developing our monitoring approach, we have explicitly considered the reliability of the monitoring results as a major requirement in contrast to related approaches. CSLAB-Mon.KOM meets this requirement in three ways. First of all, it is *location-aware* and, thus, permits differentiating between real SLA violations within the control sphere of a cloud provider and other incidents. This is realized by combining monitoring data from monitoring units deployed on the broker and the provider side. Secondly, our approach is *resource-aware*. It enables the identification of the correct SLA clause of an SLA violation based on the affected resources by combining monitoring tasks on the application-level with VM-level monitoring. Third, CSLAB-Mon.KOM provides monitoring results as *accurate* as required. For the latter, we have created two mathematical models. The first model can be applied at both, design time and runtime. At design time, the first model provides decision support for determining an appropriate monitoring frequency and the required sample size in order to verify adherence to the negotiated uptime guarantee at a certain level of confidence. At runtime, that model permits the level of confidence at which the real availability complies with the agreed uptime guarantee based on the current point estimate to be computed. Our second model provides decision support in the presence of network impairments. Specifically, it allows the calculation of a minimum timeout period in the presence of a certain level of packet loss. The estimated time serves as a guideline for adjusting the monitoring frequency, accordingly. We have evaluated the accuracy of our monitoring approach in testbed experiments based on a prototypical implementation of CSLAB-Mon.KOM in conjunction with a real cloud service. The results confirmed the applicability of our monitoring approach in practice. In detail, given an uptime guarantee of 90%, a deviation from the real availability of 1% or less is achieved at lower probing periods of 4s or 6s.

Our third major contribution comprises strategies for robust cloud monitor placement, summarized under the term CSLAB-Loc.KOM. In this regard, we have introduced the Robust Cloud Monitor Placement Problem (RCMPP). The RCMPP concerns the problem of determining a placement of the monitoring units for a given set of cloud applications on VMs in different data centers on the provider and the broker side that maximizes the robustness of the monitoring infrastructure while considering reliability values of VMs and network links, resource constraints of the VMs, and the desired redundancy factor for monitoring each application. We have formalized the RCMPP as mathematical optimization model resulting in a non-linear, multi-objective optimization problem. In order to enable to obtain an exact solution using off-the-shelf algorithms, we have proposed a set of transformations turning the RCMPP into a linear, single-objective optimization problem. For this purpose, we have adopted a worst-case perspective that minimizes the maximum risk for the monitoring units of each cloud application to fail. The corresponding exact solution approach has been denoted as CSLAB-Loc-Exa.KOM. Due to the exponential time complexity of the exact approach, we have proposed a heuristic approach, referred to as CSLAB-Loc-Start.KOM, that permits large-scale instances of the problem to be solved in practice. This heuristic constitutes an intuitive Greedy procedure, which is inspired from the steepest ascent approach. In line with that approach, our heuristic selects that location for a monitoring unit to be placed in each step that exhibits the maximum reliability without violating any of the constraints. In addition, we have developed a heuristic improvement approach, denoted as CSLAB-Loc-Imp.KOM, that permits further improvement of the solution quality of an (arbitrary) initial solution, obtained by, e.g., applying CSLAB-Loc-Start.KOM. Our improvement procedure CSLAB-Loc-Imp.KOM follows the well-known meta-heuristic Tabu Search and exploits the similarity of the RCMPP with the multi-resource agent bottleneck generalized assignment problem by building the initial neighborhood around the bottleneck application in each iteration. We have evaluated the solution quality and computational performance of our three placement strategies. In terms of solution quality, the results obtained from the exact approach CSLAB-Loc-Exa.KOM have been used as a baseline for assessing our two heuristic approaches. In addition, we have implemented a random placement approach, referred to as CSLAB-Loc-Rand.KOM in order to obtain a baseline in terms of computation time. The RCMPP instances considered in different test cases in the evaluation have been generated based on realistic data from cloud providers and Internet performance statistics. Concerning computation time, the results obtained from the evaluation confirmed the exponential complexity of the exact solution approach as well as the polynomial time complexity of the two heuristics. In detail, while CSLAB-Loc-Start.KOM is nearly close to the computation times of CSLAB-Loc-Rand.KOM, CSLAB-Loc-Imp.KOM is still able to reduce the computation times of the exact approach by around 99% or more. Concerning solution quality, all our three placement approaches achieve reductions in downtime of 92% or more in comparison to a random placement approach. CSLAB-Loc-Imp.KOM thereby only exhibits 19% of additional downtime compared to the exact solution approach CSLAB-Loc-Exa.KOM in case of a redundancy factor of 2. When further increasing the redundancy factor up to 3, the downtimes achieved with all our three placement approaches drop below one minute and further decrease to downtimes in the order of ms in case of a redundancy factor of 4.

Having developed approaches for automated Pareto-efficient SLA negotiation and reliable independent SLA monitoring in conjunction with strategies for robust monitor placement in the scope of a broker-based SLM, this thesis contributes to a foundation for market-based cloud service provisioning. By approaching our resulting SLM broker CSLAB.KOM in the market, cloud consumers become able to obtain individual quality guarantees efficiently according to their specific business constraints based on CSLAB-Neg.KOM. In addition, they obtain reliable means for verifying whether the prior negotiated guarantees are maintained by the cloud providers at runtime based on a non-provider-based assessment of cloud service quality provided by CSLAB-Mon.KOM in conjunction with a robust monitor placement achieved based on CSLAB-Loc.KOM.

9.2 Outlook

In this thesis, we have made three major contributions towards enabling an efficient and reliable control over cloud service performance from an enterprise consumer's perspective and a further step towards market-based cloud service provisioning. However, further potential for research still remains in this area. In this regard, our contributions constitute the foundation for future research work in several directions as discussed in the following.

Concerning our negotiation mechanism CSLAB-Neg.KOM, we have considered linear additive utility functions in this thesis. However, other types of utility functions could also be explored. This would contribute to a broader coverage of different consumer and provider preferences and a generalization of our negotiation approach. Further research could also focus on the consideration of data obtained from monitoring within subsequent SLA (re-)negotiations. Brokers, acting as intermediaries, could exploit their information obtained from different measurements in order to establish a ranking of recommended cloud providers and/or services. In this regard, a broker could also incorporate the consumers' experience (cf. [33]). Such an approach would extend the two SLM activities considered in this thesis towards a full control loop over cloud service performance.

With regard to our monitoring approach CSLAB-Mon.KOM, our second mathematical model provides decision support for choosing an adequate monitoring frequency in the presence of a certain level of packet loss. In this regard, the development of a mechanism for automatically adjusting the monitoring frequency at runtime accordingly could be a relevant extension of our work. For this purpose, prediction models could be developed based on, e.g, different daytimes. By developing such an adaptation mechanism, the practical applicability of our approach could be improved. Another aspect that could be of interest in future work concerns the combination of our monitoring capabilities with other network diagnostic facilities such as traceroute. This may facilitate the identification of incidents in the network and increase the location-awareness of our approach.

Regarding CSLAB-Loc.KOM, we have developed different strategies for monitor placement given a set of cloud applications to be monitored. Although our strategies are applicable at design-time and runtime, a total replacement of all monitoring units may be necessary in the worst case at runtime when for example additional cloud applications to be monitored are deployed. Therefore, potential future research may comprise mechanisms for partially adjusting the monitor placements at runtime when surrounding conditions change with the aim of re-establishing an optimal, robust monitoring infrastructure while minimizing the number of required replacements. Furthermore, we have focused on a robust monitor placement in this thesis and only implicitly considered cost constraints by restricting the number of monitoring units to be deployed based on a specified redundancy factor. As a second enhancement, cost models could be explicitly considered and incorporated into the model. This would permit the exploration of the trade-off between the level of redundancy and costs incurred. Finally, a third promising research direction may be the consideration of robust monitor placement strategies to be applied by cloud providers themselves. In this regard, placement strategies could exploit the knowledge of the data center topology. In addition, approaches from the field of software-defined networking could be beneficial for achieving robust monitor data flows.

References

[1] Giuseppe Aceto, Alessio Botta, Walter de Donato, and Antonio Pescapè. Cloud monitoring: A Survey. *Computer Networks*, 57(9):2093–2115, 2013.

[2] Jay Aikat, Jasleen Kaur, F. Donelson Smith, and Kevin Jeffay. Variability in TCP Round-trip Times. In *Proceedings of the 3rd ACM SIGCOMM Conference on Internet Measurement*, pages 279–284, 2003.

[3] Samir Aknine, Suzanne Pinson, and Melvin F. Shakun. An Extended Multi-Agent Negotiation Protocol. *Autonomous Agents and Multi-Agent Systems*, 8 (1):5–45, 2004.

[4] Gustavo Alonso, Fabio Casati, Harumi Kuno, and Vijay Machiraju. *Web Services. Concepts, Architectures and Applications*, chapter Basic Web Services Technology, pages 151–196. Springer, 2004.

[5] Amazon. Amazon ec2 service level agreement, 2013. URL http://aws.amazon.com/ec2-sla/.

[6] Bo An, Victor Lesser, David Irwin, and Michael Zink. Automated Negotiation with Decommitment for Dynamic Resource Allocation in Cloud Computing. In *Proceedings of the 9th International Conference on Autonomous Agents and Multiagent Systems (AAMAS 2010)*, pages 981–988, 2010.

[7] April K. Andreas and J. Cole. Mathematical Programming Algorithms for Two-Path Routing Problems with Reliability Considerations. *INFORMS Journal on Computing*, 20(4):553–564, 2008.

[8] Alain Andrieux, Karl Czajkowski, Asit Dan, Kate Keahey, Heiko Ludwig, Toshiyuki Nakata, Jim Pruyne, John Rofrano, Steve Tuecke, and Ming Xu. Web Services Agreement Specification (WS-Agreement). OGF Recommendation GFD-R-P.107, Open Grid Forum, 2007.

[9] Michael Armbrust, Armando Fox, Rean Griffith, Anthony D. Joseph, Randy Katz, Andy Konwinski, Gunho Lee, David Patterson, Ariel Rabkin, Ion Stoica, and Matei Zaharia. A View of Cloud Computing. *Communications of the ACM (CACM)*, 53(4):50–58, 2010.

[10] Kevin J. Barker, Kei Davis, Adolfy Hoisie, Darren J. Kerbyson, Mike Lang, Scott Pakin, and Jose Carlos Sancho. A Performance Evaluation of the Nehalem Quad-Core Processor for Scientific Computing. *Parallel Processing Letters*, 18 (4):453–469, 2008.

[11] Salman A. Baset. Cloud SLAs: Present and Future. *ACM SIGOPS Operating Systems Review*, 46(2):57–66, July 2012.

[12] Christian Baun, Marcel Kunze, Jens Nimis, and Stefan Tai. *Cloud Computing. Web-basierte dynamische IT-Services*. Springer, 2010.

[13] Yigal Bejerano and Rajeev Rastogi. Robust Monitoring of Link Delays and Faults in IP Networks. In *22nd Annual Joint Conference of the IEEE Computer and Communications Societies (INFOCOM 2003)*, volume 1, pages 134–144, March 2003.

[14] Yigal Bejerano and Rajeev Rastogi. Robust Monitoring of Link Delays and Faults in IP Networks. *IEEE/ACM Transactions on Networking*, 14(5):1092–1103, October 2006.

[15] Rainer Berbner. *Dienstgüteunterstützung für Service-Orientierte Workflows*. PhD thesis, Technische Universität Darmstadt, 2007.

[16] Eyal Bin, Ofer Biran, Odellia Boni, Erez Hadad, Eliot K. Kolodner, Yosef Moatti, and Dean H. Lorenz. Guaranteeing High Availability Goals for Virtual Machine Placement. In *31st International Conference on Distributed Computing Systems (ICDCS)*, pages 700–709, June 2011.

[17] Ken Birman, Gregory Chockler, and Robbert van Renesse. Toward a Cloud Computing Research Agenda. *ACM SIGACT News*, 40(2):68–80, 2009.

[18] André B. Bondi. Characteristics of Scalability and Their Impact on Performance. In *Proceedings of the 2Nd International Workshop on Software and Performance (WOSP '00)*, pages 195–203, 2000.

[19] Roland Böttcher. *IT-Servicemanagement mit ITIL®V3. Einführung, Zusammenfassung und Übersicht der elementaren Empfehlungen*, chapter Service Design, pages 29–79. Heise Zeitschriften Verlag, 2008.

[20] George E. P. Box and J. Stuart Hunter. *Statistics for Experimenters: Design, Innovation, and Discovery*. Wiley, 2nd edition, 2005.

[21] Ivona Brandic, Dejan Music, and Schahram. Service Mediation and Negotiation Bootstrapping as First Achievements Towards Self-adaptable Grid and Cloud Services. In *Proceedings of the 6th International Conference Industry Session on Grids Meets Autonomic Computing (GMAC '09)*, pages 1–8, 2009.

[22] Ernest Brewster, Richard Griffiths, Aidan Lawes, and John Sansbury. *IT Service Management: A Guide for ITIL®V3 Foundation Exam Candidates*, chapter Service Level Management, pages 73–82. British Informatics Society Limited, 2010.

[23] James Broberg, Srikumar Venugopal, and Rajkumar. Market-oriented Grids and Utility Computing: The State-of-the-Artrt and Future Directions. *Journal of Grid Computing*, 6(3):255–276, 2008.

[24] Paul C. Brown. *Implementing SOA: Total Architecture in Practice*, chapter 38: Process Monitoring, pages 591–598. Addison-Wesley, 2008.

[25] Rajkumar Buyya, Chee Shin Yeo, Srikumar Venugopal, James Broberg, and Ivona Brandic. Cloud Computing and Emerging IT Platforms: Vision, Hype, and Reality for Delivering Computing as the 5th Utility. *Future Generation Computer Systems*, 25(6):599–616, 2009.

[26] Rajkumar Buyya, Christian Vecchiola, and S. Thamarai Selvi. *Mastering Cloud Computing. Foundations and Applications Programming*, chapter Introduction, pages 3–28. Elsevier, 2013.

[27] Rajkumar Buyya, Christian Vecchiola, and S. Thamarai Selvi. *Mastering Cloud Computing. Foundations and Applications Programming*, chapter Virtualization, pages 71–109. Elsevier, 2013.

[28] Gion Reto Cantieni, Gianluca Iannaccone, Chadi Barakat, Christophe Diot, and Patrick Thiran. Reformulating the Monitor Placement Problem: Optimal Network-Wide Sampling. In *40th Annual Conference on Information Sciences and Systems*, pages 1725–1731, March 2006.

[29] Neal Cardwell, Stefan Savage, and Thomas Anderson. Modeling TCP Latency. In *Proceedings of the Nineteenth Annual Joint Conference of the IEEE Computer and Communications Societies (INFOCOM 2000)*, volume 3, pages 1742–1751, March 2000.

[30] Michal Chalamish and Sarit Kraus. AutoMed: an Automated Mediator for Multi-Issue Bilateral Negotiations. *Autonomous Agents and Multi-Agent Systems*, 24(3):536–564, 2012.

[31] Antonin Chazalet. Service Level Checking in the Cloud Computing Context. In *Proceedings of the 3rd IEEE International Conference on Cloud Computing*, pages 297–304, 2010.

[32] Antonin Chazalet. Service Level Agreements Compliance Checking in the Cloud Computing. Architectural Pattern, Prototype, and Validation. In *Proceedings of the Fifth International Conference on Software Engineering Advances (ICSEA)*, pages 184–189, 2010.

[33] Soon-Yong Choi, Dale O. Stahl, and Andrew B. Whinston. *The Economics of Electronic Commerce*, chapter 4 Quality Uncertainty and Market Efficiency, pages 137–174. Macmillan Technical Publishing, 1997.

[34] Yang-hua Chu, Sanjay G. Rao, Srinivasan Seshan, and Hui Zhang. Enabling Conferencing Applications on the Internet Using an Overlay Muilticast Architecture. In *Proceedings of the 2001 ACM SIGCOMM Conference on Applications, Technologies, Architectures, and Protocols for Computer Communication*, pages 55–67, 2001.

[35] Cisco. Cisco Global Cloud Index: Forecast and Methodology, 2014-2019. Whitepaper, 2015. URL `http://www.cisco.com/c/en/us/solutions/collateral/service-provider/visual-networking-index-vni/white_paper_c11-520862.pdf`.

[36] Christopher W. Clifton, Deirdre K. Mulligan, and Raghu Ramakrishnan. *Privacy and Technologies of Identity: A Cross-Disciplinary Conversation*, chapter 11. Data Mining and Privacy: An Overview, pages 191–208. Springer, 2006.

[37] Marco Comuzzi, Constantinos Kotsokalis, George Spanoudakis, and Ramin Yahyapour. Establishing and Monitoring SLAs in Complex Service Based Systems. In *IEEE International Conference on Web Services (ICWS)*, pages 783–790, July 2009.

[38] Gheorghe Cosmin, Liviu Dan Şerban, and Cristian Marius Litan. A Framework for Building Intelligent SLA Negotiation Strategies under Time Constraints. In *Proceedings of the 7th International Workshop on Economics of Grids, Clouds, Systems, and Services (GECON'10)*, pages 48–61, 2010.

[39] Les Cottrell, Warren Matthews, and Connie Logg. Tutorial on Internet Monitoring & PingER at SLAC, December 2014.

[40] Dana Crowe and Alec Feinberg, editors. *Design for Reliability*, chapter 8. Reliability Statistics Simplified, pages 8–13. CRC Press, 2001.

[41] CSA and ISACA. Cloud Computing Market Maturity. Study Results, 2012. URL `http://www.isaca.org/Knowledge-Center/Research/Documents/2012-Cloud-Computing-Market-Maturity-Study-Results.pdf`.

[42] Cloud Services Measurement Initiative Consortium (CSMIC). Service Measurement Index Framework Version 2.1, July 2014. URL http://csmic.org/downloads/SMI_Overview_TwoPointOne.pdf.

[43] Jiangbo Dang and Michael N. Huhns. Concurrent Multiple-Issue Negotiation for Internet-based Services. *IEEE Internet Computing*, 10(6):42–49, 2006.

[44] Shirlei Aparecida de Chaves, Carlos Becker Westphall, and Flavio Rodrigo Lamin. SLA Perspective in Security Management for Cloud Computing. In *Sixth International Conference on Networking and Services (ICNS)*, pages 212–217, 2010.

[45] Tharam Dillon, Chen Wu, and Elizabeth Chang. Cloud Computing: Issues and Challenges. In *24th IEEE International Conference on Advanced Information Networking and Applications (AINA)*, pages 27–33, April 2010.

[46] D.J.A. Somefun, E.H. Gerding, and J.A. La Poutré. Efficient Methods for Automated Multi-Issue Negotiation: Negotiating over a Two-Part Tariff. *International Journal of Intelligent Systems*, 21(1):99–119, 2006.

[47] Paul S. Dodd and Chinya V. Ravishankar. Monitoring and Debugging Distributed Real-time Programs. *Software – Practice and Experience*, 22(10): 863–877, October 1992.

[48] R.W. Eglese. Simulated Annealing: A Tool for Operational Research. *European Journal of Operational Research*, 46(3):271–281, 1990.

[49] Erik Elmroth, Fermín Galán Márquez, Daniel Henriksson, and David Perales Ferrera. Accounting and Billing for Federated Cloud Infrastructures. In *Eighth International Conference on Grid and Cooperative Computing (GCC '09)*, pages 268–275, August 2009.

[50] Vincent C. Emeakaroha, Ivona Brandic, Michael Maurer, and Schahram Dustdar. Low Level Metrics to High Level SLAs - LoM2HiS Framework: Bridging the Gap between Monitored Metrics and SLA Parameters in Cloud Environments. In *High Performance Computing and Simulation (HPCS), 2010 International Conference on*, pages 48–54, June 2010.

[51] Vincent C. Emeakaroha, Tiago C. Ferreto, Marco A. S. Netto, Ivona Brandic, and César A.F. De Rose. CASViD: Application Level Monitoring for SLA Violation Detection in Clouds. In *2012 IEEE 36th Annual Computer Software and Applications Conference (COMPSAC)*, pages 499–508, July 2012.

[52] Vincent C. Emeakaroha, Marco A.S. Netto, Rodrigo N. Calheiros, Ivona Brandic, Rajkumar Buyya, and César A.F. De Rose. Towards Autonomic

Detection of SLA Violations in Cloud Infrastructures . *Future Generation Computer Systems*, 28(7):1017–1029, 2012.

[53] Thomas Erl. *Service-Oriented Architecture. Concepts, Technology, and Design* , chapter Introducing SOA, pages 31–70. Prentice Hall, 2005.

[54] Thomas Erl. *Service-Oriented Architecture. Concepts, Technology, and Design* , chapter The Evolution of SOA, pages 71–154. Prentice Hall, 2005.

[55] Thomas Erl. *SOA. Principles of Service Design*, chapter Service-Oriented Computing and SOA, pages 25–66. Prentice Hall, 2008.

[56] Thomas Erl, Zaigham Mahmood, and Ricardo Puttini. *Cloud Computing. Concepts, Technology & Architecture*, chapter Understanding Cloud Computing, pages 25–50. Prentice Hall, 2013.

[57] Thomas Erl, Zaigham Mahmood, and Ricardo Puttini. *Cloud Computing. Concepts, Technology & Architecture*, chapter Cloud-Enabling Technology, pages 79–116. Prentice Hall, 2013.

[58] Peyman Faratin, Carles Sierra, and Nick R. Jennings. Negotiation Decision Functions for Autonomous Agents. *Robotics and Autonomous Systems*, 24 (3–4):159–182, 1998.

[59] Peyman Faratin, Carles Sierra, and Nicholas R. Jennings. Using Similarity Criteria to make Issue Trade-Offs in Automated Negotiations. *Artificial Intelligence*, 142(2):205–237, 2002.

[60] Kaniz Fatema, Vincent C. Emeakaroha, Philip D. Healy, John P. Morrison, and Theo Lynn. A Survey of Cloud Monitoring Tools: Taxonomy, Capabilities and Objectives. *Journal of Parallel and Distributed Computing*, 74(10):2918–2933, 2014.

[61] Shaheen Fatima, Sarit Kraus, and Michael Wooldridge, editors. *Principles of Automated Negotiation*. Cambridge University Press, 2015.

[62] Shaheen S. Fatima, Michael Wooldridge, and Nicholas R. Jennings. Multi-issue Negotiation with Deadlines. *Journal of Artificial Intelligence Research*, 27(1): 381–417, November 2006.

[63] Paul Ferguson and Geoff Huston. *Quality of Service. Delivering QoS on the IInternet and in Corporate Networks*, chapter What is Quality of Service, pages 1–24. John Wiley & Sons, 1998.

[64] Diogo A. B. Fernandes, Liliana F. B. Soares, João V. Gomes, Mário M. Freire, and Pedro R. M. Inácio. Security issues in cloud environments: a survey. *International Journal of Information Security*, 13(2):113–170, 2014.

[65] Roy Thomas Fielding. *Architectural Styles and The Design of Network-based Software Architectures*. PhD thesis, University of California, Irvine, 2000.

[66] E. C. Fieller. The Biological Standardization of Insulin. *Supplement to the Journal of the Royal Statistical Society*, 7(1):1–64, 1940.

[67] E. C. Fieller. "some problems in interval estimation". *Journal of the Royal Statistics Society. Series B (Methodological)*, 16(2):175–185, 1954.

[68] Stephan Fischer. *Towards the Internet of Services: The THESEUS Research Program*, chapter Challenges of the Internet of Services, pages 15–27. Springer, 2014.

[69] Ian Foster and Carl Kesselman. Globus: A Metacomputing Infrastructure Toolkit. *International Journal of Supercomputer Applications*, 11(2):115–128, 1997.

[70] Ian Foster and Carl Kesselman. *The Grid 2*, chapter Concepts and Architecture, pages 37–63. Morgan Kaufmann, second edition, 2004.

[71] Ian Foster, Carl Kesselman, and Steven Tuecke. The Anatomy of the Grid: Enabling Scalable Virtual Organizations. *International Journal of High Performance Computing Applications*, 15(3):200–222, August 2001.

[72] Ian Foster, Yong Zhao, Ioan Raicu, and Shiyong Lu. Cloud Computing and Grid Computing 360-Degree Compared. In *Workshop on Grid Computing Environments (GCE '08)*, pages 1–10, 2008.

[73] Armin Fügenschuh and Alexander Martin. Computational Integer Programming and Cutting Planes. In Karen Aardal, George L. Nemhauser, and Robert Weismantel, editors, *Discrete Optimization*, volume 12 of *Handbooks in Operations Research and Management Science*, pages 69–121. Elsevier, 2005.

[74] José María García, David Ruiz, Antonio Ruiz-Cortés, Octavio Martín-Díaz, and Manuel Resinas. An Hybrid, QoS-Aware Discovery of Semantic Web Services Using Constraint Programming. In *Proceedings of the Fifth International Conference on Service-Oriented Computing (ICSOC 2007)*, pages 69–80. Springer, 2007.

[75] Michael R. Garey and David S. Johnson. *Computers and Intractability: A Guide to the Theory of NP-Completeness*. W. H. Freeman and Company, 1979.

[76] GigaSpaces. Scale Up vs. Scale Out. Whitepaper, GigaSpaces Technologies, June 2011. URL http://d3a0pn6rx5g9yg.cloudfront.net/sites/default/files/private/resource/ScaleUpvsScaleOut0711.pdf.

[77] Fred Glover. Future Paths for Integer Programming and Links to Artificial Intelligence . *Computers & Operations Research*, 13(5):533–549, 1986. Applications of Integer Programming.

[78] Fred Glover. Tabu search: A Tutorial. *Interfaces*, 20(4):74–94, 1990.

[79] Fred Glover, Manuel Laguna, and Rafael Martí. *Handbook of Approximation Algorithms and Metaheuristics*, chapter 23 - Principles of Tabu Search, pages 23-1 – 23-12. Chapman & Hall/CRC, 2007.

[80] Dimitris Gouscos, Manolis Kalikakis, and Panagiotis Georgiadis. An Approach to Modeling Web Service QoS and Provision Price. In *Proceedings of the Fourth International Conference on Web Information Systems Engineering Workshops (WISEW'03)*, pages 121–130, 2003.

[81] Janusz Gozdecki, Andrzej Jajszczyk, and Rafal Stankiewicz. Quality of Service Terminology in IP Networks. *IEEE Communications Magazine*, 41(3):153–159, March 2003.

[82] H. L. Gray and T. O. Lewis. A Confidence Interval for the Availability Ratio. *Technometrics*, 9(3):465–471, August 1967.

[83] Jim Gray and Daniel P. Siewiorek. High-Availability Computer Systems. *Computer*, 24(9):39–48, September 1991.

[84] Stephan Groß, Mario Lischka, Nils Gruschka, André Miede, Meiko Jensen, Marc Mosch, Stefan Schulte, and Melanie Siebenhaar. Sicherheitsprobleme im Cloud Computing. *PIK - Praxis der Informationsverarbeitung und Kommunikation*, 34(3):126–134, August 2011.

[85] Robert L. Grossman. The Case for Cloud Computing. *IT Professional*, 11(2): 23–27, March 2009.

[86] Marc Haberkorn and Kishor Trivedi. Availability Monitor for a Software Based System. In *Proceedings of the 10th IEEE High Assurance Systems Engineering Symposium (HASE'07)*, pages 321–328, 2007.

[87] Ronny Hans, Ulrich Lampe, and Ralf Steinmetz. QoS-Aware, Cost-Efficient Selection of Cloud Data Centers. In *Proceedings of the 2013 IEEE Sixth International Conference on Cloud Computing (CLOUD 2013)*, pages 946–947, 2013.

[88] Ronny Hans, David Steffen, Ulrich Lampe, Björn Richerzhagen, and Ralf Steinmetz. Setting Priorities: A Heuristic Approach for Cloud Data Center Selection. In *Proceedings of the 5th International Conference on Cloud Computing and Services Science (CLOSER 2015)*, pages 221–228, 2015.

[89] Ronny Hans, Melanie Holloway, The An Binh Nguyen, Alexander Müller, Marco Seliger, and Jürgen Lang. Cloud-Applikationen in der Finanzindustrie - Dienstgütemerkmale und deren Überwachung (to appear). Whitepaper, Fachgebiet Multimedia Kommunikation (KOM) der Technischen Universität Darmstadt (TUD) und IBM, 2016.

[90] M.D. Harvey Motulsky. *"Intuitive Biostatistics"*. Oxford University Press, 1995.

[91] Peer Hasselmeyer and Nico d'Heureuse. Towards Holistic Multi-Tenant Monitoring for Virtual Data Centers. In *2010 IEEE/IFIP Network Operations and Management Symposium Workshops (NOMS Wksps)*, pages 350–356, April 2010.

[92] Oliver Heckmann, Ralf Steinmetz, Nicolas Liebau, Alejandro Buchmann, Claudia Eckert, Jussi Kangasharju, Max Mühlhäuser, and Andreas Schürr. Qualitätsmerkmale von Peer-to-Peer Systemen. Technical report, Technische Universität Darmstadt, 2006.

[93] John C. Henderson and N. Venkatraman. Strategic Alignment: Leveraging Information Technology for Transforming Organizations. *IBM Systems Journal*, 32(1):4–16, January 1993.

[94] Nikolas Roman Herbst, Samuel Kounev, and Ralf Reussner. Elasticity in Cloud Computing: What It Is, and What It Is Not. In *Proceedings of the 10th International Conference on Autonomic Computing (ICAC 13)*, pages 23–27. USENIX, 2013.

[95] Frederick S. Hillier and Gerald J. Liebermann. *Introduction to Operations Research*. McGraw-Hill, 8th edition, 2005.

[96] Melanie Holloway, Dieter Schuller, and Ralf Steinmetz. Customized Cloud Service Quality: Approaching Pareto-Efficient Outcomes in Concurrent Multiple-Issue Negotiations. In *Proceedings of the 8th IEEE/ACM International Conference on Utility and Cloud Computing (UCC 2015)*, 2015.

[97] Joseph D. Horton and Alejandro López-Ortiz. On the Number of Distributed Measurement Points for Network Tomography. In *Proceedings of the 3rd ACM SIGCOMM Conference on Internet Measurement*, pages 204–209. ACM, 2003.

[98] Kai Hwang and Naresh Jotwani. *Advanced Computer Architecture. Parallelism, Scalability, Programmability*, chapter 3. Principles of Scalable Performance, pages 89–130. Tata McGraw-Hill Education Private Limited, 2nd edition edition, 2010.

[99] I. Y. Kim and O. L. de Weck. Adaptive Weighted Sum Method for Multiobjective Optimization: a new Method for Pareto Front Generation. *Structural and Multidisciplinary Optimization*, 31(2):105–116, 2006.

[100] IT Governance Institute. Board Briefing on IT Governance. second edition, 2003. URL http://www.isaca.org/restricted/Documents/ 26904_Board_Briefing_final.pdf.

[101] ITU-T. Information Technology - Open Distributed Processing - Reference Model: Foundations. Recommendation ITU-T X.902 | ISO/IEC 10746-2, October 2009. URL https://www.itu.int/rec/T-REC-X.902-200910-I/en.

[102] Kamal Jain and Vijay V. An Approximation Algorithm for the Fault Tolerant Metric Facility Location Problem. *Algorithmica*, 38(3):433–439, 2004.

[103] Raj Jain. *The Art of Computer Systems Performance Analysis. Techniques for Experimental Design, Measurement, Simulation, and Modeling*, chapter Selection of Techniques and Metrics, pages 30–43. John Wiley & Sons, 1991.

[104] Nick R. Jennings, Peyman Faratin, Alessio R. Lomuscio, Simon Parsons, Michael J. Wooldridge, and Carles Sierra. Automated negotiation: Prospects, methods and challenges. *Group Decision and Negotiation*, 10(2):199–215, 2001.

[105] Paul A. Jensen and Jonathan F. Bard. Appendix A: Equivalent Linear Programs. In *Supplements to Operations Research Models and Methods*. John Wiley and Sons, 2003. http://www.me.utexas.edu/ jensen/ORMM/ supplements/units/lp_models/equivalent.pdf.

[106] Deepak Jeswani, Nakul Korde, Dinesh Patil, Maitreya Natu, and John Augustine. Probe Station Selection Algorithms for Fault Management in Computer Networks. In *Second International Conference on Communication Systems and Networks (COMSNETS)*, pages 1–9, January 2010.

[107] Jon Postel, editor. Transmission Control Protocol: Darpa Internet Program Protocol Specification. Request for Comments (RFC) 793, Information Sciences Institute, University of Southern California, September 1981.

[108] Audun Jøsang, Roslan Ismail, and Colin Boyd. A Survey of Trust and Reputation Systems for Online Service Provision. *Decision Support Systems*, 43(2): 618–644, 2007.

[109] Alexander Keller and Heiko Ludwig. The WSLA Framework: Specifying and Monitoring Service Level Agreements for Web Services. *Journal of Network and Systems Management*, 11(1):57–81, 2003.

[110] Scott Kirkpatrick, Charles Daniel Gelatt, and Mario P. Vecchi. Optimization by Simulated Annealing. *Science*, 220(4598):671–680, 1983.

[111] Leonhard Kleinrock. A Vision for the Internet. *ST Journal of Research*, 2(1): 4–5, 2005.

[112] Christos Kloukinas, George Spanoudakis, and Khaled Mahbub. Estimating Event Lifetimes for Distributed Runtime Verification. In *20th International Conference on Software Engineering and Knowledge Engineering (SEKE 2008)*, 2008.

[113] B. König, J.M. Alcaraz Calero, and J. Kirschnick. Elastic Monitoring Framework for Cloud Infrastructures. *IET Communications*, 6(10):1306–1315, July 2012.

[114] Dilip Kumar Krishnappa, David Irwin, Eric Lyons, and Michael Zink. Cloud-Cast: Cloud Computing for Short-Term Weather Forecasts. *Computing in Science Engineering*, 15(4):30–37, July 2013.

[115] Ritesh Kumar and Jasleen. Efficient Beacon Placement for Network Tomography. In *Proceedings of the 4th ACM SIGCOMM Conference on Internet Measurement*, pages 181–186, 2004.

[116] James F. Kurose and Keith W. Ross. *Computer Networking: A Top-Down Approach*. Addison-Wesley, 6th edition, 2012.

[117] Guoming Lai and Katia Sycara. A Generic Framework for Automated Multi-attribute Negotiation. *Group Decision and Negotiation*, 18(2):169–187, 2009.

[118] Guoming Lai, Katia Sycara, and Cuihong Li. A Decentralized Model for Multi-Attribute Negotiations with Incomplete Information and General Utility Functions. In Takayuki Ito, Hiromitsu Hattori, Minjie Zhang, and Tokuro Matsuo, editors, *Rational, Robust, and Secure Negotiations in Multi-Agent Systems*, volume 89 of *Studies in Computational Intelligence*, pages 39–57. Springer, 2008.

[119] Ulrich Lampe, Stefan Schulte, Melanie Siebenhaar, Dieter Schuller, and Ralf Steinmetz. Adaptive Matchmaking for RESTful Services based on hRESTS and MicroWSMO. In Walter Binder and Heiko Schuldt, editors, *Proceedings of the 5th Workshop on Enhanced Web Service Technologies (WEWST 2010)*, pages 10–17. The Association for Computing Machinery (ACM), 2010.

[120] Ulrich Lampe, Ronny Hans, Marco Seliger, Michael Pauly, and Michael Schiefer. Pricing in Infrastructure Clouds - An Analytical and Empirical Examination. In *Proceedings of the 20th Americas Conference on Information Systems (AMCIS 2014)*, 2014.

[121] Florian Lang. Developing Dynamic Strategies for Multi-Issue Automated Contracting in the Agent based Commercial Grid. In *IEEE International Symposium on Cluster Computing and the Grid (CCGrid 2005)*, volume 1, pages 342–349, May 2005.

[122] Philipp Leitner, Christian Inzinger, Waldemar Hummer, Benjamin Satzger, and Schahram Dustdar. Application-Level Performance Monitoring of Cloud Services based on the Complex Event Processing Paradigm. In *5th IEEE International Conference on Service-Oriented Computing and Applications (SOCA)*, pages 1–8, Dec 2012.

[123] Alexander Lenk, Gregory Katsaros, Michael Menzel, Jannies Rake-Revelant, Ryan Skipp, Enrique Castro-Leon, and Gopan V P. TIOSA: Testing VM Interoperability at an OS and Application Level – A Hypervisor Testing Method and Interoperability Survey. In *Proceedings of the 2014 IEEE International Conference on Cloud Engineering (IC2E)*, pages 245–252, 2014.

[124] Li Li, Marina Thottan, Bin Yao, and Sanjoy Paul. Distributed Network Monitoring with Bounded Link Utilization in IP Networks. In *22nd Annual Joint Conference of the IEEE Computer and Communications Societies (INFOCOM 2003)*, volume 2, pages 1189–1198, March 2003.

[125] Nikolaos Limnios and Vlad Stefan Barbu. *Semi-Markov Chains and Hidden Semi-Markov Models toward Applications. Their use in Reliability and DNA Analysis*, chapter Discrete-Time Renewal Processes, pages 1–25. Springer, 2008.

[126] Alessio R. Lomuscio, Michael Wooldridge, and Nicholas R. Jennings. A Classification Scheme for Negotiation in Electronic Commerce. *Agent-Mediated Electronic Commerce: A European Agent Link Perspective*, 12(1):31–56, 2003.

[127] Fumio Machida, Masahiro Kawato, and Yoshiharu Maeno. Redundant Virtual Machine Placement for Fault-Toleranto Consolidated Server Clusters. In *2010 IEEE Network Operations and Management Symposium (NOMS)*, pages 32–39, April 2010.

[128] Emmanuel Marilly, Olivier Martinot, Stéphane Betgé-Brezetz, and Gérard Delègue. Requirements for Service Level Agreement Management. In *IEEE Workshop on IP Operations and Management*, pages 57–62, 2002.

[129] Toni Mastelic, Vincent C. Emeakaroha, Michael Maurer, and Ivona Brandic. M4Cloud - Generic Application Level Monitoring for Resource-shared Cloud Environments. In *Proceedings of the 2nd International Conference on Cloud Computing and Services Science (CLOSER 2012)*, pages 522–532, 2012.

[130] Lijun Mei, W.K. Chan, and T.H Tse. A Tale of Clouds: Paradigm Comparisons and Some Thoughts on Research Issues. In *IEEE Asia-Pacific Services Computing Conference (APSCC '08)*, pages 464–469, 2008.

[131] Peter Mell and Timothy Grance. The NIST Definition of Cloud Computing. Special Publication 800–145, National Institute of Standards and Technology, September 2011.

[132] Daniel A. Menascé. QoS Issues in Web Services. *IEEE Internet Computing*, 6 (6):72–75, November 2002.

[133] Anton Michlmayr, Florian Rosenberg, Philipp Leitner, and Schahram Dustdar. Comprehensive QoS Monitoring of Web Services and Event-based SLA Violation Detection. In *Proceedings of the 4th International Workshop on Middleware for Service Oriented Computing (MWSOC '09)*, pages 1–6, 2009.

[134] Kaisa Miettinen. *Multiobjective Optimization. Interactive and Evolutionary Approaches*, volume Lecture Notes in Computer Science, chapter Introduction to Multiobjective Optimization: Noninteractive Approaches, pages 1–26. Springer, 2008.

[135] Carlos Molina-Jimenez, Santosh Shrivastava, Jon Crowcroft, and Panos Gevros. On the Monitoring of Contractual Service Level Agreements. In *First IEEE International Workshop on Electronic Contracting*, pages 1–8, July 2004.

[136] Rafael Moreno-Vozmediano, Rubén S. Montero, and Ignacio M. Llorente. Key Challenges in Cloud Computing: Enabling the Future Internet of Services. *IEEE Internet Computing*, 17(4):18–25, July 2013.

[137] Venkatesh Nandakumar, Alan Wen Jun Lu, Madalin Mihailescu, Zartab Jamil, Cristiana Amza, and Harsh V. P. Singh. Optimizing Application Downtime Through Intelligent VM Placement and Migration in Cloud Data Centers. In *Proceedings of the 25th Annual International Conference on Computer Science and Software Engineering (CASCON '15)*, pages 35–44, 2015.

[138] John Nash. The Bargaining Problem. *Econometrica*, 18(2):155–162, 1950.

[139] Maitreya Natu and Adarshpal S. Sethi. Active Probing Approach for Fault Localization in Computer Networks. In *4th IEEE/IFIP Workshop on End-to-End Monitoring Techniques and Services (E2EMON)*, pages 25–33, April 2006.

[140] Maitreya Natu and Adarshpal S. Sethi. Probe Station Placement for Robust Monitoring of Networks. *Journal of Network and Systems Management*, 16(4): 351–374, 2008.

[141] Hung X. Nguyen and Patrick Thiran. Active Measurement for Multiple Link Failures Diagnosis in IP Networks. In *5th International Workshop on Passive and Active Measurement (PAM 2004)*, pages 185–194. Springer, 2004.

[142] The An Binh Nguyen, Melanie Siebenhaar, Ronny Hans, and Ralf Steinmetz. Role-based Templates for Cloud Monitoring. In *Proceedings of the 7th IEEE/ACM International Conference on Utility and Cloud Computing (UCC 2014)*, pages 242–250, 2014.

[143] Elisabetta Di Nitto, Massimiliano Di Penta, Alessio Gambi, Gianluca Ripa, and Maria Luisa Villani. Negotiation of Service Level Agreements: An Architecture and a Search-based Approach. In *Proceedings of the 5th International Conference on Service-Oriented Computing (ICSOC 2007)*, pages 295–306, 2007.

[144] Venkata N.Padmanabhan, Sriram Ramabhadran, Sharad Agarwal, and Jitendra Padhye. A Study of End-to-end Web Access Failures. In *Proceedings of the 2nd International Conference on emerging Networking EXperiments and Technologies (CoNEXT '06)*, 2006.

[145] OASIS. Reference Architecture Foundation for Service Oriented Architecture Version 1.0. OASIS Committee Specification 01, 04 December 2012. URL http://docs.oasis-open.org/soa-rm/soa-ra/v1.0/cs01/soa-ra-v1.0-cs01.pdf.

[146] Özlem Karsu and Meral Azizoğlu. The Multi-Resource Agent Bottleneck Generalised Assignment Problem. *International Journal of Production Research*, 50(2):309–324, 2012.

[147] George Pallis. Cloud Computing: The New Frontier of Internet Computing. *IEEE Internet Computing*, 14(5):70–73, 2010.

[148] Yalian Pan, Xuesong Qiu, and Shunli Zhang. Probe Station Selection in Nondeterministic and Dynamic Virtual Network Environment. *Journal of Information & Computational Science*, 9(1):191–202, January 2012.

[149] Michael P. Papazoglou, Paolo Traverso, Schahram Dustdar, and Frank Leymann. Service-oriented Computing: A Research Roadmap. *International Journal of Cooperative Information Systems*, 17(02):223–255, 2008.

[150] Chintan Patel, Kaustubh Supekar, and Yugyung Lee. A QoS Oriented Framework for Adaptive Management of Web Service Based Workflows. In *Proceedings of the 14th International Conference on Database and Expert Systems Applications (DEXA 2003)*, pages 826–835. Springer, 2003.

[151] Dhaval Patel and Arobinda Gupta. An Adaptive Negotiation Strategy for Electronic Transactions. In *10th IEEE International Enterprise Distributed Object Computing Conference (EDOC'06)*, pages 243–252, Oct 2006.

[152] Pankesh Patel, Ajith Ranabahu, and Amit Sheth. Service Level Agreement in Cloud Computing. Technical report, Knoesis Center, Wright State University, USA, 2009.

[153] Balaji Patil, Shakti Kinger, and Vinay Kumar Pathak. Probe Station Placement Algorithm for Probe Set Reduction in Network Fault Localization. In *2013 International Conference on Information Systems and Computer Networks (ISCON)*, pages 164–169, March 2013.

[154] Cesare Pautasso, Olaf Zimmermann, and Frank Leymann. Restful Web Services vs. "Big" Web Services: Making the Right Architectural Decision. In *Proceedings of the 17th International Conference on World Wide Web*, pages 805–814, 2008.

[155] Vern Paxson, Mark Allman, H.K. Jerry Chu, and Matt Sargent. Computing TCP's Retransmission Timer. Request for Comments (RFC) 6298, Internet Engineering Task Force (IETF), June 2011.

[156] Dana Petcu and Athanasios V. Vasilakos. Portability in Clouds: Approaches and Research Opportunities. *Scientific International Journal for Parallel and Distributed Computing*, 15(3):251–271, 2014.

[157] Shuping Ran. A Model for Web Services Discovery with QoS. *ACM SIGecom Exchanges*, 4(1):1–10, March 2003.

[158] Nicolas Repp. *Überwachung und Steuerung dienstbasierter Architekturen - Verteilungsstrategien und deren Umsetzung*. PhD thesis, Technische Universität Darmstadt, 2009.

[159] Nicolas Repp, Dieter Schuller, Melanie Siebenhaar, Andre Miede, Michael Niemann, and Ralf Steinmetz. On Distributed SLA Monitoring and Enforcement in Service-Oriented Systems. In *International Journal On Advances in Systems and Measurements*, volume 2, pages 33–43, 2009.

[160] Bhaskar Prasad Rimal, Eunmi Choi, and Ian Lumb. A Taxonomy and Survey of Cloud Computing Systems. In *Fifth International Joint Conference on INC, IMS and IDC (NCM '09)*, pages 44–51, 2009.

[161] Stefanie Rinderle and Morad Benyoucef. Towards the Automation of E-Negotiation Processes Based on Web Services – A Modeling Approach. In *Proceedings of the 6th International Conference on Web Information Systems Engineering (WISE 2005)*, pages 443–453, 2005.

[162] Luigi Romano, Danilo De Mari, Zbigniew Jerzak, and Christof Fetzer. A Novel Approach to QoS Monitoring in the Cloud. In *First International Conference on Data Compression, Communications and Processing (CCP)*, pages 45–51, June 2011.

[163] Florian Rosenberg, Christian Platzer, and Schahram Dustdar. Bootstrapping Performance and Dependability Attributes of Web Services. In *International Conference on Web Services (ICWS '06)*, pages 205–212, Sept 2006.

[164] Daniel J. Rosenkrantz, Sanjay Goel, S.S. Ravi, and Jagdish. Structure-Based Resilience Metrics for Service-Oriented Networks. In *5th European Dependable Computing Conference (EDCC 5)*, pages 345–362. Springer, 2005.

[165] Jeffrey S. Rosenschein and Gilad Zlotkin. *Rules of Encounter: Designing Conventions for Automated Negotiation among Computers*. The MIT Press, 1994.

[166] Ariel Rubinstein. Perfect Equilibrium in a Bargaining Model. *Econometrica*, 50(1):97–110, January 1982.

[167] Thejendra B. S. *Practial IT Service Management: A Concise Guide for Busy Executives*, chapter Service Level Management, pages 135–148. IT Governance Publishing, second edition, 2014.

[168] Sabyasachi Saha. Improving Agreements in Multi-Issue Negotiations. *Journal of Electronic Commerce Research*, 7(1):41–49, 2006.

[169] Sabyasachi Saha and Sandip Sen. Towards Efficient Outcomes in Multi-issue Negotiation. In *Proceedings of the AAMAS Workshop on Business Agents and the Semantic Web (BASeWEB '06)*, pages 17–25, 2006.

[170] Emna Salhi, Samer Lahoud, and Bernard Cousin. Joint Optimization of Monitor Location and Network Anomaly Detection. In *35th IEEE Conference on Local Computer Networks (LCN)*, pages 204–207, October 2010.

[171] Emna Salhi, Samer Lahoud, and Bernard Cousin. Heuristics for Joint Optimization of Monitor Location and Network Anomaly Detection. In *2011 IEEE International Conference on Communications (ICC)*, pages 1–5, June 2011.

[172] K. Saravanan and M. Rajaram. An Exploratory Study of Cloud Service Level Agreements - State of the Art Review. *KSII Transactions on Internet and Information Systems (TIIS)*, 3(3):843–871, March 2015.

[173] Jens Burkhard Schmitt. *Heterogeneous Network Quality of Service Systems*, chapter Introduction, pages 3–14. Springer, 2001.

[174] Christoph Schroth. The Internet of Services: Global Industrialization of Information Intensive Services. In *2nd International Conference on Digital Information Management (ICDIM '07)*, volume 2, pages 635–642, October 2007.

[175] Christoph Schroth and Till Janner. Web 2.0 and SOA: Converging Concepts Enabling the Internet of Services. *IT Professional*, 9(3):36–41, May 2007.

[176] Dieter Schuller, Artem Polyvyanyy, Luciano García-Bañuelos, and Stefan Schulte. Optimization of Complex QoS-Aware Service Compositions. In *Proceedings of the Ninth International Conference on Service-Oriented Computing (ICSOC 2011)*, pages 452–466. Springer, 2011.

[177] Dieter Schuller, Melanie Siebenhaar, Ronny Hans, Olga Wenge, Ralf Steinmetz, and Stefan Schulte. Towards Heuristic Optimization of Complex Service-based Workflows for Stochastic QoS Attributes. In *Proceedings of the 21th International Conference on Web Services (ICWS 2014)*, pages 361–368. IEEE Computer Society, 2014.

[178] Stefan Schulte, Melanie Siebenhaar, Julian Eckert, and Ralf Steinmetz. Query Languages for Semantic Web Services. In Klaus-Peter Fähnrich and Bogdan Franczyk, editors, *Service Science - Neue Perspektiven für die Informatik - Proceedings der Informatik 2010*, volume Lecture Notes in Informatics 176, pages 109–114. Gesellschaft für Informatik, 2010.

[179] Stefan Schulte, Melanie Siebenhaar, and Ralf Steinmetz. Integrating Semantic Web Services and Matchmaking into ebXML Registry. In *4th International Workshop on Service Matchmaking and Resource Retrieval in the Semantic Web (SMR2 2010) at the 9th International Semantic Web Conference (ISWC2010)*, volume 667, pages 69–83, 2010.

[180] Jin Shao and Qianxiang Wang. A Performance Guarantee Approach for Cloud Applications Based on Monitoring. In *2011 IEEE 35th Annual Computer Software and Applications Conference Workshops (COMPSACW)*, pages 25–30, July 2011.

[181] Jin Shao, Hao Wei, Qianxiang Wang, and Hong Mei. A Runtime Model Based Monitoring Approach for Cloud. In *Proceedings of the 3rd IEEE International Conference on Cloud Computing (CLOUD)*, pages 313–320, July 2010.

[182] Vivek Shrivastava, Petros Zerfos, Kang won Lee, Hani Jamjoom, Yew-Huey Liu, and Suman Banerjee. Application-aware Virtual Machine Migration in Data Centers. In *Proceedings of the 30th IEEE International Conference on Computer Communications (INFOCOM 2011)*, pages 66–70, April 2011.

[183] Melanie Siebenhaar, Ulrich Lampe, Tim Lehrig, Sebastian Zöller, Stefan Schulte, and Ralf Steinmetz. Complex Service Provisioning in Collaborative Cloud Markets. In Witold Abramowicz, Ignacio M. Llorente, Mike Surridge, Andrea Zisman, and Julien Vayssière, editors, *Proceedings of the 4th European Conference ServiceWave*, volume Lecture Notes in Computer Science, pages 88–99. Springer, 2011.

[184] Melanie Siebenhaar, Hsin-Yi Tsai, Ulrich Lampe, and Ralf Steinmetz. Analyzing and Modeling Security Aspects of Cloud-based Systems. In *1. GI/ITG KuVS Fachgespräch "Sicherheit für Cloud Computing"*, 2011.

[185] Melanie Siebenhaar, The An Binh Nguyen, Ulrich Lampe, Dieter Schuller, and Ralf Steinmetz. Concurrent Negotiations in Cloud-based Systems. In Kurt Vanmechelen, Jörn Altmann, and Omer Rana, editors, *Proceedings of the 8th International Workshop on Economics of Grids, Clouds, Systems, and Services (GECON2011), in conjunction with ICSOC 2011*, volume Lecture Notes in Computer Science. Springer, 2012.

[186] Melanie Siebenhaar, Olga Wenge, Ronny Hans, Hasan Tercan, and Ralf Steinmetz. Verifying the Availability of Cloud Applications. In Matthias Jarke and Markus Helfert, editors, *Proceedings of the 3rd International Conference on Cloud Computing and Services Science (CLOSER 2013)*, pages 489–494. SciTe Press, 2013.

[187] Melanie Siebenhaar, Ulrich Lampe, Dieter Schuller, and Ralf Steinmetz. Robust Cloud Monitor Placement for Availability Verification. In Markus Helfert, Frédéric Desprez, Donald Ferguson, Frank Leymann, and Víctor Méndez Muñoz, editors, *Proceedings of the 4th International Conference on Cloud Computing and Services Science (CLOSER 2014)*, pages 193–198. SciTe Press, 2014.

[188] Melanie Siebenhaar, Dieter Schuller, Olga Wenge, and Ralf Steinmetz. Heuristic Approaches for Robust Cloud Monitor Placement. In Xavier Franch, Aditya K. Ghose, Grace A. Lewis, and Sami Bhiri, editors, *Proceedings of the*

12th International Conference on Service Oriented Computing (ICSOC 2014), volume Lecture Notes in Computer Science, pages 321–335. Springer, 2014.

[189] Carles Sierra, Peyman Faratin, and Nick R. Jennings. A Service-Oriented Negotiation Model between Autonomous Agents. In Julian A. Padget, editor, *Collaboration between Human and Artificial Societies*, volume 1624 of *Lecture Notes in Computer Science*, pages 201–219. Springer, 1999.

[190] Kwang Mong Sim. Agent-based Interactions and Economic Encounters in an Intelligent InterCloud. *IEEE Transactions on Cloud Computing*, PP(99):1–1, 2015.

[191] Vijendra P. Singh and S. Swaminathan. Sample Sizes for System Availability. In *Proceedings of the Annual Reliability and Maintainability Symposium*, pages 51–55, 2002.

[192] Michael Smit, Bradley Simmons, and Marin Litoiu. Distributed, Application-Level Monitoring for Heterogeneous Clouds using Stream Processing. *Future Generation Computer Systems*, 29(8):2103–2114, 2013.

[193] Reid G. Smith. The Contract Net Protocol: High-Level Communication and Control in a Distributed Problem Solver. *IEEE Transactions on Computers*, 29 (12):1104–1113, 1980.

[194] Koye Somefun, Enrico Gerding, Sander Bohte, and Han La Poutré. Automated Negotiation and Bundling of Information Goods. In Peyman Faratin, David C. Parkes, Juan A. Rodríguez-Aguilar, and William E. Walsh, editors, *Agent-Mediated Electronic Commerce V. Designing Mechanisms and Systems*, volume 3048 of *Lecture Notes in Computer Science*, pages 1–17. Springer, 2004.

[195] Seokho Son and Kwang Mong Sim. Adaptive and Similarity-based Tradeoff Algorithms in a Price-Timeslot-QoS Negotiation System to establish Cloud SLAs. *Information Systems Frontiers*, 17(3):565–589, 2015.

[196] Barrie Sosinsky. *Cloud Computing Bible*, chapter Understanding Service Oriented Architecture, pages 271–296. John Wiley & Sons, 2011.

[197] Ilango Sriram and Ali Khajeh-Hosseini. Research Agenda in Cloud Technologies, 2010. URL http://arxiv.org/pdf/1001.3259v1.

[198] Ralf Steinmetz. *Multimedia-Technologie*. Springer, 2000.

[199] Ralf Steinmetz and Klara Nahrstedt. *Multimedia Systems*. Springer, 2004.

[200] Ralf Steinmetz and Klaus Wehrle. *Peer-to-Peer Systems and Applications*. Springer, 2005.

[201] Kyoungwon Suh, Yang Guo, Jim Kurose, and Don Towsley. Locating Network Monitors: Complexity, Heuristics, and Coverage. In *24th Annual Joint Conference of the IEEE Computer and Communications Societies (INFOCOM 2005)*, volume 1, pages 351–361, March 2005.

[202] Katia Sycara. Utility Theory in Conflict Resolution. *Annals of Operations Research*, 12(1):65–83, 1988.

[203] Hsin-Yi Tsai, Melanie Siebenhaar, André Miede, Yu-Lun Huang, and Ralf Steinmetz. Threat as a Service?: Virtualization's Impact on Cloud Security. *IT Professional*, 14(1):32–37, January 2012.

[204] Astrid Undheim, Ameen Chilwan, and Poul Heegaard. Differentiated Availability in Cloud Computing SLAs. In *Proceedings of the 12th IEEE/ACM International Conference on Grid Computing*, pages 129–136, 2011.

[205] Luis M. Vaquero, Luis Rodero-Merino, Juan Caceres, and Maik Lindner. A Break in the Clouds: Towards a Cloud Definition. *SIGCOMM Computer Communication Review*, 39(1):50–55, 2009.

[206] Srikumar Venugopal, Xingchen Chu, and Rajkumar Buyya. A Negotiation Mechanism for Advance Resource Reservations Using the Alternate Offers Protocol. In *16th International Workshop on Quality of Service (IWQoS 2008)*, pages 40–49, June 2008.

[207] Jeffrey Voas and Jia Zhang. Cloud Computing: New Wine or Just a New Bottle? *IT Professional*, 11(2):15–17, 2009.

[208] William Voorsluys, James Broberg, Srikumar Venugopal, and Rajkumar Buyya. Cost of Virtual Machine Live Migration in Clouds: A Performance Evaluation. In *Proceedings of the First International Conference on Cloud Computing (CloudCom 2009)*, pages 254–265, 2009.

[209] William Voorsluys, James Broberg, and Rajkumar Buyya. *Cloud Computing. Principles and Paradigms*, chapter Introduction to Cloud Computing, pages 3–42. Wiley, 2011.

[210] Qingyang Wang, Yasuhiko Kanemasa, Jack Li, Deepal Jayasinghe, Motoyuki Kawaba, and Calton Pu. Response Time Reliability in Cloud Environments: An Empirical Study of n-Tier Applications at High Resource Utilization. In *Proceedings of the 2012 IEEE 31st Symposium on Reliable Distributed Systems (SRDS)*, pages 378–383, 2012.

[211] Wendai Wang and D. B. Kececioglu. Confidence Limits on the Inherent Availability of Equipment. In *Proceedings of the Annual Reliability and Maintainability Symposium*, pages 162–168, 2000.

[212] Zheng Wang. *Internet QoS. Architectures and Mechanisms for Quality of Service*, chapter The Big Picture, pages 1–14. Morgan Kaufmann, 2001.

[213] Yi Wei and M. Brian Blake. Service-Oriented Computing and Cloud Computing: Challenges and Opportunities. *IEEE Internet Computing*, 14(6):72–75, Nov 2010.

[214] Susanne Wied-Nebbeling and Hartmut Schott. *Grundlagen der Mikroökonomik*, chapter Bedingungen für optimale Allokation, pages 261–279. Springer, 3rd edition, 2005.

[215] Linlin Wu and Rajkumar Buyya. *Performance and Dependability in Service Computing: Concepts, Techniques and Research Directions*, chapter Service Level Agreement (SLA) in Utility Computing Systems, pages 1–25. Information Science Reference - Imprint of: IGI Publishing, 2011.

[216] Linlin Wu, Saurabh Kumar Garg, Rajkumar Buyya, Chao Chen, and Steve Versteeg. Automated SLA Negotiation Framework for Cloud Computing. In *13th IEEE/ACM International Symposium on Cluster, Cloud and Grid Computing (CCGrid)*, pages 235–244, May 2013.

[217] Jun Yan, Ryszard Kowalczyk, Jian Lin, Mohan B. Chhetri, Suk Keong Goh, and Jianying Zhang. Autonomous Service Level Agreement Negotiation for Service Composition Provision. *Future Generation Computer Systems*, 23(6): 748–759, 2007.

[218] Haibo Yang and Mary Tate. A Descriptive Literature Review and Classification of Cloud Computing Research. *Communications of the Association for Information Systems*, 31(2):35–60, July 2012.

[219] Qinghe Yin, Peng-Yong Kong, and Haiguang Wang. Quantitative Robustness Metric for QOS Performances of Communication Networks. In *Proceedings of the 17th Annual IEEE International Symposium on Personal, Indoor and Mobile Radio Communications (PIMRC'06)*, pages 1–5, 2006.

[220] Lamia Youseff, Maria Butrico, and Dilama Da Silva. Toward a Unified Ontology of Cloud Computing. In *Grid Computing Environments Workshop (GCE '08)*, pages 1–10, Nov 2008.

[221] Qi Zhang, Lu Cheng, and Raouf Boutaba. Cloud Computing: State-of-the-Art and Research Challenges. *Internet Services and Applications*, 1(1):7–18, 2010.

[222] Ronghuo Zheng, Nilanjan Chakraborty, Tinglong Dai, and Katia. Multiagent Negotiation on Multiple Issues with Incomplete Information. In *Proceedings of the 2013 International Conference on Autonomous Agents and Multi-agent*

Systems, pages 1279–1280. International Foundation for Autonomous Agents and Multiagent Systems, 2013.

[223] Ronghuo Zheng, Nilanjan Chakraborty, Tinglong Dai, Katia Sycara, and Michael Lewis. Automated Bilateral Multiple-Issue Negotiation with No Information About Opponent. In *46th Hawaii International Conference on System Sciences (HICSS)*, pages 520–527, Jan 2013.

[224] Xianrong Zheng, Patrick Martin, and Kathryn Brohman. Cloud Service Negotiation: Concession vs. Tradeoff Approaches. In *12th IEEE/ACM International Symposium on Cluster, Cloud and Grid Computing (CCGrid)*, pages 515–522, May 2012.

[225] Xianrong Zheng, Patrick Martin, and Kathryn Brohman. Cloud Service Negotiation: A Research Roadmap. In *IEEE International Conference on Services Computing (SCC)*, pages 627–634, June 2013.

[226] Minqi Zhou, Rong Zhang, Dadan Zeng, and Weining Qian. Services in the Cloud Computing Era: A Survey. In *4th International Universal Communication Symposium (IUCS)*, pages 40–46, Oct 2010.

[227] Farhana Zulkernine, Patrick Martin, Chris Craddock, and Kirk Wilson. A Policy-Based Middleware for Web Services SLA Negotiation. In *Proceedings of the 7th International Conference on Web Services*, pages 1043–1050, 2009.

All electronic references stated in the bibliography have been checked in July 2016. However, the locations of the online sources may change due to the dynamic nature of the Internet.

A Appendix

A.1 TCP Behavior in the Presence of Packet Loss

Figure A.1 depicts the Wireshark[1] trace of a sample monitoring request which has been sent to the Kaltura[2] cloud service used in the evaluation of our monitoring approach (cf. Section 8.3). This trace has been compiled in order to validate the values specified by Paxson et al. [155] for the initial RTO of the handshake phase of TCP and the RTO before the data transfer phase in case of lost SYNs or SYN+ACKs. These values correspond to the variables T_S and T_D in our mathematical model in Section 6.2.4.

	ip.addr == 130.83.245.97 and tcp					
No.	Time	Source	Destination	Protoc	Length	Info
28	4.828991	192.168.0.10	130.83.245.97	TCP	66	62454 → 8020 [SYN] Seq=414062777 Win=8192 Len=0 MSS=1260 W
37	7.828948	192.168.0.10	130.83.245.97	TCP	66	[TCP Retransmission] 62454 → 8020 [SYN] Seq=414062777 Win=
38	7.840168	130.83.245.97	192.168.0.10	TCP	66	8020 → 62454 [SYN, ACK] Seq=2778128307 Ack=414062778 Win=2
39	7.840539	192.168.0.10	130.83.245.97	TCP	54	62454 → 8020 [ACK] Seq=414062778 Ack=2778128308 Win=66780
40	7.843150	192.168.0.10	130.83.245.97	HTTP	402	GET /api_v3/?ks=OGQ5NzA1NmI5YTk3MWI2ODVjYTdmOTcxMzg2MTM2ZD
46	10.843127	192.168.0.10	130.83.245.97	TCP	402	[TCP Retransmission] 62454 → 8020 [PSH, ACK] Seq=414062778
123	16.843323	192.168.0.10	130.83.245.97	TCP	402	[TCP Retransmission] 62454 → 8020 [PSH, ACK] Seq=414062778
172	28.843852	192.168.0.10	130.83.245.97	TCP	402	[TCP Retransmission] 62454 → 8020 [PSH, ACK] Seq=414062778

Figure A.1: Excerpt of a Wireshark trace showing TCP's retransmissions

A.2 Additional Results of the Evaluation of CSLAB-Neg.KOM

In the following, we provide further results of the evaluation of our negotiation mechanism CSLAB-Neg.KOM described in Chapter 8.2. In detail, further results are depicted with regard to the impact of the risk factor, the greed factor, and the patience on the Pareto-efficiency in other time-dependent strategy settings. Their impact is also illustrated in comparison with a pure Alternate Offers-based approach. Furthermore, additional results are provided concerning the impact of the number of providers and the patience on the number of exchanged messages and on the execution time at other deadline intervals.

---

[1]   http://www.wireshark.org
[2]   http://corp.kaltura.com

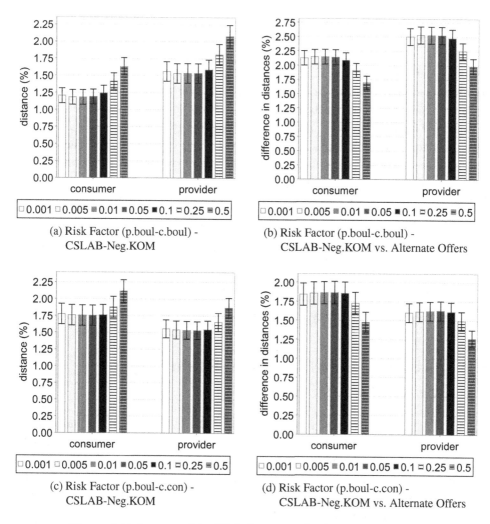

(a) Risk Factor (p.boul-c.boul) -
CSLAB-Neg.KOM

(b) Risk Factor (p.boul-c.boul) -
CSLAB-Neg.KOM vs. Alternate Offers

(c) Risk Factor (p.boul-c.con) -
CSLAB-Neg.KOM

(d) Risk Factor (p.boul-c.con) -
CSLAB-Neg.KOM vs. Alternate Offers

Figure A.2: Impact of the Risk factor on the Pareto-efficiency

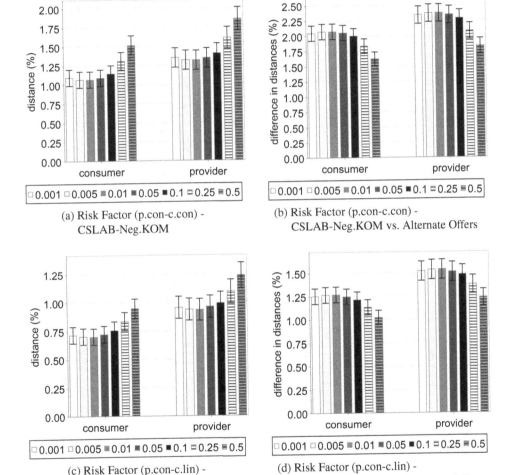

(a) Risk Factor (p.con-c.con) -
CSLAB-Neg.KOM

(b) Risk Factor (p.con-c.con) -
CSLAB-Neg.KOM vs. Alternate Offers

(c) Risk Factor (p.con-c.lin) -
CSLAB-Neg.KOM

(d) Risk Factor (p.con-c.lin) -
CSLAB-Neg.KOM vs. Alternate Offers

Figure A.3: Impact of the Risk factor on the Pareto-efficiency (cont'd)

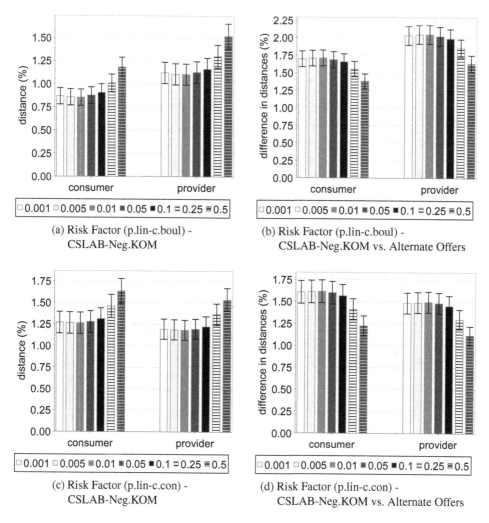

Figure A.4: Impact of the Risk factor on the Pareto-efficiency (cont'd)

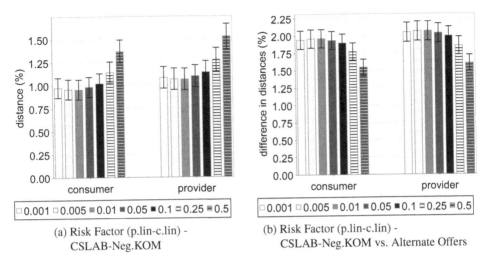

(a) Risk Factor (p.lin-c.lin) -
CSLAB-Neg.KOM

(b) Risk Factor (p.lin-c.lin) -
CSLAB-Neg.KOM vs. Alternate Offers

Figure A.5: Impact of the Risk Factor on the Pareto-Efficiency (cont'd)

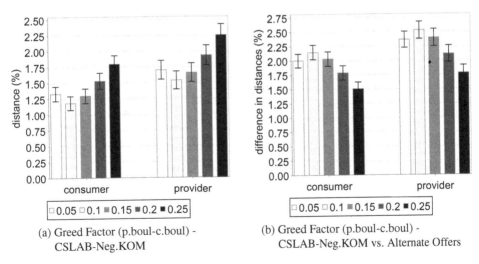

(a) Greed Factor (p.boul-c.boul) -
CSLAB-Neg.KOM

(b) Greed Factor (p.boul-c.boul) -
CSLAB-Neg.KOM vs. Alternate Offers

Figure A.6: Impact of the Greed factor on the Pareto-efficiency

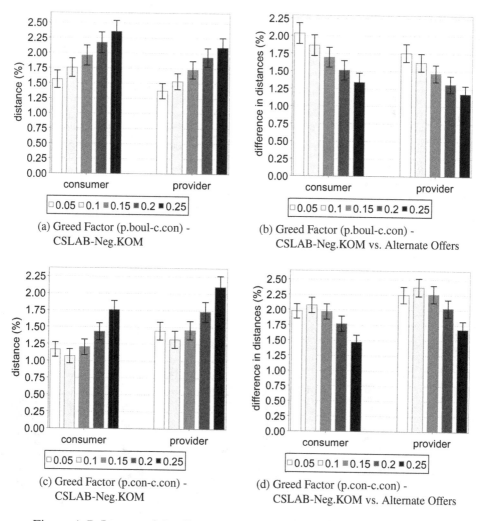

(a) Greed Factor (p.boul-c.con) -
CSLAB-Neg.KOM

(b) Greed Factor (p.boul-c.con) -
CSLAB-Neg.KOM vs. Alternate Offers

(c) Greed Factor (p.con-c.con) -
CSLAB-Neg.KOM

(d) Greed Factor (p.con-c.con) -
CSLAB-Neg.KOM vs. Alternate Offers

Figure A.7: Impact of the Greed factor on the Pareto-efficiency (cont'd)

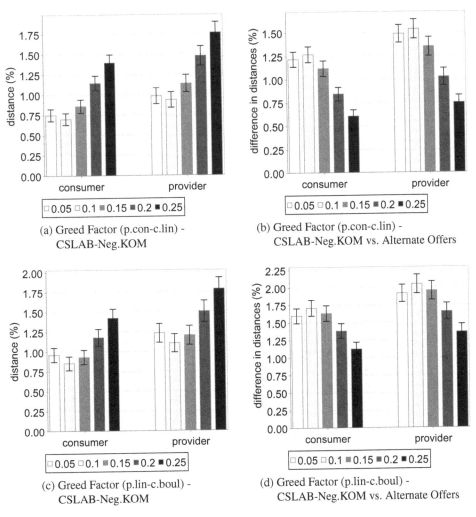

Figure A.8: Impact of the Greed factor on the Pareto-efficiency (cont'd)

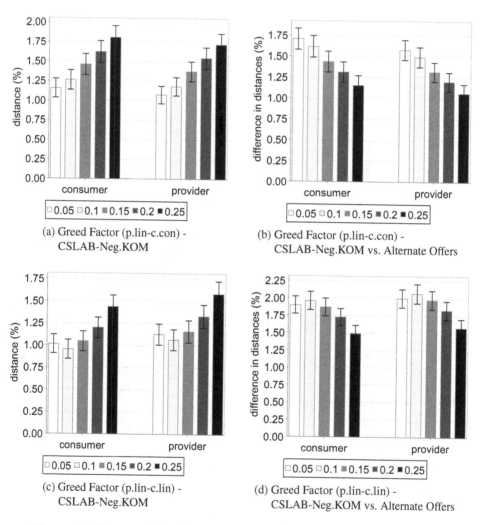

(a) Greed Factor (p.lin-c.con) -
CSLAB-Neg.KOM

(b) Greed Factor (p.lin-c.con) -
CSLAB-Neg.KOM vs. Alternate Offers

(c) Greed Factor (p.lin-c.lin) -
CSLAB-Neg.KOM

(d) Greed Factor (p.lin-c.lin) -
CSLAB-Neg.KOM vs. Alternate Offers

Figure A.9: Impact of the Greed factor on the Pareto-efficiency (cont'd)

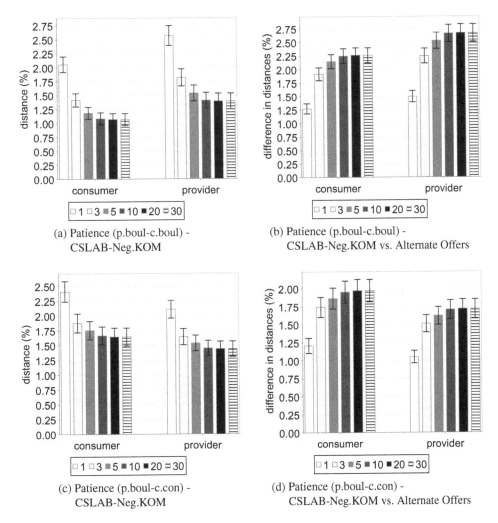

(a) Patience (p.boul-c.boul) -
CSLAB-Neg.KOM

(b) Patience (p.boul-c.boul) -
CSLAB-Neg.KOM vs. Alternate Offers

(c) Patience (p.boul-c.con) -
CSLAB-Neg.KOM

(d) Patience (p.boul-c.con) -
CSLAB-Neg.KOM vs. Alternate Offers

Figure A.10: Impact of the Patience on the Pareto-efficiency

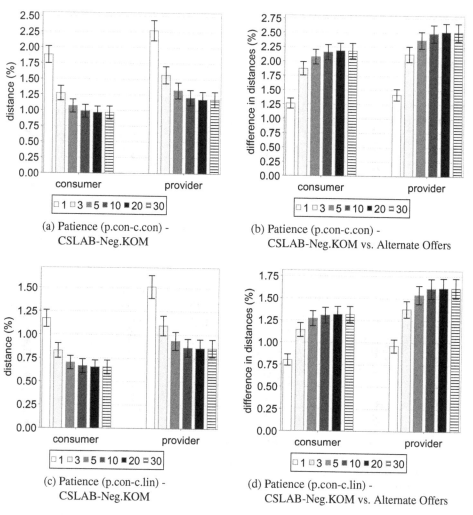

(a) Patience (p.con-c.con) -
CSLAB-Neg.KOM

(b) Patience (p.con-c.con) -
CSLAB-Neg.KOM vs. Alternate Offers

(c) Patience (p.con-c.lin) -
CSLAB-Neg.KOM

(d) Patience (p.con-c.lin) -
CSLAB-Neg.KOM vs. Alternate Offers

Figure A.11: Impact of the Patience on the Pareto-efficiency (cont'd)

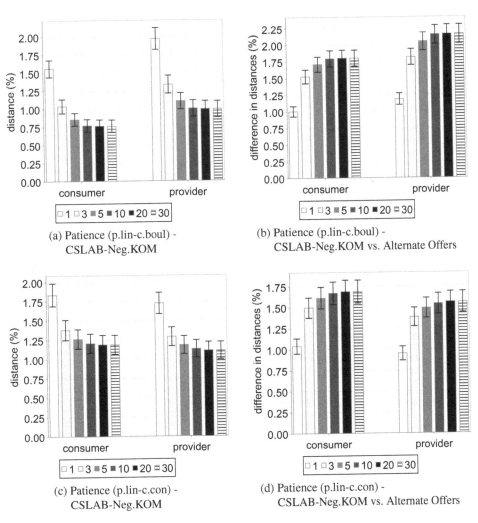

(a) Patience (p.lin-c.boul) -
CSLAB-Neg.KOM

(b) Patience (p.lin-c.boul) -
CSLAB-Neg.KOM vs. Alternate Offers

(c) Patience (p.lin-c.con) -
CSLAB-Neg.KOM

(d) Patience (p.lin-c.con) -
CSLAB-Neg.KOM vs. Alternate Offers

Figure A.12: Impact of the Patience on the Pareto-efficiency (cont'd)

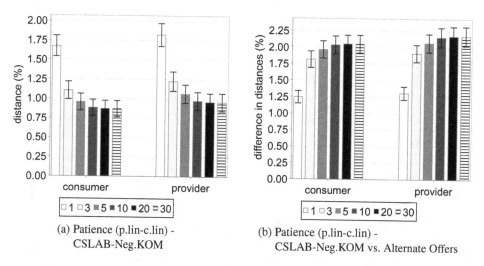

(a) Patience (p.lin-c.lin) -
CSLAB-Neg.KOM

(b) Patience (p.lin-c.lin) -
CSLAB-Neg.KOM vs. Alternate Offers

Figure A.13: Impact of the Patience on the Pareto-efficiency (cont'd)

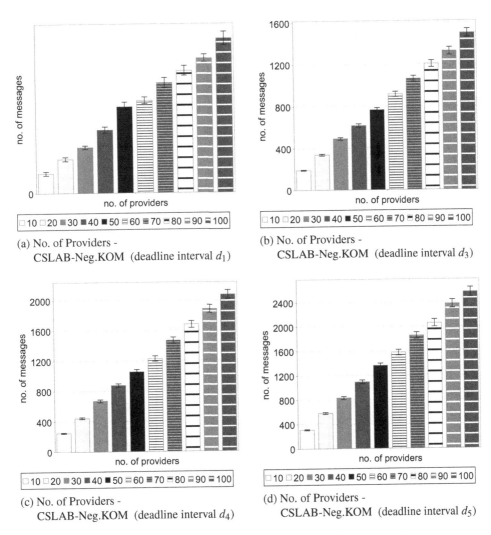

(a) No. of Providers -
      CSLAB-Neg.KOM (deadline interval d_1)

(b) No. of Providers -
      CSLAB-Neg.KOM (deadline interval d_3)

(c) No. of Providers -
      CSLAB-Neg.KOM (deadline interval d_4)

(d) No. of Providers -
      CSLAB-Neg.KOM (deadline interval d_5)

Figure A.14: Impact of the no. of providers on the no. of exchanged messages over different deadline intervals

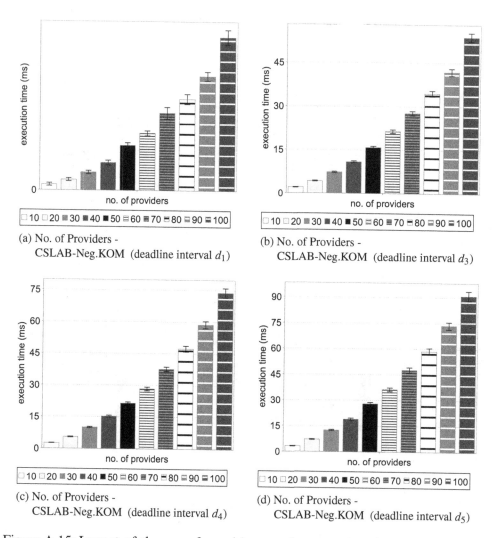

(a) No. of Providers -
    CSLAB-Neg.KOM (deadline interval d_1)

(b) No. of Providers -
    CSLAB-Neg.KOM (deadline interval d_3)

(c) No. of Providers -
    CSLAB-Neg.KOM (deadline interval d_4)

(d) No. of Providers -
    CSLAB-Neg.KOM (deadline interval d_5)

Figure A.15: Impact of the no. of providers on the execution time over different
           deadline intervals

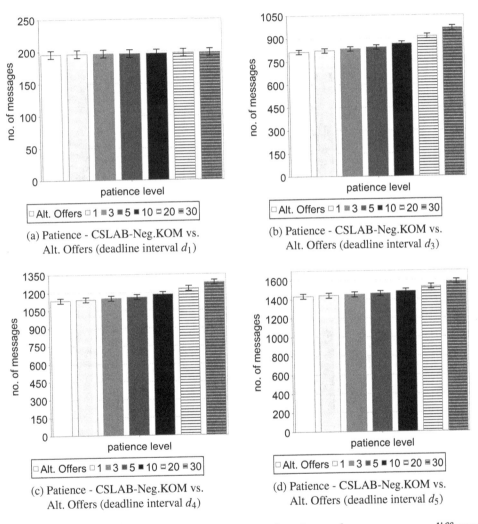

(a) Patience - CSLAB-Neg.KOM vs.
Alt. Offers (deadline interval d_1)

(b) Patience - CSLAB-Neg.KOM vs.
Alt. Offers (deadline interval d_3)

(c) Patience - CSLAB-Neg.KOM vs.
Alt. Offers (deadline interval d_4)

(d) Patience - CSLAB-Neg.KOM vs.
Alt. Offers (deadline interval d_5)

Figure A.16: Impact of the Patience on the no. of exchanged messages over different
deadline intervals

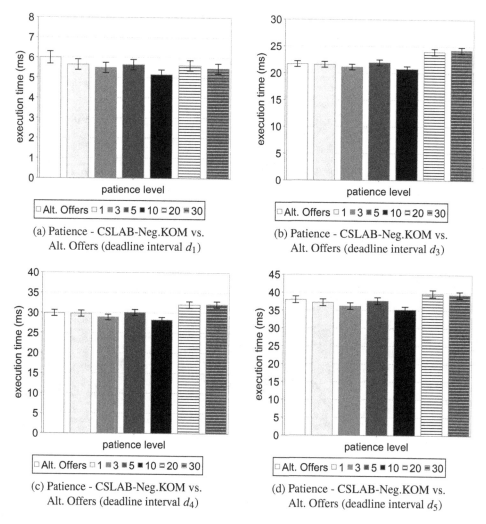

(a) Patience - CSLAB-Neg.KOM vs.
Alt. Offers (deadline interval d_1)

(b) Patience - CSLAB-Neg.KOM vs.
Alt. Offers (deadline interval d_3)

(c) Patience - CSLAB-Neg.KOM vs.
Alt. Offers (deadline interval d_4)

(d) Patience - CSLAB-Neg.KOM vs.
Alt. Offers (deadline interval d_5)

Figure A.17: Impact of the Patience on the execution time over different deadline
intervals

Printed in the United States
By Bookmasters